CRICUT

Kimberly Johnson

Table of Contents

CRICUT FOR BEGINNERS

A Beginner's Guide to Mastering Your Cricut Machine. A Step-by-Step Guide with Illustrated and Detailed Practical Examples and Project Ideas.

Kimberly Johnson

Introduction

Cricut machines offer creativity you might never have experienced before. For many people who are interested in learning how to build projects that they love, a Cricut machine can be their new best friend.

But what's so special about this machine? Why do people buy them?

Well, read on to find out. This book offers a beginner's guide on how to get started using a Cricut machine, and how to get the most out of your Cricut machine experience. For many, Cricut machines can be daunting to work with, but here's the thing: it can help you put images on practically anything – if you're someone who likes to make cool pieces, this is the item for you.

And there's lots more that you can do with Cricut! Let us help you get started.

What Can I Make with This?

The short answer is anything, but some of the cool design elements you can make include the following:

- Logos

- Designs for shirts and pillows

- Drawings

- Vinyl appliques

- Designs for faux leather

So, the short answer is a lot of great things. If you are an artistic person, you perhaps heard about these bad boys back in college, where you'd use cartridges of ink to make designs. Well, gone are the days of doing that – you'll learn in this book what you can do with your Cricut machine.

We'll help you build the best designs out there and suggest some cool ideas you can try, both for beginners and for using more advanced tools, as well.

Chapter 1: What Is a Cricut Machine

Cricut machines, at the core, are really cool printers. Technically, they die cutters and creative planners that help you put together cool designs for various items that you want to make. There are a lot of models out there, and many great types to choose from.

The Explore series of machines contain software called Cricut Design Space, which allows for you to design in the space whatever you want to make, and then literally print it out.

If you're sick and tired of making the same images each time, or you're looking to cut out a design in vinyl without tearing your hair out, then a Cricut machine could really help you.

Models Overview

There are four main types of Cricut machines, all of which are used to cut out various designs. There are also the Legacy machines, such as the Cricut Expression, the Cricut Expression 2, and the Cricut Explore. You can also find the Cricut Cuttlebug, but this is a machine that's primarily used for embossing and die-cutting, and as of spring 2019, this item is discontinued.

Cricut Maker

So, you have the Cricut maker – the newest cutting machine – and it has a lot of new features. You can cut unbonded fabric with this, so you won't need to buy a stabilizer or a tiny rotary blade. It can also cut thicker materials, even balsa wood or thicker leather, and it can score items with a scoring wheel. This system is used with a variety of tools, which we'll get into. It is the priciest option at $399, but for that price, you'll be able to do a whole lot with it.

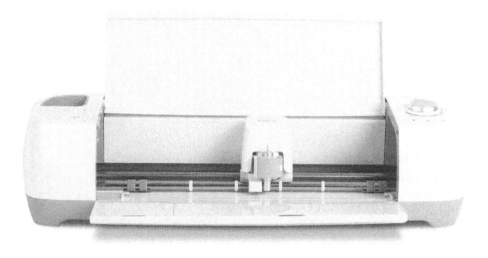

Cricut Explore One

The second model we'll tackle here is the cheapest one, which is the Explore One. It's pretty basic, but for under $200, you're getting a great machine to start with. Personally, this is my favorite for beginners, since you can cut precisely, score, write, and do a lot more with it, and you don't need to use cartridges. It isn't Bluetooth-enabled like the other devices, so you need to run a cord from the device you are using to create the design to the Cricut machine. Again, this is not really a problem, especially if you're someone who uses your machine a lot. This also isn't wireless, but if you won't be using your computer or iPad in another room, this isn't an issue.

It isn't a double tool cartridge, either, so you won't be able to score and cut at the same time, but it can be done separately. However, this isn't a problem unless you have to do both.

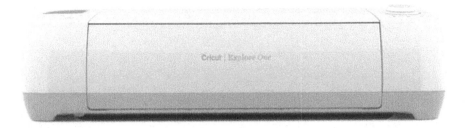

Cricut Explore Air

Then, there is the Cricut Explore Air, which is literally one step up from the first model. It has Bluetooth compatibility, and also has a second tool holder, basically doing what the first model couldn't. It is a nice upgrade, and for only $50 more, you really can't complain.

Cricut Explore Air 2

Your next step up is the Cricut Explore Air 2, which again, is another $50 increase from the previous model discussed. This one is another small model, and it is super-fast – faster than the Air 1. This is great for most of the materials that you want to cut, and the best part is that it doesn't take long to get the job done.

The primary difference with this one is that it's also pretty to look at, as well. If you like pastel colors, this might be one to consider – but again, the price could be a little hefty for those just starting out with Cricut machines.

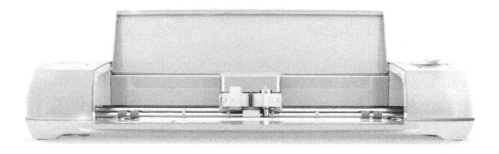

Tools

Cricut machines can also be used with a ton of tools, and most of them are pretty straightforward to use. Here are some of the best tools to consider for your machine:

· Wavy tool: Helps you cut waves into your design.

· Perforation tool: Helps to make perforated markings in your design.

· Weeding tool: This is one of the best tools to use when working with vinyl because it helps with peeling vinyl from the backing sheets.

· Scraping tool: This helps remove any tiny pieces off of the design and prevents the material from moving around.

· Spatula: This is a great one because it helps with moving the design off the backing without tearing material, and can keep it free of debris.

· Tweezers: These are good for pulling the tiny pieces of vinyl or other design elements from the middle without pulling the edges or tearing them.

· Scissors: Cricut scissors are durable, made of stainless steel with micro-tip blades – perfect for detailed work.

· Paper trimmer: This is really convenient with straight cuts, so you don't need to use scissors or a ruler. It's essential for working with vinyl.

·   Brayer: If you're using fabric or larger pieces of vinyl, this is actually one of the best tools to keep the material stabilized on your mat so the mat itself isn't damaged.

·   Backup mats: This should be obvious, but if you're going to work with larger projects, the mats do lose their stickiness after a while. This can prevent you from having to leave your project to pick up more.

·   Easypress Tool: This is awesome for iron-on vinyl that you don't want to iron. It also holds the vinyl much better, even if you wear it a lot, and eliminates the temperature and time guesswork you may otherwise have to do. It's a little pricey, but there are beginner options.

·   Brightpad: Finally, you have a Brightpad, which helps make the lines that you need to cut more visible. If you are doing more than just one cut, this is handy, since it will help with tracing, and with adapting the patterns, too.

These tools are essential, and to pick up the first few on the list, you'll want to get the toolset, since it's much cheaper. But if you're going to be using your machine a lot, I highly recommend spending a little extra by picking up tools to use with it.

Accessories

The accessories and tools often do overlap in some ways, since a lot of these tools are accessories, such as the perforation tool and scraping tools. However, there is more available than just that, and below, you'll learn of the important accessories that can help you make the most of your machine.

·   Deep cut blade: This helps you cut wood and leather, and you can buy these individually.

·   Bonded fabric blade: This can cut through fabric that's been bonded with stabilizers such as Heat N Bond.

·   Cutting Mats: These will be used for crafting pretty much anything, and if you're using lighter materials or heavier lines, you should get both a LightGrip and a strong grip cutting mat. These are useful for a variety of projects.

· Toolsets: We discussed tools in the previous section, but they are essential to help you with your Cricut projects.

· Scoring Stylus: While the Maker model has this included, picking up scoring stylus accessories for other models can help you make anything requiring precise folding. These can help you fold pretty much any project by giving you neat score lines, taking out all the guesswork!

· Pens: These are useful for not just for scoring and cutting, but also writing –you can address letters and cards directly from your Cricut machine. No more signing a bunch of cards!

· Aluminum Foil Ball: Hey, look – a Cricut accessory that isn't something you need to go to a craft store or Amazon for! This will keep your blades clean and sharp, so you don't need to spend extra money buying replacements. Plus, you don't have to travel far to find it, you may even have some in your kitchen!

· Fabric Marking Pen: If you plan on using your Cricut machine for cutting fabric, this is something that you should consider buying. It will save you a bunch of time.

These accessories are items that you either already have or items that you may not have even thought about. But purchasing a few of these will certainly help you use your Cricut machine, that's for sure.

Cricut Access

Cricut Access is the software that gives you access to images, fonts, and the like. You will need to purchase this if you plan on using your Cricut machine, period, and if you don't have the software already, I suggest purchasing it.

The monthly option is perfect for beginners and offers over 400 different fonts and 90,000 different images. And it comes with a 10% savings on any additional Cricut purchases you need, as well as a 10%

savings on premium images and fonts, such as Disney fonts. You'll also have access to a priority member line.

The next membership option is annual, which is exactly the same as the basic, but you don't have to pay as much – just $7.99 per month, upfront. It's good if you're serious about getting into Cricut.

Finally, you have the premium option, which is the same price as monthly and offers unlimited access to the same fonts and images, savings on both products and licenses, and a 50% extra savings on licensed images and fonts, along with some ready-to-make projects. If you spend over $50 on the Cricut store, you earn free shipping. Personally, I think this is the best option if you plan on spending a lot of money on Cricut items, and you're in it for the long haul. However, if you're just beginning, the monthly membership is probably a better choice, because you can cancel this at any time.

Membership allows you to save a little bit on premium ideas and licensed designs – the more you make with your Cricut machine, the more you save, and you'll realize that you could save a lot really fast. On average, customers say that they make up the subscription costs with the money they save, and the coolest thing is that there is so much to choose from, you can find some beautiful designs. It is definitely great if you want exclusive content.

Cartridges

The final item you'll need is, of course, Cricut cartridges. These are little cartridges that you put into the machines that are loaded with different fonts, images, and graphics. You can buy themed cartridges, too, with the idea to create the design that the Cricut machine will make for you.

There are many different ways to use just one cartridge, even though the designs are limited.

Now, if you are getting the Cricut access package, this might not be worth it, but for those of us who don't want to pay for a subscription service yet and just want to cut things, this could be a good option to try out.

You can also import images, of course, with the Cricut design space on the most current machines, and these machines also work with Cricut cartridges. For crafters who don't want to design their cuts, this is ideal. You can also use both together, and there are benefits to this, too.

To use the cartridge, you just put it into the machine, go to Design Space, and then follow the steps. Once they're linked up, you can essentially choose the cartridge you want to work on, and you're ready to go. The advantage of this system is that there are a lot of cartridges you can get, each with unique designs, and once they're linked up, you can mix and match them quite easily.

For newbies, these especially great as you learn how to get better at designing. They are a bit bare-bones, but they're worth it.

The cartridges are a little more expensive than the Design Space and Cricut access alternatives. They're about $20 each unless you're lucky enough to find them on clearance, but here's the thing – you could get hundreds of designs out of that small investment, and if you're not yet sure how to use your Cricut machine, these are great for you to work with.

These aren't used as much these days when compared to the Cricut Access option, but if you're just starting out, this is a really good way to learn. However, you'll soon realize that the ability to do different designs is limited on a Cricut machine with just cartridges, and in truth can be almost a bit boring, so you may want to consider an alternative.

With Cricut, there are many materials you can use. While it might seem like a lot, getting them early on or buying even just the basic toolset is a great option. That way, you can learn how to use them better and pick up cool tricks that you can use to get the most out of your Cricut experience.

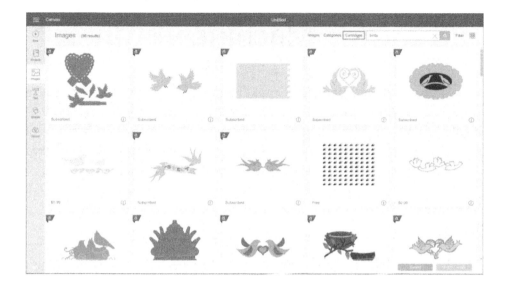

Chapter 2: Materials That Can Be Worked on Using a Cricut Machine

When you look at what Cricut makers can do, you're going to realize there are a ton of materials to choose from. But, which ones do you really need? Which ones are kind of useless? Well, here are some of the main materials you should consider buying, and the materials that you don't necessarily need when using your Cricut machine.

Main Materials

Iron-On Vinyl and Adhesive Vinyl

This is one of the best materials for a Cricut blade, especially fine-point Cricut blades. You can adjust the settings and design the image onto the vinyl. Then, by ironing it on or using the Cricut press, you can design shirts and other appliques for outfits. You'll want to make sure that the iron-on setting is on your Cricut, however, before you think about using this.

You will realize that when you start to look for vinyl, the ideal type to choose is heat-transfer vinyl since you can simply iron or press it on. There are many different options, including fuzzy locked or glitter vinyl, that you can purchase.

Adhesive vinyl is another good one, and there are many different ways to use this. Containers, ornaments, and the like benefit immensely from this material. You can get permanent outdoor and removable indoor options. Again, Cricut machines are known for cutting vinyl, and this material is worth it if you're thinking about making decals, as well.

Cardstock

If you're doing any scrapbooking or making cards, you'll want to consider crafting your items with cardstock. You can choose some great 65-pound cardstock for your crafting projects, and the nice part about this option is that it's pretty cheap.

Paper

Cereal boxes, construction paper, embossed paper, even freezer paper can be used with your Cricut machine. Some users have had a lot of luck with the poster board, too, but you'll want to make sure you clean your blades if you plan on using this material since the poster board can be quite trying on them. Your blades could end up dulling over time, so make sure you clean them with aluminum foil.

Craft paper is another option, as well, and if you're creating personalized boxes, this is a good material to consider – it can help bring a more personalized touch to your finished product.

Fabric

With some fabrics, you'll need a lighter grip board, such as for silk or polyester, but if you're working with heavy fabrics such as leather, burlap, or canvas, make sure that you have StrongGrip cutting boards. But the fabric is another great option for your Cricut experience, since they are wonderful for cutting fabrics, and fabrics can also be printed on. You will want to make sure you use a stabilizer, such as Heat N Bond or Wonder Under before you cut them, to prevent the fabric from getting messed up. Different cuts can be made to fabric and textiles with the Cricut Explore machine. Cricut maker machines work best with fabric, though there is the consideration that it could be a bit pricey.

Alternative Materials

While those are the main materials, you also have some other alternative options. If you're working with light material, typically the Explore series of machines are ideal.

One great material you could try is the chipboard. If you're working with a chipboard thicker than what your blades can handle, then you can insert the material into the Cricut machine and let it work its magic.

Rubber is another option that a lot of people don't think about when they're using a Cricut machine. If you're trying to create custom-designed stamps, such as for pottery or other projects, consider this option. You'll want a deep-cut blade for this, but it works.

Wood veneer works well with your Cricut machine, but you'll want to make sure that you have both a fine-point and a deep-point blade, depending on the project. This material will also take a little longer to cut.

What about magnets? That's right, you can actually make your own customized magnets with a Cricut machine. These are great for gifts for teachers or friends, and the best part is you don't have to sit around, trying to cut out intricate designs on your own. They're wonderful and super fun.

Craft foam is really good for arts and crafts with children, but if you don't want to spend all your time cutting out various shapes for the kids to use, just insert the design into the Cricut machine and let it do the work. This is wonderful for art teachers who want to put together a project but don't want to deal with the hassle of spending all their time prepping the materials.

Finally, you have a mat board. This will require a deep-point blade, but if you want a strong material for a durable art project, this is a wonderful option.

The craziest part of Cricut machines is that it can cut items you wouldn't ever expect – tissue paper, stencil paper to make your own stencils, sticker paper to make stickers, plastic packages, adhesive foil, and even aluminum foil can be used with this! So, yes, there are so many options for your Cricut experience and so many designs that you can take advantage of that it's worth checking out, that's for sure.

To put it simply, Cricut machines can handle a ton of materials. The general idea is that if the machine can cut it, chances are you can use it, so don't be afraid to try some of your crazy ideas – Cricut machines are quite wonderful for just about everything.

Chapter 3: How to Use a Cricut Machine

So, you have all your materials on hand, which is awesome, but how do you actually *use* a Cricut machine? Well, that's what you're about to find out. If looking at your Cricut machine makes you feel all sorts of confused, then continue reading – here, we'll tell you how to use your new Cricut machine in a simple, yet effective manner.

Setting Up the Machine

First, you'll want to set up the Cricut machine. To begin, create a space for it. A craft room is the best place for this, but if you're at a loss of where to put it, I suggest setting it up in a dining room if possible. Make sure you have an outlet nearby or a reliable extension cord.

Next, read the instructions. Often, you can jump right in and begin using the equipment, but with Cricut machines, it can be very tedious. The best thing to do is to read all the materials you get with your machine – while we'll go over the setup in this book, if you're still stumped, take a look at the manual.

Make sure that you do have ample free space around the machine itself, because you will be loading mats in and out and you'll need that little bit of wiggle room.

The next thing to set up is, of course, the computer where the designs will be created. Make sure that whatever medium you're using has an internet connection, since you'll need to download the Cricut Design Space app. If it's a machine earlier than the Explore Air 2, it will need to be plugged in directly, but if it's a wireless machine like the Air 2, you can simply link this up to your computer, and from there, design what you need to design.

Now, once you have this bad boy initially set up, you'll want to learn how to use Design Space – and that's what we'll talk about next.

Using Cricut Software

So, Cricut machines use a program called Cricut Design Spaces, and you'll need to make sure that you have this downloaded and installed when you're ready. Download the app if you plan to use a smartphone or tablet, or if you're on the computer, go to http://design.cricut.com/setup to get the software. If it's not hooked up already, make sure you've got Bluetooth compatibility enabled on the device, or the cord plugged in. To turn on your machine, hold the power button. You'll then go to settings, where you should see your Cricut model in Bluetooth settings. Choose that, and from there, your device will ask you to put a Bluetooth passcode in. Just make this something generic and easy to remember.

Once that's done, you can now use Design Space.

So, what I love about Design Space is that it's incredibly easy to use. They know you're a beginner, so you'll notice it's very easy to navigate.

Now, I personally like to use the app for Design Space, since this will allow you to have every design uploaded to the cloud so you can reuse your designs. However, if you want to use them without having an internet connection, you'll want to make sure that you download them and save them to the device itself, rather than relying on the cloud.

When you're in the online mode, you'll see a lot of projects that you can use. For the purpose of this tutorial, I do suggest making sure that you choose an easy one, such as the "Enjoy Card" project you can get automatically.

So, you've got everything all linked up – let's move onto the first cut for this project.

Imputing Cartridges and Keypad

The first cut that you'll be doing does involve keypad input and cartridges, and these are usually done with the "Enjoy Card" project you get right away. So, once everything is set up, choose this project, and from there, you can use the tools and the accessories within the project.

You will need to set the smart dial before you get started making your projects. This is on the right side of the Explore Air 2, and it's basically the way you choose your materials. Turn the dial to whatever type of material you want, since this does help with ensuring you've got the right blade settings. There are even half settings for those in-between projects.

For example, let's say you have some light cardstock. You can choose that setting, or the adjacent half setting. Once this is chosen in Design Space, your machine will automatically adjust to the correct setting.

You can also choose the fast mode, which is in the "set, load, go" area on the screen, and you can then check the position of the box under the indicator for dial position. Then, press this and make your cut. However, fast mode is incredibly loud, so be careful.

Now, we've mentioned cartridges. While these usually aren't used in the Explore Air 2 machines anymore, they are helpful with beginner projects. To do this, once you have the Design Space software and everything is connected, go to the hamburger menu and you'll see an option called "ink cartridges." Press that bad boy, and from there, choose the Cricut device. The machine will then tell you to put your cartridge in. Do that, and once it's detected, it will tell you to link the cartridge.

Do remember, though, that once you link this, you can't use it with other machines – the one limit to these cartridges.

Once it's confirmed, you can go to images, and click the cartridges option to find the ones that you want to make. You can filter the cartridges to figure out what you need, and you can check out your images tab for any other cartridges that are purchased or uploaded.

You can get digital cartridges, which means you buy them online and choose the images directly from your available options. They aren't physical, so there is no linking required.

Loading and Unloading Your Paper

To load paper into a Cricut machine, you'll want to make sure that the paper is at least three inches by three inches. Otherwise, it won't cut very well. You should use regular paper for this.

Now, to make this work, you need to put the paper onto the cutting mat. You should have one of those, so take it right now and remove the attached film. Put a corner of the paper to the area where you are directed to align the paper corners. From there, push the paper directly onto the cutting mat for proper adherence. Once you do that, you just load it into the machine, following the arrows. You'll want to keep the paper firmly on the mat. Press the "load paper" key that you see as you do this. If it doesn't take for some reason, press the unload paper key, and try this again until it shows up.

Now, before you do any cutting for your design, you should always have a test cut in place. Some people don't do this, but it's incredibly helpful when learning how to use a Cricut. Otherwise, you won't get the pressure correct in some cases, so get in the habit of doing it for your pieces.

Is there a difference between vinyl and other products? The primary difference is the cutting mats. Depending on what you're cutting, you may need some grip or lack thereof. If you feel like your material isn't fully sticking, get some Heat N' Bond to help with this since often, the issue with cutting fabrics comes from the fact that it doesn't adhere. But you may also need mats that are a bit thicker, too, to help get a better grip on these.

Selecting Shapes, Letters, And Phrases

When you're creating your design in Design Space, you usually begin by using letters, shapes, numbers, or different fonts. These are the basics, and they're incredibly easy.

To make text, you just press the text tool on the left-hand side and type out your text. For example, write the word hello, or joy, or whatever you want to use.

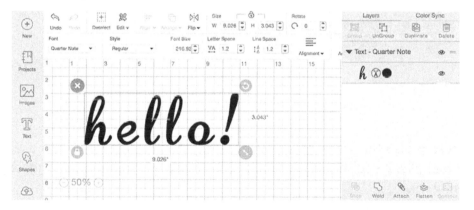

You can change the font size by pressing the drag and drop arrow near the corner of the text box, or by going to the size panel near the top to choose actual font sizes. You can also choose different Cricut or system fonts, too. Cricut ones will be in green, and if you have Cricut Access, this is a great way to begin using this. You can sort these, too, so you don't end up accidentally paying for a font.

The Cricut ones are supposed to be made for Cricut, so you know they'll look good. Design Space also lets you put them closer together so they can be cut with a singular cut. You can change this by going to line spacing and adjusting as needed. To fix certain letters, you go to the drop-down advanced menu to ungroup the letters, so everything is separate as needed.

Cricut also offers different writing styles, which is a great way to add text to projects. The way to do this is to choose a font that's made with a specific style and choose only the Cricut ones, and then go to writing. This will then narrow down the choice so you're using a good font for writing.

Adding shapes is pretty easy, as well. In Design Space, choose the shapes option. Once you click it, the window will then pop out, and you'll have a wonderful array of different shapes that you can use with just one click. Choose your shape, and from there, put it in the space. Drag the corners in order to make this bigger or smaller.

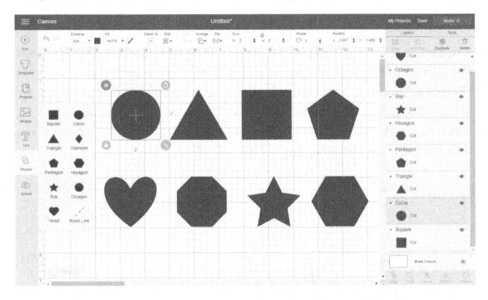

There is also the scoreline, which creates a folding line for you to use. Personally, if you're thinking of trying to make a card at first, I suggest using this.

You can also resize your options by dragging them towards the right-hand side, and you can change the orientation by choosing that option, and then flipping it around. You can select exact measurements as well, which is good for those design projects that need everything to be precise.

Once you've chosen the design, it's time for you to start cutting, and we'll discuss this next step below.

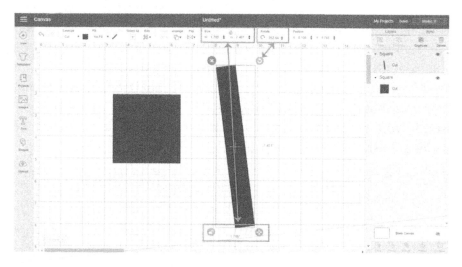

How to Remove Your Cut from The Cutting Mat

Removing your cut from the mat is easy, but complicated. Personally, I ran into the issue of it being more complicated with vinyl projects since they love to just stick around there. But we'll explain how you can create great cuts and remove them, as well.

The first thing to remember is to make sure that you're using the right mat. The light grip ones are good for very light material, with the pink one being one of the strongest, and only to be used with the Cricut Maker. Once the design is cut, you'll probably be eager McBeaver about removing the project directly from the mat, but one of the problems with this is that often, the project will be ruined if you're not careful. Instead of pulling the project from the mat itself, bend the mat within your hand, and push it away from the project, since this will loosen it from the mat. Bend this both horizontally and vertically, so that the adhesive releases the project.

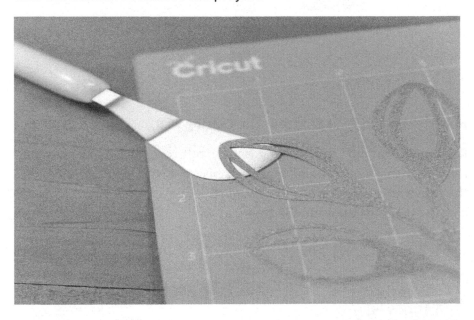

Remember the spatula tool that we told you to get with your Cricut machine early on? This is where you use it. Use this spatula to lightly pull on the vinyl, until you can grab it from the corner and lift it up. Otherwise, you risk curling it or tearing the mat, which is what we don't want.

Now, with the initial cuts, such as the paper ones, this will be incredibly easy. Trust me, I was surprised at how little effort it took, but one of the biggest things to remember is that with Cricut machines, you have to go slow when removing the material. Do this slowly, and don't get rushed near the end. Taking your time will save you a lot of problems, and it will even save you money and stress, too!

You will notice that Cricut mats are incredibly sticky, and if you don't have a Cricut spatula on hand or don't want to spend the money, metal spatulas will work, too. You can put the paper on a flat surface and then lightly remove it. But always be careful when removing these items.

Cricut machines are pretty easy to use, and the beauty is that with the right understanding and ideas, you can make any items you want to.

Chapter 4: Complex Operations

Cricut machines are pretty straightforward with what you need to do in order to make simple designs, but you might wonder about some of the more complex operations. Here, we'll tell you how to accomplish these with just a few simple button presses.

Blade Navigation and Calibration

The blades that come with a Cricut machine are important to understand, and you will need to calibrate your blades every single time you use your machine.

Each blade needs this because it will help you figure out which level of depth and pressure your cut needs to be. Typically, each blade needs to be calibrated only once, which is great, because then you don't have to spend time doing this each time. Once you've done it once, it will stay calibrated, but if you decide to change the housings of the blades or if you use them in another machine, you'll need to calibrate it again.

So, if you plan on using a knife blade and then a rotary blade, you'll want to make sure that you do recalibrate – and make sure you do this before you start with your project. It is actually incredibly easy to do this though, which is why it's encouraged.

To calibrate a blade, you just launch the Design Space, and from there, you open the menu and choose calibration. Then, choose the blade that you're going to put in. For the purpose of this explanation, let's say you're using a knife blade.

Put that blade in the clamp B area and do a test cut, such as with copy paper into the mat, and then load that into the machine.

Press continue, then press the go button on the machine. It will then do everything that you need for the item itself, and it will start to cut.

You can then choose which calibration is best for your blade, but usually, the first one is good enough.

You can do this with every blade you use, and every time you use a new blade on your machine, I highly recommend you do this - for best results, of course.

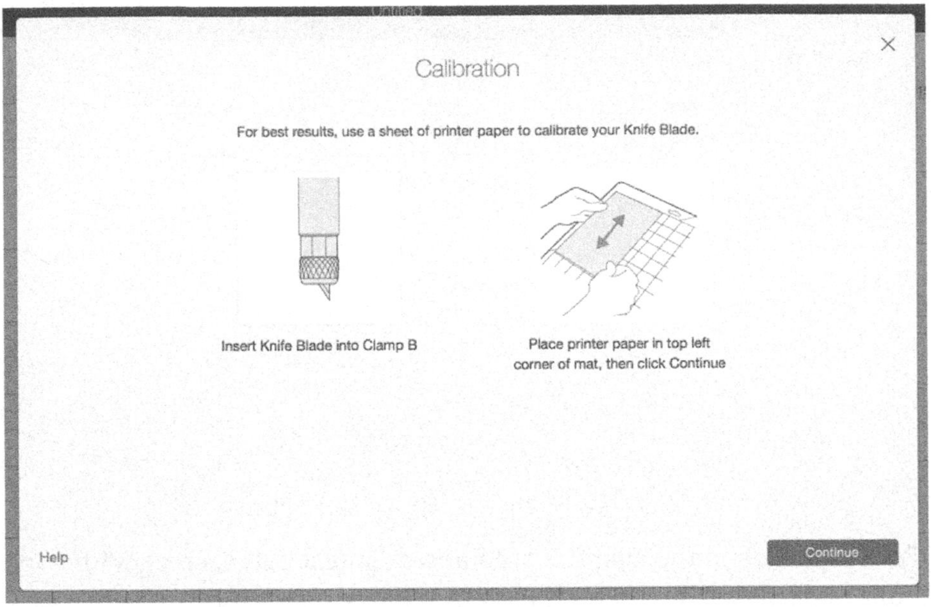

Calibration

For best results, use a sheet of printer paper to calibrate your Knife Blade.

Insert Knife Blade into Clamp B

Place printer paper in top left corner of mat, then click Continue

Help

Continue

Set Paper Size

Setting paper size in a Cricut machine is actually pretty simple. You will want to use this with either cartridge or with Design Space for what you'd like to make. This also comes with a cutting mat, and you'll want to load this up with paper so that you can use it. To do this, you'll want to make sure that you have it plugged in, then go to the project preview screen. If you choose a material that's bigger than the mat size, it will automatically be changed, and it'll be adjusted as necessary based on the size of the material that you select.You can choose the color, the size of the material, whether or not it'll mirror – and you can also choose to fully skip the mat, too, if you don't want that image printed just yet.

Note that the material size menu does offer sizes that are bigger than the largest mat available.

If you're planning on using the print then cut mode, do understand that it's limited to a print area of 8.5x11 inches, but again, you can choose these settings for yourself.

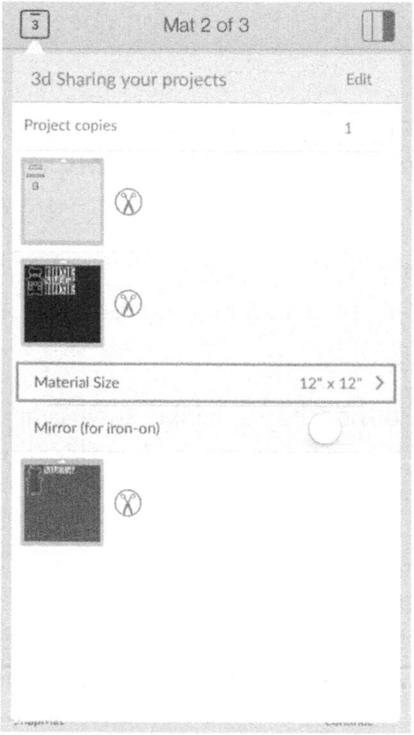

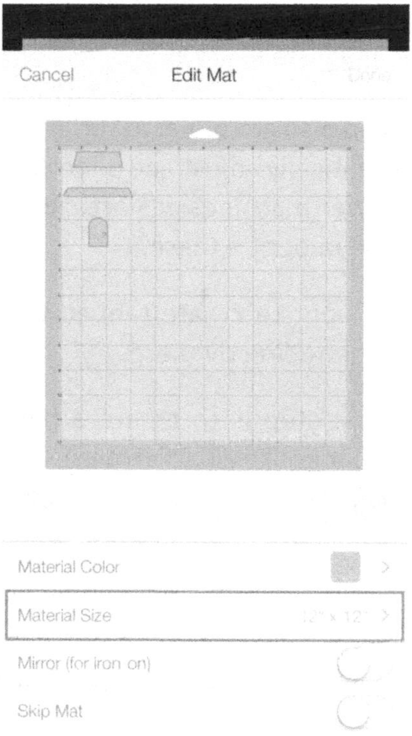

3d Sharing your projects   Edit

Project copies   1

Material Size   12" x 12" >

Mirror (for iron-on)

Cancel   Edit Mat

Material Color

Material Size   12" x 12" >

Mirror (for iron on)

Skip Mat

Load Last

To load that paper and image last is pretty simple. Remember the preview we discussed in the previous section? Remember that "skip this mat" step? Literally, press that, and then go. You'll be able to skip this quite easily. It's one of those operations that's definitely a little different from what you may be used to, but if you want to skip design and don't want to work with it just yet, this is probably the best option for you to use. If you're worried about forgetting it, don't worry – Cricut will remind you.

Paper Saver

Saving paper is something you'll want to consider doing with a Cricut machine because it loves to eat up the paper before you even start decorating. The Explore Air 2 definitely will appreciate it if you save paper, and there are a few ways to do so.

The first one is, of course, to halve your mats. But you don't need to do only that.

You can also go to the material saver option on the machine, which will automatically adjust and align your paper as best it can. Unfortunately, on newer machines, it's actually not directly stated, but there is a way to save paper on these.

You'll want to create tabbed dividers to organize your projects and save them directly there.

The first step is to create a background shape. Make sure that the paper looks like a background. Go to shapes, and then select the square to make the square shape.

Next, once you've created squares to represent the paper, arrange this to move to the back so that the shapes are organized to save the most space on each mat. Then organize the items that are on top of where the background is and arrange them so they all fit on a singular mat.

Rotating is your best friend – you can use this feature whenever you choose objects, so I do suggest getting familiarized with it.

Next, you hide the background at this point, and you do this by choosing the square, and in Design Space, literally hiding this on the right side. Look at the eyeball on the screen, and you'll see a line through the eyeball. That means it's hidden.

Check over everything and fine-tune it at this point. Make sure they're grouped around one object, and make sure everything has measurements. Move these around if they're outside of the measurements required.

Once they're confirmed, you then attach these together on the right-hand side of Design Space, which keeps everything neatly together – they're all cut from the same sheet.

From here, repeat this until everything is neatly attached. It will save your paper, but will it save you time? That's debatable, of course.

Speed Dial

So, the speed dial typically comes into play when you're setting the pressure and speed. Fast mode is one of the options available on the Explore Air 2 and the Maker machines, which make the machine run considerably faster than other models. You can use this with vinyl, cardstock, and iron-on materials. To set this, go to the cut screen. You'll have a lot of speed dials here, and various different settings. If you have the right material in place when choosing it, you'll be given the option to do it quickly with fast mode. From there, you simply tap or click on that switch in order to toggle this to the position for on. That will activate fast mode for that item.

It will make everything about two times faster, which means that if you're making complex swirl designs, it will take 30 seconds instead of the 73-second average it usually takes.

However, one downside to this is that because it's so fast, it will sometimes make the cuts less precise – you'll want to move back to the regular mode for finer work.

This is all usually set with the smart-set dial, which will offer the right settings for you to get the best cuts that you can on any material you're using. Essentially, this dial eliminates you having to manually check the pressure on this.

To change the speed and pressure for a particular material that isn't already determined with the preset settings, you will need to select custom mode and choose what you want to create. Of course, the smart-set dial is better for the Cricut products and mats. If you notice that the blade is cutting too deep or not deep enough, there is a half-settings option on each material that you can adjust to achieve the ideal cut.

Usually, the way you do this with the pre-set settings is to upload and create a project, press go, and load the mat, then move the smart-set dial on the machine itself to any setting. Let's select custom and choose the speed for this one.

In Design Space, you then choose the material, add the custom speed, and you can adjust these settings. You can even adjust the number of times you want the cut to be changed with the smart-set dial, too. Speed is something you can adjust to suit the material, which can be helpful if you're struggling with putting together some good settings for your items.

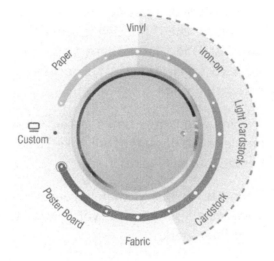

Pressure Dial

Now, let's talk about pressure. Each piece of material will require different pressure settings. If you're not using enough pressure, the blade won't cut into the material, and if you use too much pressure, you'll end up cutting the mat, which isn't what you want to do.

The smart-set dial kind of takes the guesswork out of it. You simply choose the setting that best fits your material, and from there, you let it cut. If you notice you're not getting a deep enough cut, then you'll want to adjust it about half a setting to get a better result. From there, adjust as needed.

But did you know that you can change the pressure on the smart-set dial for custom materials? Let's say you're cutting something that's very different, such as foil, and you want to set the pressure to be incredibly light so that the foil doesn't get shredded. What you do is you load the material in, and you choose the custom setting. You can then choose the material you plan to cut, such as foil – and if it's not on the list, you can add it.

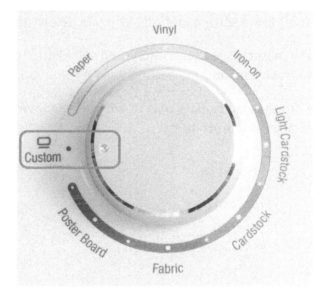

From here, you're given pressure options. Often, people will go too heavy with their custom settings, so I do suggest that you go lighter for the first time and change it as needed. There is a number of draggers that goes from low to high. If you need lots of pressure, obviously let it go higher. If you don't need much pressure, make sure it's left lower. You will also want to adjust the number of times the cut is done on a multi-cut feature item.

This is a way for you to achieve multiple cuts for the item, which can be incredibly helpful for those who are trying to get the right cut, or if the material is incredibly hard to cut. I don't suggest using this for very flimsy and thin material, because it'll just waste your blade and the mat itself.

That's all there is to it! This is a great way to improve on your Cricut designs. Personally, I love to work with custom cuts, and you can always delete these if you feel like they don't work. You just press the change settings button to adjust your pressure, speed, or how many cuts you want, and then choose to save when you're done.

What if you don't like a setting, period? You can delete it, of course!

To delete, go to materials settings, and you'll see a little trash can next to it. Press the trash can, and the setting will be removed.

Adjusting the pressure and cuts is part of why people love using Design Space, and it's a great feature to try.

Cricut Design Space

Design Space lets you do many things with your Cricut machine. Here are a few things you can do with this convenient app:

- Aligning various items right next to one another.

- Attaching items to hold images in place, and lets you use score lines.

- Arranging these to make them sit on the canvas in different layers.

- Canvas, a tool that lets you arrange prints and vectors so you can use the various tools with them.

- Contouring, which is a tool that lets you hide image layers quickly, so they're not cut out.

- Color sync, which lets you use multiple colors in one project to reduce the material differences.

- Cut buttons, which will start cuts.

- Make it button: this is the screen that lets you see the designs being cut.

- Draw lines: lets you draw with the pen to write images and such.

- Fill: lets you fill in a pattern or color on an item.

- Flipping items flip it horizontally or vertically by 180 degrees.

- Group: puts different text and images on a singular layer, and everything is moved at once so that it doesn't affect the layout.

- Linetype: an option that you can do with your piece, whether you want to cut a line, draw a line, or score a line.

- Mirrored image: reverses it, which is very important with transfer vinyl, so everything reads correctly.

- Print then Cut: it's an option that lets you print the design, and from there, the machine cuts it.

- Redo: does an action again and reverses it.

- Reverse Weeding: removes the vinyl that's left behind, and it's used mostly for stencil vinyl

- Score lines: helps you make creases in the papers so you can fold it.

- SVG: this is a scalable vector graphic that lets you cut a file that's scaled to be larger or smaller so that the resolution is kept, and made up of lines that consist of infinite white dots.

- Texts and fonts: let you use put specialized fonts and words within Design Space.

- Weeding: lets you remove the excess vinyl from designs. Press this when you're cutting vinyl.

- Welding: a tool you use when you want to combine two line shapes into one shape, and it's used to make seamless cursive words.

These are most of the functions you can do in Design Space. To use these, simply choose an image or font that you want to use and put it in Design Space. From there, you can do literally whatever you need to do with it – within reason, of course – and then put the image onto the material that you're using. For the purposes of learning, I suggest not getting in too deep with vinyl just yet, and get used to using these tools. You also have pens, which can be implemented to help you write images with a tool that looks sharp and crisp. We'll go over the purpose of pens and what you can do with them in the next section.

Cricut Pens

Pens for your Cricut machine are essentially another way to get creative with your projects. I love to use them for cards, handmade tags for gifts, or even fancy invites and labels.

Now, each pen offers a little different finish and point size. They aren't toxic, and they are permanent once they're dried. You've got the extra-fine points for small lettering, up to a medium tip for making thicker lines. There are also glitter and metallic pens, so you have a lot of options to choose from!

But do you have to use them? Well, the answer is no. You can use different pens, but test them on paper first and get adapters to use with them. Cricut pens are your best option.

To use these, choose the wording or design, or whatever you want to do. You want to go to the layers panel that's on the right-hand side, and choose the scissors icon – change that to the write icon. From there, you'll want to choose the pen color that you would like to use.

You can then have the design printed out on the material you're using.

Some people like to use different fonts, whether it be system fonts or Cricut fonts, or the Cricut Access fonts. However, the one thing with Design Space is that it will write what will normally be cut, so you'll get an outline of that font rather than just a solid stroke of writing.

This can add to the design, however – you essentially change the machine from cut to write, and there you go.

You can also use the Cricut writing fonts, which you can choose by going to a blank canvas, and then choosing the text tool on the left-hand side, along with the wording you'd like for this to have.

Once you're in the font edit toolbar, you are given a font selection. You choose the writing font filter, so you have fonts that you can write with. From there, choose the font, and then switch from the scissors to the pen icon, and then select the pen color. That's all there is to it!

You can also use this with Cricut Access – if you're planning on using this a lot, it might be worth it.

To insert the pens into the Cricut machine, you want to choose to make it, and from there, you'll then go to the prepare mat screen. It will say draw instead of writing in the thumbnail this time around, so you press continue in the bottom right-hand corner, then put the pen into clamp A – you just unlock it and then put it in. Wait until it clicks, and that's it!

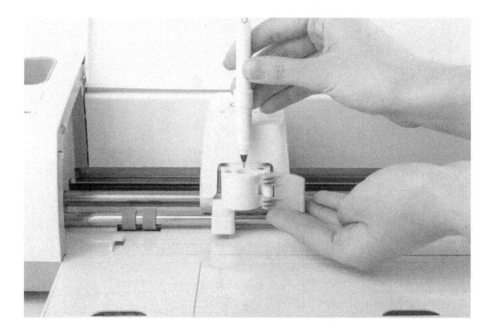

Cricut pens are super easy, and it's a great idea to consider trying these out.

As you can see, there are many different Cricut features and a lot of functions that may seem complex, but as you can see are really not that hard. There are tons of options for your Cricut projects, and a lot that you can get out of this machine.

Chapter 5: Maintenance of the Cricut Machine

Every Cricut machine needs to be cleaned and taken care of in order to keep it working for as long as possible. Here, you'll learn about the maintenance required for Cricut machines, and what you can do to keep your machine working efficiently.

Cleaning and Care

Cleaning your machine is very important, and you should do it regularly to keep everything in tip-top shape. If you don't take care of your machine, that's just money down the drain.

But what can you do to care for your machine? Well, I do suggest initially that you make sure to run maintenance on it as much as you can and keep it clean. There are a few other tips and tricks that can help prolong the machine's life. For starters, keep liquids and food away from the machine – never drink or eat while you use your Cricut machine. Set up your machine in a location that's free of dust and try to keep it away from excessive coolness or heat, so don't just throw it in the attic or an especially cold basement. If you're transporting your machine to use it at a different location, never leave it in the car.

Excessive heat will melt the machine's plastic components, so be careful.

Finally, make sure the machine is stored away from sunlight. Keep it out of places in the home where sunlight hits it directly. For example, if you have an office that is very bright and the sun warms the machine for a long period of time, you'll want to move it so that it doesn't get damaged.

Be gentle with your machine. Remember, it is a machine, so you'll want to make sure that you do take some time and try to keep it nice and in order. Don't be rough with it, and when working with the machine parts, don't be too rough with them, either.

Caring for your machine isn't just about making sure that the parts don't get dirty, but you should also make sure that you keep everything in good working order.

Cleaning the Machine Itself

In general, the exterior is pretty easy to clean – you just need a damp cloth. Use a soft cloth to wipe it off, and keep in mind that chemical cleaners with benzene, acetone, or carbon tetrachloride should never be used on your Cricut machine. Any cleaner that is scratchy, as well, should be avoided at all costs.

Make sure that you never put any machine components in water. This should be obvious, but often, people may use a piece of a damp cloth, thinking that it'll be fine when in reality, it isn't.

You should consider getting some non-alcoholic wipes for cleaning your machine. Always disconnect the power before cleaning, as you would with any machine. The Cricut machine can then be lightly wiped down. Some people also use a glass cleaner sprayed on a cloth but do be careful to make sure no residue builds up. If you notice there is some dust there, you can typically get away with a cloth that's soft and clean.

Sometimes, grease can build up – you may notice this on the cartridge bar if you use cartridges a lot. Use a swab of cotton or a soft cloth to remove it.

Greasing the Machine

If you need to grease your machine, first make sure that it's turned off and the smart carriage is moved to the left. Use a tissue to wipe this down, and then move it to the right, repeating the process again.

From there, move the carriage to the center and open up a lubrication package. Put a small amount onto a Q-tip. Apply a thin coating, greasing everything evenly, and also clean any buildup that may have occurred. This is usually the issue if you hear grinding noise when cleaning the machine itself.

There are a few other important places that you should make sure to clean, besides the outside and the carriage. Any places where blades are should be cleaned; you can just move the housing unit of the blade to clean it. You should also check the drawing area, to make sure there isn't any excessive ink there.

Never use spray cleaner directly on the machine, for obvious reasons. The bar holding the housing shouldn't be wiped down, but if you do notice an excessive grease, please take the time to make sure that it's cleaned up. Remember to never touch the gear chain near the back of this unit, either, and never clean with the machine on, for your own safety.

When caring for a Cricut machine, try to do this more frequently if you're using the machine a lot, or twice yearly. If you notice strange noises coming from the machine, do get a grease packet. You can always contact Cricut and they'll help you figure out the issue, if there is one, with your machine.

Cricut machines are great, but you need to take care in making sure that you keep everything in rightful order.

Cutting Blade

Your blades will tend to dull over time, but this is usually a very slow process. The best way to prevent it is to have different blades to cut different materials. Having a different blade for each material is a really good idea.

You can get fine-point ones which are good for smaller items; deep-cut, which is great for leather and other fabrics; bonded fabric, so great for fabric pieces; a rotary blade for those heavy fabrics; and finally, a knife blade, which is good for those really thick items.

In order to maintain your blades, you should clean the housing area for every blade after each use, since they get gunky fast. Squirting compressed air into the area is a wonderful way to get the dust out of there.

As for the blades, remember foil? Use a little bit of that over the edges of the blade to help clean and polish them up. To polish them, you should put them on the cutting mat and from there, cut small designs on it. It actually does help with sharpening them, and it doesn't require you to completely remove them. You can do this with every single blade, too!

To change the blades in their housings, just open the clamps, pull up, and remove the housing within the machine. Put a new blade in, and then close it. That's all it takes.

Storing them is also pretty simple. There is a drop-down doorway at the front area of the machine. It's made for storing the blades within their housings. Put your loose blades in there first, then utilize the magnet to keep them in place. The best part about this storage is that your blades are always with the Cricut, even if you take the machine somewhere else.

There is also a blade organizer that you can use, too, made out of chipboard with some holders attached. This is also a wonderful means to store all of your items. Organizing your Cricut blades is very important, and understanding the best places to keep them is, of course, essential.

Cutting Mat

Your cutting mats need to be cleaned because if you don't clean them frequently, they will attract dirt and lose adhesiveness. That means you'll have to spend more money on mats, which isn't ideal. There are different ways to clean them, and we'll go over a few of the different means to clean your mats so you can use them for longer.

Cleaning the Mat Itself

First, if your mat is completely filthy, you need to clean it. Of course, you'll also want to do this for just general maintenance, too. Once it's been cleaned, you'll notice it's sticky again.

Typically, washing it down with either a magic eraser or a kitchen scrubber can do it. Sometimes, if it's really dirty, you might want to get some rubbing alcohol onto a wipe. If you notice a chunk of the debris left behind, however, is fabric oriented, then get some lint rollers or even just stick some scotch tape on there and pull it off. This can eliminate the issue.

But what about the really tough grime? Well, get some Goo Gone cleaner. Put a little bit on the troublesome spots and wipe it around, and then let the goo stick on there. From there, get an old card or something to get it off, and then wash the mat. Once it's dry, check to see if it's sticky. If it is, then great – you don't need to do anything more. But what if you notice that it's still not sticky? Well, why not restick the cutting mat itself!

Resticking The Mat

To do this, you need to make sure that you tape the edges, so you don't get adhesive near the edges, and mess with the rollers of the machine. Once that's there, use either spray adhesive or glue stick, and then let it dry. If you notice that it's still not sticky enough when you're finished applying the first coat, apply a second coat.

There are great adhesives out there, such as simple spray adhesive, easy tack, quilt basting, bonding, and also repositionable e glue. All of these are fairly effective, and if you notice that the mat is actually sticking pretty well, then you're in luck.

However, always make sure that you let this fully dry. If you don't let the adhesive dry and you start using the mat again, you will run into the problem of the material being stuck to it.

Once it's dried, try it out with some test material. If you find it too sticky at this point, but either your hands or a shirt on there to help reduce the tackiness.

Caring for Machines and Mats

Here are a couple of other tips to use with your cutting mats.

The first, use different mats. You may notice that you can get more out of one type of mat than another kind, which is something many people don't realize. Often, if you notice that you get a lot more out of the firmer grip mats, buy more of those.

Finally, halve your mats. You can save immensely by making sure that they're cut in half. This does work, and it helps pretty well.

You can expect anywhere from about 25 to 40 different cuts before you'll need to replace the mat, but cleaning after about half of that can definitely help with improving the quality of your cuts. The life of the mat, of course, does vary based on the settings and what materials you cut. When you can't get it to stick, try cleaning and resticking it, but if you notice that it's still not doing the job, you're going to need to get a replacement.

Taking care of your Cricut machine will get you more use out of it, so make sure you perform regular maintenance on all your machine's components so it can be used for years.

Chapter 6: Cricut Project Ideas to Try!

With Cricut, the ideas for projects are so vast, you'll be amazed at how much you can do. So, what are some ideas that could work for you? Here are a few that you can consider, and some of the best project ideas for those who are stumped on where to begin!

Easy Projects

Custom Shirts

Custom shirts are incredibly easy. The beauty of this is, you can use the Cricut fonts or system options, and from there, you can simply print it on. Personally, I like to use the iron-on vinyl, because it's easy to work with. Just take your image and upload it into Design Space. Then, go to the canvas and find the image you want. Once you've selected the image, you click on the whitespace that will be cut – remember to get the insides, too. Make sure that you choose cut image, not print from cut image, and then place it on the canvas to the size of your liking. Put the iron-on vinyl shiny side down, turn it on, and then select iron-on from the menu. Choose to cut, and make sure you mirror the image. Once done, pull off the extra vinyl to remove the vinyl between the letters. There you go! A simple shirt.

Vinyl Decals

Vinyl can also be used to make personalized items, such as water bottle decals. First, design the text – you can pretty much use whatever you want for this. From here, create a second box and make an initial, or whatever design you want. Make sure that you resize this to fit the water bottle, as well.

From here, load your vinyl, and make sure that you use transfer tape on the vinyl itself once you cut it out. Finally, when you adhere the lettering to the bottle, go from the center and then push outwards, smoothing as you go. It takes a bit, but there you have it – simple water bottles that children will love! This is a wonderful, simple project for those of us who aren't really that artistically inclined but want to get used to making Cricut items.

Printable Stickers

Printable stickers are the next project. This is super simple and fun for parents and kids. The Explore Air 2 machine works best.

With this one, you want the print then cut feature, since it makes it much easier. To begin, go to Design Space and download images of ice cream or whatever you want, or upload images of your own. You click on a new project, and on the left side that says images, you can choose the ones you like, and insert more of these on there.

From here, choose the image and flatten it, since this will make it into one piece rather than just a separate file for each. Resize as needed to make sure that they fit where you're putting them.

You can copy/paste each element until you're done. Once ready, press saves, and then choose this as a print then cut image. Click the big button at the bottom that says make it. Make sure everything is good, then press continue, and from there, you can load the sticker paper into the machine. Make sure to adjust this to the right setting, which for sticker paper is the vinyl set. Put the paper into there and load them in, and when ready, the press goes – it will then cut the stickers as needed.

From there, take them out and decorate. You can use ice cream or whatever sticker image you want!

Personalized Pillows

Personalized pillows are another fun idea and are incredibly easy to make. To begin, you open up Design Space and choose a new project. From here, select the icon at the bottom of the screen itself, choosing your font. Type the words you want, and drag the text as needed to make it bigger.

You can also upload images, too, if you want to create a huge picture on the pillow itself.

From here, you want to press the attach button for each box, so that they work together and both are figured when centered, as well.

You then press make it – and you want to turn to mirror on, since this will, again, be on iron-on vinyl. From here, you load the iron-on vinyl with the shiny side down, the press continues, follow the prompts, and make sure it's not jammed in, either.

Let the machine work its magic with cutting and from there, you can press the weeding tool to get the middle areas out.

Set your temperature on the easy press for the right settings, and then push it onto the material, ironing it on and letting it sit for 10 to 15 seconds. Let it cool, and then take the transfer sheet off.

There you have it! A simple pillow that works wonders for your crafting needs.

Cards!

Finally, cards are a great project idea for Cricut makers. They're simple, and you can do the entire project with cardstock.

To make this, you first want to open up Design Space, and from there, put your design in. If you like images of ice cream, then use that. If you want to make Christmas cards, you can do that, too. Basically, you can design whatever you want to on this.

Now, you'll then want to add the text. You can choose the font that you want to use, and from there, write out the message on the card, such as "Merry Christmas." At this point, instead of choosing to cut, you want to choose the right option – the make it option. You don't have to mirror this, but check that your design fits properly on the cardstock itself. When choosing material for writing, make sure you choose the cardstock.

From there, insert your cardstock into the machine, and then, when ready, you can press go and the Cricut machine will design your card. This may take a minute, but once it's done, you'll have a wonderful card in place. It's super easy to use.

Cricut cards are a great personalized way to express yourself, creating a one-of-a-kind, sentimental piece for you to gift to friends and family.

Medium Projects

Cricut Cake Toppers

Cricut cake toppers have a little bit of added difficulty because they require some precise scoring. The Cricut maker is probably the best piece of equipment for the job, and here, we'll tell you how to do it. The scoring tool is your best bet since this will make different shapes even easier, as well. You will want to make sure you have cardstock and the cutting mat, along with a fine-point blade for cutting. The tape is also handy for these.

First, go to Design Space and choose the rosettes you want. From there, the press makes it and follow the prompts. It will then ask you whether you want the single or double wheel. Scoring shells are meant to create extra-deep score lines in materials, to get the perfect fold. The single wheel will make one crease, and the double wheel will make a parallel wheel that will crease – perfect for specialty items. Plus, the double wheel is thicker, so it's easier to fold.

Once you score everything, you remove it and replace the scoring wheel with the fine-point blade.

From here, you simply fold everything and just follow the line. This should make the rosette, and you can then use contrasting centers and create many of these to form a nice backdrop.

Cricut Gift Bags

Next, are gift bags. Remember to put the foil poster board face-down on the mat itself, to help prevent the material from cracking and showing through to the white backdrop, when you fold them together after you score them.

To make these, you want to implement the template that you'd like to use in Design Space. From here, I do suggest cutting out the initial design first, and then putting it back in to create scoring lines, following the same steps. After that, you can then take your item and fold along the score lines, and then use adhesive or glue to help put it all together. This is a great personalized way to do it but can be a bit complicated to work with at first.

Cricut Fabric Coasters

Fabric coasters with a Cricut maker are great, and they need only a few supplies. These include the maker itself, cotton fabric, fusible fleece, a rotary cutting mat or some scissors, a sewing machine, and an iron.

Cut the fabric to about 12 inches to fit the cutting mat – if it's longer, you can hang it off, just be careful.

From here, go to Design Space, then click shapes and make a heart. You can do this with other shapes, too. Resize it to about 5 inches wide. Press make it, and you'll want to make sure you create four copies. Press continue, and then choose medium fabrics similar to cotton. You then load the mat and cut, and then you do it again with the fusible fleece on the cutting mat, changing it to 4.75 inches. This time, when choosing the material, go to more, and then select fusible fleece. Cut the fusible fleece, and then attach these to the back of the heart with the iron and repeat with the second.

Sew the two shapes together, leaving a gap for stitching and the turning. Clip the curves, turn it inside out, and then fold in the edges and stitch it.

There you go – a fusible fleece heart coaster. It's a little bit more complicated, but it's worth trying out.

Difficult Projects

Giant Vinyl Stencils

Vinyl stencils are a good thing to create, too, but they can be hard. Big vinyl stencils make for an excellent Cricut project, and you can use them in various places, including bedrooms for kids.

You only need the explore Air 2, the vinyl that works for it, a pallet, sander and, of course, paint and brushes. The first step is preparing the pallet for painting, or whatever surface you plan on using this for.

From here, you create the mermaid tail (or any other large image) in Design Space. Now, you'll learn immediately that big pieces are hard to cut and impossible to do all at once in Design Space.

What you do is section of each design accordingly, and remove any middle pieces. Next, you can add square shapes to the image, slicing it into pieces so that it can be cut on a cutting mat that fits.

At this point, you cut out the design by pressing make it, choosing your material, and working in sections.

From here, you put it on the surface that you're using, piecing this together with each line, and you should have one image after piecing it all together. Then, draw out the line on vinyl and then paint the initial design. For the second set of stencils, you can simply trace the first one and then paint the inside of them. At this point, you should have the design finished. When done, remove it very carefully.

And there you have it! Bigger stencils can be a bit of a project since it involves trying to use multiple designs all at once, but with the right care and the right designs, you'll be able to create whatever it is you need to in Design Space so you can get the results you're looking for.

Cricut Quilts

Quilts are a bit hard to do for many people, but did you know that you can use Cricut to make it easier? Here, you'll learn an awesome project that will help you do this. To begin, you start with the Cricut Design Space. Here, you can add different designs that work for your project. For example, if you're making a baby blanket or quilt with animals on it, you can add little fonts with the names of the animals, or different pictures of them, too. From here, you want to make sure you choose the option to reverse the design. That way, you'll have it printed on correctly. At this point, make your quilt. Do various designs and sew the quilt as you want to.

From here, you should cut it on the iron-on heat transfer vinyl. You can choose that, and then press cut. The image will then cut into the piece.

At this point, it'll cut itself out, and you can proceed to transfer this with some parchment paper. Use an EasyPress for best results and push it down. There you go, an easy addition that will definitely enhance the way your blankets look.

Cricut Unicorn Backpack

If you're making a present for a child, why not give them some cool unicorns? Here is a lovely unicorn backpack you can try to make. To make this, you need ¾ yards of a woven fabric – something that's strong, since it will help with stabilizing the backpack. You'll also need half a yard of quilting cotton for the lining. The coordinating fabric should be around about an eighth of a yard. You'll need about a yard of fusible interfacing, some strap adjuster rings, a zipper that's about 14 inches and doesn't separate, and some stuffing for the horn.

To start, you'll want to cut the main fabric, and you should use straps, the loops, a handle, some gussets for a zipper, and the bottom and side gussets.

The lining should be done, too, and you should make sure you have the interfacing. You can use fusible flex foam, too, to help make it a little bit bulkier.

From here, cut everything and then apply the interfacing to the backside, and the flex foam should be adjusted to achieve the bulkiness you are looking for. You can trim this, too. The interfacing should be one on the backside, and then add the flex foam to the main fabric. The adhesive side of this will be on the right-hand side of the interfacing.

Fold the strap pieces in half and push one down, on each backside. Halve it, and then press it again, and stitch these closer to every edge, and also along the short-pressed edge, as well.

From here, do the same thing with the other side but add the ring for adjustment, and stitch the bottom of these to the main part of the back piece.

Then add them both to the bottom.

At this point, you have the earpieces that you should do the backside facing out. Stitch, then flip out and add the pieces.

Add these inner pieces to the outer ear, and then stitch these together.

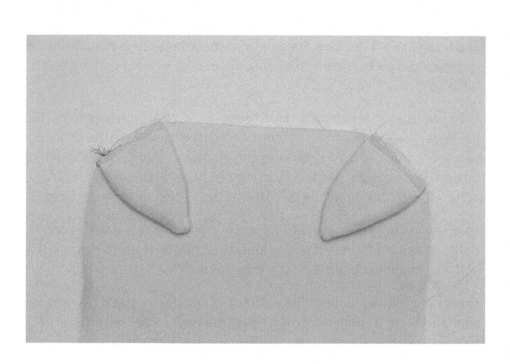

At this point, you make the unicorn face in the Design Space. You'll notice immediately when you use this program everything will be black, but you can change this by adjusting the desired layers to each color. You can also just use a template that fits, but you should always mirror this before you cut it.

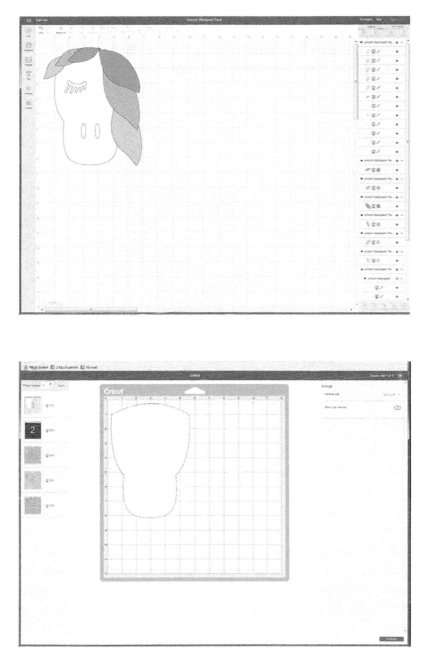

Choose vinyl, and then insert the material onto the cutting mat. From there, cut it and remove the iron-on slowly.

You will need to do this in pieces, which is fine because it allows you to use different colors. Remember to insert the right color for each cut. At this point, add the zipper, and there you go!

Diamond Planters

Finally, we have some diamond planters. These are a bit complicated, but there is a pattern to do it. Essentially, you create the diamond design and the trapezoids on top and then cut them into the chipboard. Make sure to choose a chipboard in your materials. From there, cut them, and then use masking tape to hold these pieces as you glue. When done, you essentially do the same with the trapezoid pieces and put them on top. Then, just get the outside seams. Once dried, remove the tape. This project is more complicated due to the extra steps you need to take with assembling it and getting the Cricut measurements right.

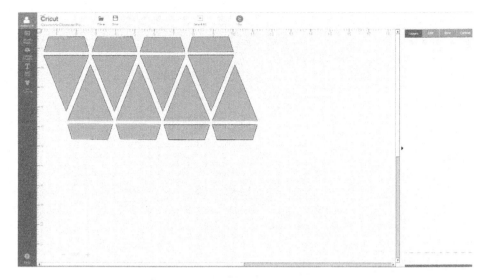

Cricut projects are fun, and with the instructions in this section of the book, you should have everything you need to get started with some of the easier, more popular projects. There are tons more out there to choose from, so once you've got a handle on the ones we've suggested, take a look and see what else you might be interested in creating. Your options are almost limitless, thanks to your Cricut machine.

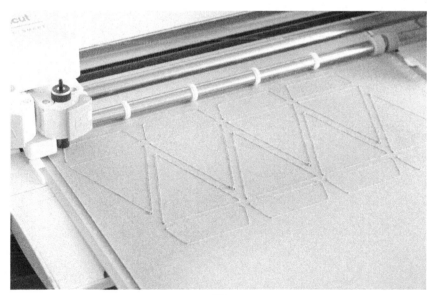

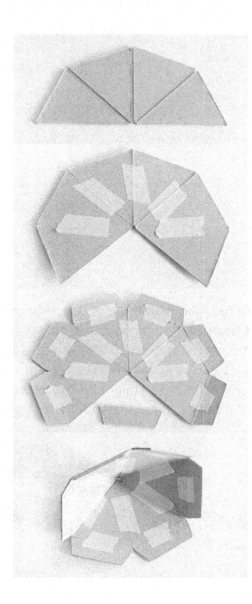

Conclusion

Cricut may seem complicated at first, but there is a lot you can do with this machine – and a lot that you can get out of it. If you feel confused by Cricut, then take your time, get familiar with the buttons, and start having fun with it.

With Cricut, anything is possible. If you've been wondering what you can do with your machine, the simple answer is almost anything. For designers, for those who like to make precise cuts, and for those who like to print their own shirts, this is a wonderful option to consider. If you are thinking of getting a Cricut machine, you'll see here that there is a lot that you can do with this unique tool, and endless creative possibilities.

The next step is simple – if you have a Cricut machine, get familiar with it. Learn more about it and see for yourself some of the fun things you can do with Cricut, and the cool basic projects you can try now.

CRICUT DESIGN SPACE™

A Beginner's Guide Illustrated and Detailed. A Step by Step Guide to Design Space and Use every Tool and Function. Basic Keyboard Shortcuts and Advanced Tips and Tricks

Kimberly Johnson

Introduction

Perhaps you've just purchased your first Cricut or you've had one for some time but haven't tried it out yet, or you are fairly skilled but aren't sure how to use the Design Space.

This book will teach you everything you need to know about using Cricut Design Space™ like a pro.

Cricut has come a long way since it was first introduced in 2006 by Provo Craft & Novelty, Inc, and has undergone many changes. The company has released many versions of its die-cutting machine as its popularity among crafters has soared.

From its inception, the Cricut has provided many ways for a crafter to make beautiful things and sell them for a nice profit.

Most of us, whether we're Cricut pros or a beginner, have seen the many items for sale at craft shows and in specialty stores. Everything from popular saying and quotes stenciled on wood signs to monogrammed water tumblers and most everything in between.

Some Cricut users have mastered the machine and they can make vinyl letters look as if they were painted onto the wood. The vinyl meshes so well that with the naked eye you won't be able to find a spot to lift one of the vinyl letters. That's how realistic it can look. And, most vinyls are weather-resistant. That means you can make all kinds of awesome things for outside as well as inside.

Cricut has come so far since the days of die-cutting for scrapbooking, and although scrapbooking is still popular, you don't see as many sheets of stickers in stores, and in some stores, the scrapbooking section has shrunk since Cricut has become so much more than your scrapbooking partner.

And that's not to say scrapbooking isn't fun, but it is to say that ideas are endless and you can make almost anything you can think of.

Best of all, many Cricut models are Bluetooth enabled, making it easy to communicate with your other devices.

One of the nice features of a Cricut machine is that it doesn't take up too much space. It's about the size of a home printer; however, you will most likely want a large workspace for your tools and materials.

What machine should I buy?

Before we get started on how to use the Design Space feature, let's review the types of machines available. There are many to choose from and for first-time buyers, it can be daunting to select the right one. We'll focus on the more recent models.

Your budget and how you intend to use the machine are big factors; however, you'll find most Cricut machines are around the same price with the exception of the Cuttlebug Machine.

This is a small, portable hand-crank machine that has a maximum cutting width of six inches. It only works with dies and embossing folders; however, it's perfect for those who are looking for a machine they can use for scrapbooking and card making.

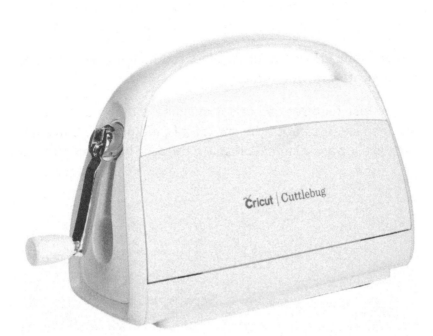

The hand-crank machine has been a staple in the Cricut family and you can usually find a new one for under $100. A used hand-crank can be far less money. If it's in good condition and that's what you want, you can sometimes find them for as low as $25 at garage sales and garage sale sites.

This year, a new model was released called The Cricut Maker™. This has all the bells and whistles to do most anything. It has the capability of cutting more materials than any previous models and the company boasts its fast, precise cutting.

The Cricut Maker can be used with your own images, which is a plus for those who prefer to use their own or don't want to buy a subscription or pay for individual images. It allows you to personalize your items and make your own statement. You can make personalized cards, signs, and anything your heart desires. The ability to personalize your items with multiple lines and fonts broadens your horizon, and if you make products to sell, you can offer personalization.

The Cricut Maker is supposed to be better than the Cricut Explore Air 2, and is considered the top-of-the-line. The Explore is promoted as being easier to use than the Maker. It works with paper, vinyl and cardstock, which is a plus.

Of course, you'll need the tools of the trade and these are sold in what are called "Bundles." There are many bundles available, and you can purchase them alone or with your machine, with the exception of the hand-crank model.

A bundle includes the machine and a set of accessories. The bundles vary; however, many include printable sticker paper, cardstock, trimmers and cutting tools, pens, and usually free project ideas. Each model comes with a different bundle.

Once you have your machine, you'll need dies. There are two options— Cricut Access and Cricut Design Space.

The two are often confused, so let's touch briefly on the differences.

Cricut Access

When you purchased your Cricut, you may have been offered a 30-day free trial for Cricut Access.

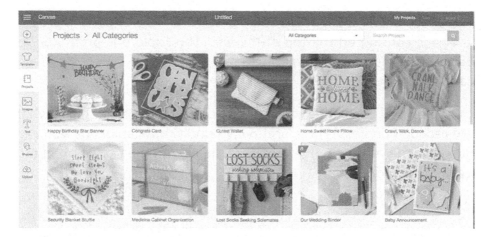

Cricut Access is a subscription-based program that gives you access to images and fonts without an extra charge, provided your subscription is up-to-date. The images and fonts are only available to those with an active subscription and if you don't pay, you'll no longer have access. The subscription is use-only; it does not allow you to keep the images and fonts. That is a common misconception.

How much you use your machine will determine if it's worth it for you to subscribe. If you're a heavy user and make a lot of different items, then a monthly or annual subscription might be right for you. This is a good choice if you're a crafter making a variety of items to sell.

Country stores and those selling folk art sometimes can't keep up with the demand for wooden or chalkboard signs. Sayings and inspirational quotes are popular right now, and if you're one of the lucky ones profiting from the craze, you'll get your money's worth from the subscription.

If you've decided a subscription is the way to go, there are three options:

The monthly basic plan currently costs $9.99 per month and is billed monthly. The annual plan is $7.99 per month with a one-time annual billing of $95.88. The premium plan costs $119.88 annually.

Of course, you might be able to find a coupon code online and save a few dollars, and the premium subscription will give you 50% off on images and fonts not included in the basic subscription.

Cricut Access is used with Design Space.

Design Space

Cricut Design Space is an app that is used with the Cricut Explore and Cricut Maker™ machines. What makes Design Space unique is that it lets you wirelessly cut your designs.

You can get Cricut Design Space from the Apple™ store as a free download.

The app offers you access to Make It Now™ projects and fonts in the Cricut Image Library along with thousands of images, according to Apple's promo.

Apple describes Cricut Design Space as an app offering the following features:

- Design and cut DIY projects with Cricut Explore and Cricut Maker cutting machines

- Choose from over 50,000 images, fonts, and projects in the Cricut Image Library—or use your own images and fonts for free

- Upload and clean up your own images

- Design and cut without an Internet connection using fonts and images downloaded to your device

- Cut quick and easy predesigned Make It Now™ projects

- Make home and party décor, cards, and invitations, scrapbooking, fashion, jewelry, kids' crafts, and more

- Cut a wide variety of materials including paper, vinyl, iron-on, cardstock, poster board, fabric—even thicker materials like leather

- Use the built-in camera on your device to position, and visualize your projects on a real-life background

- Sign in with your Cricut ID to access your images and projects and for easy checkout when making purchases on Cricut.com or in Design Space

- Bluetooth wireless capability

By now, you've probably downloaded an app from the Apple Store, so we'll bypass instructions as to how to do so. If you've never done it before, use the Apple Store help menu and it'll be self-explanatory.

With these explanations behind us, let's begin taking the steps you'll need to successfully use Cricut Design Space.

Now that we've been introduced, let's get started!

***

If you are a Windows user, Design Space is typically installed on your PC through the new machine setup process, but you can manually install it through the steps below:

Open an internet browser and go to design.cricut.com.

When the page has loaded, sign in with your Cricut ID, or create one if you don't have one.

Once signed in, select the **New Project** tile. You will receive a prompt to download and install the Design Space plugin.
Select **Download**. Watch for the screen to change as the plugin file is downloaded.

When the file is downloaded, select the file or find it in your Downloads folder to Open or Run it. If you receive a message asking if you want to allow this app to make changes to your device, select **Yes.** You may be required to enter your **computer's** "Admin" password to continue.

When you receive a notice that the Setup wizard is ready to begin installing Cricut Design Space, select **Next** to begin the installation.

The setup wizard will display the installation progress and notify you when the installation is complete. Select **Finish. Now you can** begin using Design Space.

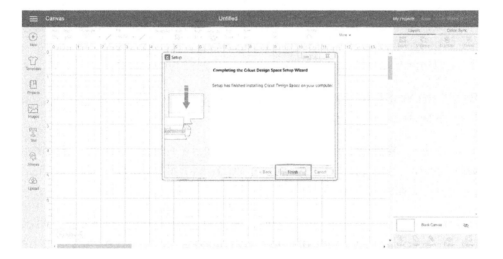

Chapter 1: Getting to Know Design Space

If you're new to Cricut or have little experience using one, it can be quite intimidating. I've had friends tell me they can't figure out how to use theirs, or they feel they aren't getting the full benefits of the machine.

That's what led me to write this book and clear up the confusion. Yes, the Cricut can be daunting, especially for the newbie or inexperienced.

I'm sure you're anxious to start your first project, and understandably so. You've seen all the amazing things it can do and ideas are swirling in your mind. Cards, gifts, home decorations... you can't wait!

But wait! You want to prevent disasters and, yes, they can happen, so let's start from the beginning.

The Cricut Design Space is cutting software that has a canvas area where you'll do your design work, such as uploading images. It also provides a plethora of fonts.

Before you do anything, you'll need to go to the Cricut website and set up an account. This will provide you with a homepage that will be unique to you. Sign-up is simple and free. You'll need to create an access ID and password.

Once you've set up your account, you'll want to go to your page, which is broken down into six areas: canvas, design panel, edit and text edit bar, layer panel and color sync panel.

The design panel allows you to start a new project, complete a project, add images and upload your own images. There is also an edit bar so you can undo an action and redo it if necessary.

72

The tool bar at the top gives you plenty of options to layout your work by aligning it, size, rotate, etc. You'll find almost all the same tools as you would in a Microsoft Word toolbar.

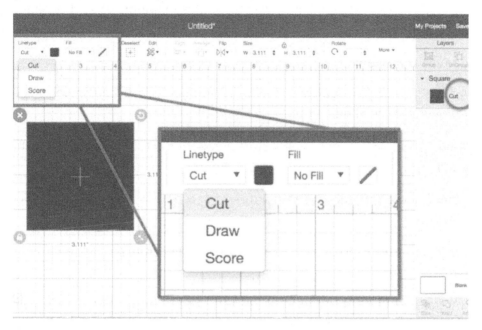

These are user-friendly and self-explanatory, so you shouldn't have any problem learning them.

Next, well look at some important words and terms to know.

Cheat Sheets

There are many cheat sheets available on the internet and you simply need to type "Design space cheat sheets" into the search bar. You'll have many options to explore that will help you with any of the six areas mentioned above.

The cheat sheets are filled with tips and tricks from getting you up and running to doing complex projects.

The cheat sheets are free from most sites, and Pinterest has many to choose from. You can also purchase them on Etsy. They aren't expensive, but chances are you can find what you're looking for at no cost. It's just a matter of searching through the hundreds or thousands available online.

Canvas Overview

As we noted, the canvas is where you'll do your designing. The following tips will help you get to know the canvas.

New - This icon is where you'll start a new project. Simply click on it to begin.

Templates - You can use templates to see how your finished project will look.

Projects - You can use this icon for browsing projects, including your own.

Images - This is where you can select images from the Cricut Image Library and insert them into your canvas. You can also upload your own images.

Text - This icon allows you to add text to your design.

Shapes - You can add shapes by clicking this icon.

Upload - The upload icon allows you access to Cut What You Want and upload what you want for free in your desired file format.

Tip: Remember that by clicking the Cricut icon, you will return to your homepage.

Cricut Vocabulary

These are some of the most common technical terms you'll hear when discussing Cricut. They are provided courtesy of HTV Addict, and they are written in simple terms.

Design Space – The cloud based Cricut software for making your projects accessed at https://us.cricut.com

Siser Easyweed – Most popular manufacturer of Heat Transfer Vinyl.

631 – Removable vinyl (Indoor, used for stencils, temporary wall designs, and window cling).

651 – Permanent vinyl (Outdoor, weatherproof).

951 – Permanent vinyl (Marine grade – the higher the number the stronger grade of adhesive!).

Oracal – Oracal is a manufacturer of adhesive vinyl (631, 651, 951, etc.) commonly used by crafters.

Printable vinyl – vinyl you can put through your inkjet or laser printer (make sure you use the correct type for your printer!!) usually used with Print and Cut function in Design Space.

There are also the less technical terms to assist you in getting to know your Cricut compiled by ShopCraftables.

Attach

You'll find the attach tool in Design Space. This tool holds your cuts in the same position on the cutting mat as they are on the design screen.

AutoBlade

The Silhouette cutting blade automatically adjusts to the recommended cut settings based on the material type the user has selected from the Send > Material panel in Silhouette Studio. This blade is only compatible with the CAMEO 3 and the Portrait 2. The Autoblade can only be used in the left carriage of the CAMEO 3.

Contour

If you want to hide part of an image, the Contour tool will remove any unwanted cut lines. You can use this feature in Design Space.

Compound path

When all of the cut lines are grouped together. To edit a design with compound paths right click and then click "release compound path."

Cut lines

Cut lines are the lines that outline the shape you are trying to cut. They are red or gray lines that indicate where the machine will cut. Without cut lines, the Silhouette will not cut. Cut lines also indicate where the sketch pens will draw when using the sketch function.

Decal

The end result when you cut shapes into vinyl.

Designer Edition

The paid upgrade of Silhouette Studio that allows the user access to more features and tools.

Edit Points

The dots on lines in a design that indicate where the line curves and moves to form a shape. You can manipulate edit points to change the shape of the design.

Firmware

The program that exists on your cutting machine. Firmware updates can be done by plugging your machine into your computer.

Floating Panels

Windows that open with options and controls when a right sidebar tool icon is selected. Multiple floating panels can be kept open in the work area at the same time. Panels can also be moved around, snapped together, and collapsed while remaining in the work area.

Force

Or the "thickness" setting, the force setting determines how much pressure the blade will use to cut.

Group / Ungroup

A command that enables you to bunch multiple layers, images, or text together. This is helpful to do when arranging your workspace so that all the elements you are working with stay together when you move them and won't affect how your images are laid out on the cutting mat. You can ungroup layers, images, or text so that they move and size independently.

Heat Transfer Vinyl

HTV for short, is a specialty vinyl that can be used on certain fabrics/materials to create designs. It is a thin, flexible vinyl with an adhesive backing that is activated with heat. It comes in roll or sheet form with an adhesive backing and a carrier sheet so it can be cut, weeded, and placed on fabric.

Inkscape

Inkscape is a free graphic design software that can be used to trace images, create vectors, and SVG files. You can find it at: https://inkscape.org/en/

JPG & PNG Files

Types of files. You can tell if a file is a JPEG if it ends in .jpg and PNG will end in .png. You can use these files in Design Space or Silhouette Studio by tracing them and turning them into SVGs. This will be an easy process with clip art/black and white images but might require outside software if it is a photograph.

Kiss cut

When the cut made by the machine only cuts through the top layer- such as when only the top vinyl layer is cut when making a decal.

License Key

The 16 digit code that can be purchased to upgrade Silhouette Studio to one of the three upgraded versions of the software: Designer Edition, DE+, or Business Edition. License Keys can be activated through the Help menu in Silhouette Studio and are stored in the My Account tab in the user's Silhouette America account.

Mirrored Image

A necessary step before you cut any HTV. All images that have been mirrored will appear reversed when cut.

Offset

The act of creating an equal distance border - at any distance of your choosing - around the border of a design. Offsets are automatically welded in Silhouette Studio when possible. Offsets can be used to make a border for a design or text and even to thicken fonts for easier cutting and weeding. You can also create an internal offset which creates an offset at the selected distance inside the design rather than around the outside.

Print then cut

A feature in both Silhouette and Cricut design software which allows you to use your home printer to print a design and your cutting machine to die cut your design.

Printable vinyl

Vinyl that can be sent through your inkjet/home printer. You can print on it from DS or Silhouette Studio and then have your machine die cut it, also called print and cut function. Comes in heat transfer and adhesive varieties.

Registration Marks

Marks that are printed on printable vinyl when using the print then cut function. These marks are then read on your Cricut or Silhouette when cutting inkjet printable vinyl.

Reveal Grid

Exposing the grid lines, from the Page Set-Up window, on the work area in Silhouette Studio. Grid lines on the virtual mat correspond to grid lines on the Silhouette cutting mat to make placement of material easier and more accurate.

Reverse Weeding

The act of removing the area of the vinyl that would normally be left behind. This technique is mostly used when creating stencils.

Scraper/Squeegee

A flat tool used to smooth or secure decals or transfer tape. A credit card makes a great squeegee/scraper!

Shear

A feature in Silhouette Studio Designer Edition that slants the design or text by an exact degree.

Silhouette Studio

The free program that comes with Silhouette. You can download or update this program here: https://www.silhouetteamerica.com/software

Sketching

An action that can be performed by your machine if the blade is replaced with a sketch pen.

Slice

The slice tool creates new cut paths from two images, resulting in three or more completely new shapes. Each of the new shapes will show up in the Layers panel as individual layers.

Software

The program that exists on your computer, whether it be Silhouette Studio or Design Space.

Spatula

A tool used to help remove small pieces of vinyl or paper from the mat.

SVG

A type of file that is a scalable vector. That means that it is a traced image that can be made larger or smaller without losing resolution. These types of files are editable in Design Space and the Design Edition of Silhouette Studio.

Trace

A function in Silhouette Studio which reads JPEGs, GIFs, PNGs and PDFs and traces them, therefore creating SVGs/cut files.

Teflon

A thin, waxy sheet that can be used when ironing HTV. A teflon sheet should always be placed between an iron/heat press and HTV to protect your iron or heat press.

Text to Path

The action of manipulating text by forcing it to curve around another object or shape such as a circle. When the text is converted to a path, it will keep its new shape.

Transfer Tape

Transfer tape is the sticky material that is used to transfer adhesive vinyl from the carrier sheet to the surface of your project.

Weeding

The process of removing unwanted vinyl from a decal.

Weeding Lines

Cut lines put around a design to make the weeding process easier.

Weld

You'll need to use the weld tool when you want to join shapes to create a single image by removing any overlapping cut lines in your design. Welding is a necessary step when cutting cursive letters.

Work Area

The virtual mat area where designing takes place in Silhouette Studio.

Zip File

A compressed, or smaller sized file. It is usually a folder with files inside. You will need to Unzip the file to get access to the contents. Windows has an unzip feature built in- right click on zip file and choose Open With > Windows Explorer. Mac OS X users can unzip a zip file by double-clicking the file.

I hope that putting these in one place for you helps so that you aren't searching all over the World Wide Web for one definition. A Google search brings back hundreds of results and it can be overwhelming to find one specific thing. You likely won't memorize all of these terms right away, but over time, you may realize that you speak the Cricut language fluently.

There is a learning curve with the Cricut machine, no matter which model you choose, and there are many things with the Cricut that you'll acclimate to with time. You can't expect to learn everything at once, and a lot of it will come as you work on your projects.

It's important that you don't feel overwhelmed and become frustrated. Using your Cricut is like learning anything else; the more you do it and the more familiar you become with it, the easier it will be for you. Soon, you'll be a master and will be able to make anything and everything you want. Just hang in there as you go through the learning curve.

Tip: Cricut Design Space will not work with a Chromebook. You need either a Mac or Windows operating system, and that can be a PC, MacBook, tablet, or mobile device.

Chapter 2: Project Design

You know the vocabulary and where to locate icons on your canvas. Now, you're ready to design your first project, but where do you begin?

At the beginning, of course! Let me walk you through it.

Starting a New Project - The Basics

When starting a new project, you'll want to know what that project will be and what materials you will be using before doing anything else.

For example, if you want to cut vinyl letters to place on wood, you'll need to know all of your dimensions so your letters fit evenly and centered on the wood. You'll need wood that vinyl can adhere to without the risk of peeling. And you'll want to make certain that your wood is sanded and finished to your desire because you don't want any imperfections. You may find even with store-bought wood pieces advertised as ready-to-use, there are tiny imperfections.

You want to make sure when working with fabric that you know what inks or vinyls will adhere to the surface. You don't want any peeling or cracking to happen to your beautiful design.

When working with any kind of fabric, including canvas bags, you'll want to prewash for sizing because shrinkage after your design has been set can cause the design to become distorted.

If you aren't sure exactly what you want to do, have something in mind so that you aren't wasting a lot of materials by trial and error. The cost of crafting materials can add up, so you'll want to eliminate as much potential waste as possible.

If you're new to Cricut Design Space, start with something simple. You don't want to get in over your head. That's the worst thing you can do when you learn any new craft. There are many used Cricut machines for sale, and while some users sell because they upgraded, others are users who gave up. You made the investment and you'll want to get a return on that investment.

Ready to conquer Cricut Design Space?

Before we begin, it's important to note that Cricut has announced some changes to Design Space as of January 2019. " ...we moved Linetype (Cut, Draw, Score), Print Then Cut, and color selection from the layers panel to the edit toolbar."

To keep up with any changes, you should subscribe to the company email list or check the Cricut website often.

Let's begin by clicking on "New" from our menu options. It's at the very top of the canvas in the left corner.

An empty canvas will appear. You might have previously started a project, and in that case, the machine will detect it in the queue, and you'll be asked if you want to replace the project. If you don't want to replace it, be sure you save all of your changes or you might lose them, and you don't want to lose all of your hard work. It's important to not rush so that you don't accidentally delete a project you want to be saved. When you've completed that action, you'll be returned to your new blank canvas.

First, you want to name your project. Use a name that closely relates to it so you aren't getting projects confused. If you have a lot of projects, and you don't use a system to identify them, you might want to consider it.

As you can see from our illustration, everything you need is on the left, under the "new" icon.

You can review different templates by clicking on the templates icon, however, these are only for viewing to get an idea of how your final project will look.

- Here's a brief overview of each icon. They are pretty self-explanatory, but they are worth reviewing for the new Cricut user.

- Projects allows you to access the Make It Now™ platform. There are so many to choose from and you might find yourself spending a lot of time looking at them all.

- Images is just what it says. This is the icon you need to add an image or images to your project.

- Text is for writing the text if your project has words.

- Shapes allows you to add different shapes such as circles, squares and hearts.

- Upload your images and/or begin cutting. This is the final design step!

If you know what your project is going to be, you can go to the "projects" icon and begin to customize it or start cutting.

We have talked about subscriptions, and it should be noted that you can purchase a one-time design for a nominal fee. You can also purchase designs from Etsy and other craft sites.

When you've done your design, don't forget to save it. You will get the option of "save" or "save as." You will get a message letting you know that your project was successfully saved. "Save as" will save your project as a new one and keep the old one under its name. You will need to rename your project with the save as feature.

It's easy to get so caught up in the design process and anxious to see our finished project that we can forget to hit "save." Your project should automatically save in cloud, but if it doesn't, you'll have it. It's always better to be safe than sorry.

Now, you've brought your design to your screen. You want to give it a final look and make certain everything is where you want it. If you're ready to cut, click "Make It."

If your Cricut machine isn't turned on, do it now and have all your materials ready. You'll want to follow the prompts. Set your material and load your tools and mat. Press the go icon and wait. When the cutting is done, press unload and carefully remove the mat.

Viola! Your project is finished. Wasn't that easy?

Machine Reset

The Cricut machine is like any other machine, and it can have problems. You may need to do a hard reset if you can't resolve the problem any other way. When troubleshooting, it's critical to follow the manufacturer's instructions. To do otherwise can damage your machine and void your warranty. For that reason, I am giving you the specific instructions from the manufacturer's website.

You want to make certain that you follow these steps in the proper order and use the instructions that are specific to your model.

The Cricut website recommends you do the following to reset the Expression, Create, Personal, Cake, and Cake Mini:

1. Turn the machine on with NO cartridge loaded.

2. Roll all of the gray dials down to their lowest setting.

3. Grasp the blade assembly and use it to pull the entire carriage car along its track to the far left of the machine.

4. Back where the carriage car usually sits there is a red button. Press that button and hold it down for about 3 seconds.

5. Move the gray carriage car back into place.

6. Roll all of the gray dials all the way up and all the way down three times - three times for each dial.

7. Press the Cut button, then turn the machine off.

8. Set the Speed, Pressure, and Size for the type of paper.

9. Load a cartridge, turn the machine on, select a simple image and attempt a practice cut.

To reset the Expression 2 machine, the official website recommends the following:

1. Power off the Expression 2 machine.

2. Hold down the magnifying glass, pause, and power buttons all at the same time.

3. Hold until the machine gives a rainbow screen; then release the buttons.

4. Follow the on-screen directions.

5. Repeat this process one more time.

Basic Object Editing

The canvas comes equipped with an editing toolbar that allows you to make corrections.

If you make a mistake, you can easily fix it. You can use the "undo" and "redo" buttons by clicking them the required number of times.

The undo icon will let you get rid of something you don't like. It acts like an eraser, and each click will undo the previous action.

If you accidentally delete something, you can use the redo button. This will restore your work.

Another editing tool is the linetype dropdown that will let you change to a cut, draw, or score object. It communicates with your machine so it knows what tools you're going to be using.

Cut is the default linetype you'll use unless you've uploaded a JPEG or PNG image. When you click on the "make it" icon, those designs will be cut.

Use Draw if you want to write on your design. You'll be prompted to select a pen, and you'll use this to write or draw.

Tip: This option won't color your designs.

You can use the score feature to score or dash your design.

The edit icon lets you cut, copy, and paste from the canvas. It functions with a dropdown menu and you use it by selecting the elements you want to edit from your canvas.

The program also features an align tool that will let you move your design around on the canvas. If you've used a design program before, this should be easy for you to do. If you haven't, it can be tricky.

Functions of the alignment tool

The following are the functions you can use to move your design on the canvas. You might want to practice using these until you're comfortable with them.

Align allows you to align all of your designs by selecting two or more elements on your canvas.

Align Left will move everything to the left.

Center Horizontal will align horizontally and will center text and images. This brings everything to the center.

Align Right will move everything to the right.

Align Top will move the designs you select to the top of the canvas.

Center Vertically will align your selections vertically.

Align Bottom will bring your selections to the bottom.

Center will bring everything to the center, vertically and horizontally.

You can also distribute vertically and horizontally. This will give you some space between your design elements.

You can also flip, arrange, rotate, and size your design. All of these features are handy, and once you master them you can quickly align your design to your preference.

Chapter 3: Using Images in Design Space

Selecting the image, you want to use can be fun. There are so many to choose from and you'll enjoy browsing the library.

You'll want to start by browsing the Cricut Image Library. There you will find cartridges, called image sets, where you can choose your designs.

How to Browse and Search for Cartridges

To begin, select the "images" icon in the design panel to the left of the canvas. A new window should appear with the Image Library. You'll next select the "cartridges" tab at the top of the screen to browse all the available cartridges. There are over 400 cartridges to choose from. You should see the cartridge name and a sample of the image. It will tell you if the cartridge is free or if it can be purchased individually or is a part of the subscription plan.

You don't have to search alphabetically. You can type all or part of a cartridge name into the search bar and click on the magnifying glass icon. You then click "view all images" to browse your search results.

Once you've made your selection, simply click the "Insert Images" button and they will be added to the canvas. Once added to the canvas, you can size your image(s) and move them around on the canvas. You can get an idea of where you want your image and how it will look on your final project.

It can be more cost effective to purchase entire cartridges than to purchase individual images if your selection isn't included in the free offerings.

Searching for Cartridge with Filters

If you want to search for cartridges with filters, you simply click on the cartridge icon and select the Filters menu in the top right corner of the screen. This will bring up all available filters.

There are three ways to search: alphabetical order, cartridge type, or by specific cartridge. When you find the filter you want, select "Apply" to transfer it to your canvas.

How to Purchase Images

- My Cartridges – This includes all cartridges that are free, linked, purchased, and part of Cricut Access. You must be a member to have access to these.

- Free – These cartridges can be used without a subscription or a one-time purchase.

- Cricut Access – These cartridges are accessible with your subscription.

- Purchased – These are the cartridges you've already purchased and are added to your canvas.

These are your four options for obtaining images. I've included how to access them for free for those who don't want to spend money on images or have their own.

We did cover the subscription plans in Chapter 1, and it's good to check the Cricut website for any price changes and the features each subscription entitles you to.

Uploading Your Own Images

You can upload your own images in the file formats .jpg, .gif, .png, .bmp, .svg, and .dxf.

Design Space will let you upload your images for free and will convert them into shapes that you can cut.

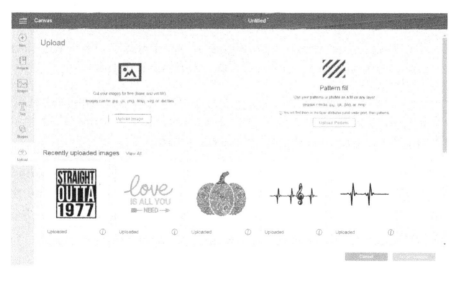

There are two different ways your images are uploaded, depending on the file type.

Basic images are compatible with .jpg, .gif, .png, and .bmp file types. These files are uploaded as a single layer, and you have the ability to edit the images during the upload process.

Vector images include .svg and .dxf file types. These files are designed before you upload to your canvas. They will automatically be separated into layers after uploading and saving.

To begin a basic upload, click Upload from the Design Panel on the left side of the screen. A window will open and prompt you to choose image or pattern to upload. Click the image you want, and click the upload icon again. It's that simple!

How to Edit Images using the Slice Tool

Many Cricut users do all their editing separately because it seems too difficult to do on the machine. Let's walk through the process, so you'll be able to do this with ease once you've had a little practice.

First, you need to add your uploaded image to your canvas by clicking on the image and then clicking "Insert Images." You can add one more image at this time.

You can make your image a bit bigger if you need to. Click the right-bottom corner and drag it down so you can see it better.

There's no erase option, so if there's something in your image that you don't want, you'll have to use the Slice tool. This can be a bit more difficult than simply erasing with the eraser tool.

You'll need to click on "Shapes" on the left side, and click the square. You'll see a lock icon on the left-bottom of the circle just below the square. This will unlock it and give you the freedom to move it wherever you'd like.

Place it over the part of the image you want to erase. This should bring up a bubble. Your square and your image should be highlighted. Make sure they are and click the Slice tool. You'll find it in the bottom-right corner.

You can begin to pull away the pieces and delete them. You may have to repeat this several times before you've erased the parts of the image that you want gone. This will depend on the size of your erasure.

Be sure to save your changes.

Editing Images in Upload Mode

This is an easy process for editing your uploaded image. But first, you need to upload an image from your computer.

When it's uploaded, click on the complete icon and a window should open. Look to the top-left corner of your canvas and you should see a wand. Place it over the part of the image you want to erase and click once. Click continue and you'll need to type in a name for your image and click the save button. That part of the image should be gone. You'll repeat the steps for each part of the image you want erased.

When you have erased everything you want, you need to make sure it's named before you save it and close it.

Insert both images on to your Cricut Design Space canvas. Once you have them there you can put them back together.

95

The nice thing about this feature is that you can do more than erase. If you want to change a color, the same process applies.

Editing doesn't have to be a difficult task, and the more you get to know your Circuit and the Design Space, the easier it will be to upload and edit your own images.

Create Layers and Separate Objects

There are many features for creating layers. This can be complex if you're not accustomed to using the many features your Cricut offers. We will review them separately so you can understand each one. You will want to practice before cutting your project.

Group/Ungroup - You can group multiple layers, images, or text together using the group function. They will move and size together on your design canvas.

The ungroup function will let you move and size layers, images, or text separately.

Duplicate – To duplicate an object, you simply copy and paste to create multiples of the same object.

Delete – Deleting will remove your selected object from the canvas. If you do this in error, you can undo this action.

Slice - Slicing will split two overlapping layers.

Weld - When you want to join multiple layers to create one object, use the meld function.

Attach/Detach - When you attach, you hold your objects in position so that objects will cut, draw, or score separately from the other layers.

Flatten/Unflatten - When you want to convert an image into a printable image, use the flatten feature. This will merge the layers you selected into a single layer. Unflatten does the opposite, separating layers from one printable image into separate printable layers.

Contour - Contouring will hide or show contour lines or cut paths on a layer. If your image uses more than one layer, be sure to Ungroup first for Contour to work.

Visible/Hidden Layer - When the eyeball icon is open, it indicates that the layer is visible on the canvas and it's safe to cut, draw, score, or print. Hidden layers will not cut, draw, score, or print and you simply click the icon to hide them. Click again to unhide.

In the next chapter I'll explain some imaging tips if you want to upload any images from Photoshop and other illustration programs. You can upload your artwork from these programs to Design Space easily.

Chapter 4: Advanced Tips and Tricks

There are so many advanced tricks you can do with Cricut Design Space, and the more proficient you become with your machine, the more you'll want to dive into some of the more complex features.

I'll review mirrored images and how to shadow letters. We'll look at some illustration programs and how you can make them work in Cricut Design Space.

Some of these features are more advanced, and as you've probably learned by now, there's a lot to learn if you want to use all of them. It will take a lot of time and patience to get to know all Cricut Design Space does, and you'll want to take it slow unless you can find a class locally. Some areas offer classes at libraries, craft shops, or community colleges. Yes, there is that much to learn, and with new features being added from time to time, it can feel as if you can't keep up with the changes.

As I mentioned in Chapter 1, there are many levels of Cricut users. Some are so intimidated by it, that they order one and it will sit in the box for months. This book was written to help you have the courage to open the box and start enjoying your machine.

For those with minimal skills, this book can help you to become more experienced.

For those who are experienced and know the Cricut like the back of their hand, this book will offer some new tips (hopefully) and will serve as a handy reference guide.

So, before we conclude, let's explore more features...some simple, some a bit more difficult.

Working with Text

There is a lot to working with text and at first glance, it looks dizzying, but really, it's not. Let's start with adding text so you can personalize your projects.

Adding text

You'll want to begin by inserting text onto the design screen. You do that by clicking the "Text Tab" located in the design panel on the left. You should get a blank text box with a text edit field. If you've worked with PDF editing, you'll know how to use this feature. Type your text into the text edit field. It will appear in the edit field. Once you've typed the text you want, you can size it, move it, or rotate it.

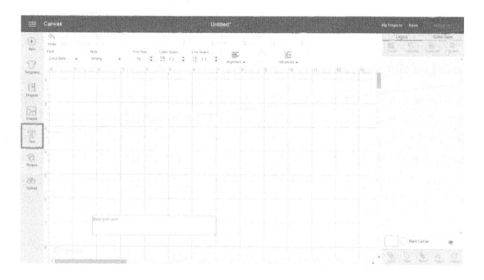

Now you can move, size, and rotate the text by clicking the black area of any letter. The "Bounding Box" appears around your text when it is selected and you can make an edit in each corner if you prefer to do any editing. You can then click the solid area of any letter to view the Bounding Box.

By clicking the red "x" in the top-left corner of the Bounding Box, you can remove text from the design screen.

Click and hold the circular arrow icon on the top-right corner of the Bounding Box if you want to rotate the text. You'll have to drag it to where you want it.

If you want to change the width and height while keeping the text proportional, use the closed lock icon at the bottom-left corner. If you want to Unlock the aspect ratio, click the lock of the same name. Unlocking the aspect ratio will let you resize the image.

The Sizing Handle is used to size the text by clicking and holding its icon in the bottom-right corner of the Bounding Box. You can drag it in any direction to see the text change.

The Rotation Handle allows you to change the orientation of the text in 45-degree increments.

Text Edit Bar Overview

The Text Edit Bar is located at the top of the canvas. The Font menu allows you to change your text to one of the hundreds of font choices, depending on whether or not you have Cricut Access. Cricut Access fonts are identified by a green "a" symbol. There are also fonts that you can purchase individually. You can filter the font library so you know which are System Fonts, Cricut Fonts, or All Fonts.

The program also allows you to search for fonts by name, if you know the name. To do so, simply type the name in the search bar in the upper right-hand corner. You can also search by style. For example, if you want a font that is available in bold, simply type "Bold" into the search bar.

A neat feature is that you can mouse over some sample text to preview the alphabet and numerals for that particular font.

The Style menu allows you to select your style from regular, bold, italic, or bold Italic. Not all fonts have all styles. You may find some that are only available in regular or only regular and bold. You can adjust the size of the font with the "Font Size" menu.

With the "Letter Space" menu, you can adjust the spacing between each letter within the text. The up and down arrows are for increasing or decreasing the amount of space between each letter. You will be able to see how this looks on your canvas. You can adjust paragraph spacing with the Line Space menu.

With the "Alignment" menu, you can align a paragraph to the left, right, centered, or justified.

If you've used MS Word or Apple Pages, you'll notice the toolbars and functions are almost identical. If you regularly use these features on a word processing program, you should have no problem using them with your Cricut Design Space.

For more advanced features, head to the "Advanced" menu. There are many options for you to choose such as rotating, resizing, coloring, and deleting.

Selecting a Font

I mentioned that there are hundreds of fonts and we talked about them briefly. You might think that it's overwhelming to search for a font and pick the right one for your project. You will be surprised to learn how easy it is. As we noted above, you can tell which are the free fonts and which are a one-time purchase or a subscription-based purchase.

When your text has been added to your project, you can go to the Font menu to make your selection. Next, click on the drop-down menu in the Text Edit Bar. This will allow you to view the available fonts.

You might want to practice searching for different font styles and sizes. For example, you can search "Georgia" or "Comic Sans." You can then filter your search results by "All," "System (the fonts on your computer)," or "Cricut."

You can't accidentally purchase a font, as you'll be asked if you want to buy the font. You can decline this and you won't have to worry about being charged.

The filter will allow you to narrow your search results even more by selecting single-layers, which are fonts with one layer; multi-layer with more than one layer; writing style, which is similar to handwritten text; and "My Fonts," which are your subscription-based fonts or your pre-purchased fonts.

When you find the font you want to use, you'll need to position your mouse over the row. After viewing your sample, you can then make your selection.

Text Sizing

You'll be using the Bounding Box around the text to define the image size. When sizing, you can keep the size ratio consistent so the length and width stay proportional. You can also size the length and width separately. There are three options you can choose from to size your text with a constant ratio, or keeping it proportional.

● Size text using the Bounding Box (in a Locked state)

● Size text by changing the dimensions in the Edit Panel

● Size text by changing the point size in the Edit Panel. Select a solid portion of the text so the Bounding Box appears around it. The Sizing Handle will appear in the lower right corner of the Bounding Box.

Click the Sizing Handle and drag it diagonally to make the image larger or smaller. As you make changes, the text dimensions will be shown near the text.

Once image sizing is complete, the Edit Panel will show the updated image size.

Size Text by Changing the Dimensions in the Edit Panel

Click on the text so the Bounding Box appears. Select your image and you will see the size in the Edit Panel. Next, you need to click in the box next to "Width" or "Length." You will then type in a size. This will change your size within the Edit Panel.

Size Text in the Edit Panel

Click on the text to bring up the Bounding Box. Selected your image and you will see the point size (pt) in the Edit Panel. Click in the point size field and type in the number that you want.

Working with Multiple Lines of Text

Another nice feature of Design Space is that you can add multiple lines of text to your project, allowing to personalize with a favorite quote, the names and dates of birth of your children, your surname and the names of all your family members, the names of your pets, and most anything that will fit in your designated space.

If your child plays a sport, you can add their team name and jersey number and even their stats or a quote related to the sport they're playing.

With the adhesive vinyls, you can decorate water bottles, mason jars, calendars, phone cases, plates, tote bags, beer koozies, and the list goes on and on. You can sell personalized beer koozies, calendars, etc. to businesses and make a tidy profit. You can make ornaments for your family and friends as gifts.

With so much you can do with your Cricut, you want to take advantage of all the features and with the ability to add multiple-line text, it opens a whole new world whether you Cricut for profit or for yourself.

What's even more fun is that you can edit text using a single font style or with multiple styles. Here's an example:

Merry Christmas

from

Susan and Stephen

So, you see how we can change the font on our example. Of course, you can make yours better looking than my example. I just wanted to give you an idea of how you can switch it up.

Here's how:

To edit text using a single text box and only one font style, you must first go to the "Add Text" box to bring it to your screen. Your text should appear as a single image in the Layers panel.

By default, the text will align to the left, just as with any word processing program. You can realign the text by clicking on the Edit tab, and that will open your Edit panel. Choose the alignment option that you prefer.

Your text will appear on the Mat Preview and should show as you arranged it.

Next, we will explore how to edit text using multiple text boxes and multiple font styles.

First, you need to click the add text icon to add a text box to your screen.

Type your first line and each subsequent line. Each text box should appear in the Layers Panel. You can arrange them here if you'd like.

Next, open the text edit bar and select your font and make all your adjustments. You can adjust the alignment and the size or style. If you want to move your letters, you can also do so now using the letter spacing option.

While your text is in the Layers Panel it is attached and you'll no longer be able to edit. If you are ready to cut, you can begin the process by clicking the "Make It" icon. Be sure you have everything as you want it. Your text should be exactly as you arranged it on the mat and should cut in the same manner.

Writing on Your Project

Design Space has fonts designed to be drawn with a pen. They will look like handwriting, and it provides a nice, homemade look to your finished product.

These script-style fonts can be found by searching "writing" in the font search bar. You'll be able to pick a style and color from the drop-down menu. Your new font will be displayed.

Using the attach feature, you need to select which layer the text should be written on. When your images have been selected, click "Attach." At this point, your text should be converted to an image and written on the layer it's attached to. You can now click the "Make It" icon to go to your preview screen.

Your images should appear on the preview screen in the same manner as you have them arranged on your project.

When you begin the cutting process, you will need to insert your pen.

Working with Color

You can visualize your final project by selecting the colors for your individual image layers. The images are separated by color and placed on the mats. Layers with the same color should be positioned on the same mats.

The image color can be changed from either the Color Sync Panel or the Layer Attributes Panel.

Using the Color Sync Panel

If you want to consolidate the colors of your project, you can do that easily with the Sync Panel. This will help you to reduce the number of different materials needed. To sync layer colors, you need to drag an image layer and drop it onto another layer in the color you want to match.

The Sync Panel helps you consolidate colors within your project to reduce the number of different materials needed and also the number of cutting mats. When syncing colors, you can change a single layer individually or all layers of a specific color at once.

Changing a single layer color individually

To open the Sync Panel, you first need to click the Sync Tab. The panel should show your layers sorted by color. You want to drag a layer thumbnail to a different color so it will move to the new color. If done correctly, the new color will change on the canvas.

Changing a Color Row to a Different Color

Again, we begin by clicking the Sync Tab to open the Sync Panel. The panel should show your layers sorted by color. Click the color bar on the left side of the row. Hold and drag your color bar to a different color. All the tiles on the row should move to the new color. If done properly, these will show on the canvas.

Custom Color Picker

Adding colors to your design makes them pop, and if you want to be colorful, you'll want to use the custom color picker. It gives you plenty of color options.

Begin by clicking on the layer thumbnail in the Layers Panel. Once there, you need to go to the Layer Attributes Panel. You'll see the eye-dropper icon, and when you click on that the Custom Color Selector will appear.

To change the color across the spectrum, you need to move the vertical slider up or down. When you stop moving the slider, the color will be reflected on the canvas and in the Layers Panel.

You can then select a specific hue within the color spectrum by moving the circle within the square color area.

When you have the color that you want, click anywhere outside of the Layer Attributes Panel to close it.

Hex Values

We will do a brief overview of Hex values. They are codes that represent color. The six-digit Hex value may include numbers, letters, or both. In the custom color picker, Hex values allow you to select a very specific color for your images.

To begin, click the layer thumbnail in the Layers Panel. The Layer Attributes Panel will appear and display the Hex Value Field. From there, you can enter the hex code.

Once you've typed the six-digit hex value into the field at the bottom of the Layer Attributes Panel, the new color will be reflected on the Canvas and in the Layers Panel.

You can click anywhere outside of the line type panel when you're ready to close it.

When you select the colors for individual image layers, you can see what your final project will look like and determine how the images will be laid out on the cutting mats.

The Cricut blog suggests that "all changes to layer colors need to be made prior to flattening the image. If you would like to change the colors of a flattened image, you will need to unflatten it first."

There are three ways to select new colors for images with a Print line type: basic colors swatches, custom color picker, and Hex values.

Basic Colors Swatches

To quickly select a color of an image layer with a Print line type, use one of the 30 Basic Colors offered in the Basic Colors swatches.

Click the layer thumbnail in the Layers Panel.

You'll find the Basic Colors swatches on the Layer Attributes Panel under Colors.

Select a color by clicking on one of the Basic Colors swatches. The new color is reflected on the Canvas and in the Layers Panel. Click outside of the Layer Attributes Panel to close it.

Custom Color Picker

You have many more color options for your designs when you use the Custom Color picker.

Click the layer thumbnail in the Layers Panel.

You'll find the Custom Color picker on the Layer Attributes Panel under Colors.

Click on the eyedropper icon for the Custom Color selector to appear.

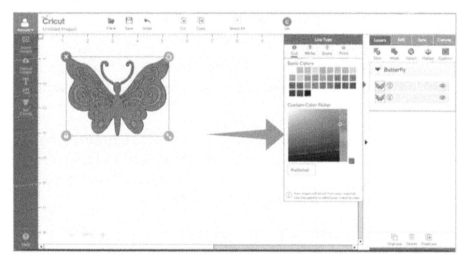

Move the vertical slider up or down to change the color across the spectrum. The new color is reflected on the Canvas and in the Layers Panel.

Select a specific hue within the color family by moving the circle within the square color area. Click outside of the Layer Attributes Panel to close it.

Hex values are codes that represent color. The 6-digit hex value may include numbers, letters, or a combination of both. In the Custom Color picker, hex values allow you to select a very specific color for your images.

Click on the layer "thumbnail" in the Layers Panel.

The Layer Attributes Panel appears and displays the Hex Value Field where you can enter the hex code.

Type the six-digit hex value into the field just above the Custom Color picker. The new color is reflected on the Canvas and in the Layers Panel. Click outside of the Layer Attributes Panel to close it again.

How to Make Multiple Layer Vinyl

You can layer vinyl by uploading a multi-colored image to your Design Space. When it's uploaded, you will need to select an image type. There are options available that allow you to choose one that's closest to your image.

An image with a lot of detail and color can become distorted or the colors can change, so it's important to select the image type closest to your image.

The next step is layering. You want to layer from the bottom to the top. Look closely at your image and visualize the finished product. Is the look of the image exactly as you want it? If so, you can keep your image as is without tweaking and rearranging the layers.

You will have the option of a "Print and Cut" image or a "Cut" image. For vinyl, you'll want to choose the "cut" option. You can name your image if you'd like. It can be beneficial to do so. You can name it with the colors of vinyl you'll be using, or with the first letter or few letters of each color. For example, you can name it R,Blu,Gre,O,P for red, blue, green, orange and purple. You'll want them in the order that you will be cutting your vinyl.

If you want to separate your colors, you want to use the magic wand tool. This will allow you to separate your colors.

When your vinyl is sorted by color, weed to remove all the excess vinyl. Start with the bottom later and place your image. Next, you will add the second layer. This can be tricky and clear vinyl transfer tape can help you to see what you're doing. Place the second layer on top of the first layer. Repeat the process, being careful as you layer.

Once you've added your layers and haven't made any errors, you're done! You have a beautiful layered vinyl project.

The more you do this, the easier it will become. For vinyl layering you need a good eye or magnifier and a steady hand.

Using the Contour Feature

Before getting into more complex areas, I'd like to give a quick overview of the contour feature.

This feature allows you to hide part of an image layer by removing unwanted cut lines.

Start by making sure you ungroup your image if it has multiple layers. This is an important step.

On Windows and Mac, you'll select the image and click the ungroup icon at the top of the layers panel. If you're using iOS/Android, you'll select the image and click the ungroup icon in the actions menu.

You next want to select the layer you want to remove the cut lines from and on Windows or Mac, click the contour icon in the layers panel, and on iOS/Android, you'll do the same under the action menu.

So far, it's easy. You just need to be sure you follow the instructions for the device you're using.

When you've completed these steps, the "hide contour" window will appear.

For Windows and Mac, you'll notice that the lines on the image are the individual cut lines. You now want to click on the cut line you want to hide or select the contour to be hidden. You will find that to the right of your window.

When the hidden contour changes to a lighter shade, that part of the image will not show and it won't cut.

You need to repeat this process with each cut line you want to hide.

If you're using an iOS/Android, you'll see dark gray lines that represent the cut lines. As with Windows or Mac, the line will lighten to let you know the part of the image you selected will not show, hence, it will not cut.

You need to repeat these steps to continue hiding the cut lines you desire.

When you're finished hiding all the cut lines you choose, click the "X" in the right-hand corner or click outside the window. The hidden cut lines will no longer appear.

This is an easy method to hide the cut lines you no longer want. Following these steps will give you an error-free cut.

How to Add Shadows to Letters

Decorative shadows can add such beauty to a product. Have you ever wondered how it's done?

For those using programs such as Photoshop, it can be simple, but not everyone has an illustration program.

Fortunately, it can be done with Cricut Design Space and a smartphone app called Phonto, available on the Apple Store.

Phonto is a free, easy-to-use app with over 400 fonts and interchangeable text sizes. You can also add your own fonts if you'd like.

Don't let the "free" part scare you into thinking there won't be much you can do with it. On the contrary, it has amazing features and so much you can do with it that it's worth the small amount of space it will take up on your device.

There's a video tutorial available and it's worth watching. It will walk you through all the features.

To begin, open Phonto and click the camera at the bottom of the screen. You'll see options and you'll want to select "plain image."

You will see a white square in the top right-hand corner. It's next to a black square and it can be hard to see. Select the white square and click the "upload icon" in the top right-hand corner of your screen. Next, you want to select "use." You will now see a white square in the middle of your screen.

You need to tap on the white square, then tap "add text."

Write your text and click done once you've added what you want it to say. The next step is to click on "style." Three options will appear: text, stroke, and background.

A gray highlighted area will appear and this is where you'll start.

The next part might make you nervous because you're going to change the text color to white in the color box. Your text will turn white and you might not be able to see it. Don't panic! It's still there.

Now it's time to add the shadow. To do so, you need to select the "stroke" box. It should be highlighted in gray. You want to change the stroke to black.

Scroll to the bottom of the screen until you see the "width" slider and slide it upward until you get your desired shadow. Select the shadow you want and click "done." Next, click the "upload icon" in the bottom right corner and save the image.

Your shadow is saved, so now it's time to save the text inside of the shadow.

Click on your letters and select "style" again. This time go to "stroke" and pull the "width slider" back down to remove the shadow.

After you remove the shadow, select "text" again and turn your text back to black. Select "done" and then select the "upload icon" to save your image.

You now have two images and you need to transfer them from your phone to your computer, or you can transfer to the Cricut app.

Open Cricut Design Space and upload your images to a new project.

Cricut advises the following: "Make sure you're only deleting the white background around the shadow and not the inner white part. For the word you'll delete the white background and all the inner parts of the letters just like normal." This is important, as you don't want to delete the inner white part. If you do it by accident, undo should restore it.

With your new project started, you'll want to make any adjustments such as resizing or rearranging. You can select your colors and you're ready to cut. Your letters should be shadowed as you selected, and your finished project should be awesome.

The Phonto app makes shadowing very simple to do on your phone, and you shouldn't have any instability when transferring to your computer or Cricut app.

You can now make beautiful shadowed letters, just like the Cricut pros make!

Mirroring Images for Iron-on

You'll want to avoid the mistake of having your mirrored image be wrong when you go to iron it on, so I'll explain how to prevent this.

Iron-on material is fun to work with and you can do so many projects with it. Nothing is more frustrating than ironing a design onto fabric and having it reversed. For some designs, you might think "Hey, this doesn't look so bad" because the image does look good either way, but for letters, there's obviously only one way to go!

So, let's begin to design our iron-on images. You'll design it the way you design your other images, and when finished, double check the direction of the image and click the "Make It" icon in the top-right of the design screen.

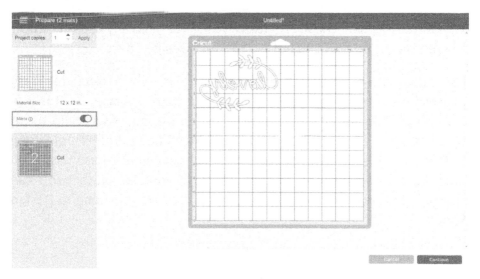

Next, select the mat you will use, and check the "Mirror Image" box and make certain it's for iron-on. You'll need to repeat these steps for each mat that will be used with iron-on material.

Once you select the mirror option, the images will reflect the change on the "Mat Preview." If you set the Smart Set dial to iron-on, but didn't mirror your images on the Mat Preview, you will get an alert on the cut screen. If you want to mirror the images, go back to the Mat Preview pane, and check "Mirror." You can now continue and your image will reproduce correctly.

Tips for Using Images from an Art Program

Cricut Design Space is compatible with many file types, such as .jpg, .gif, .png, .bmp, .svg, and .dxf images and lets you upload and convert them into cuttable shapes. There's generally no problem uploading any of these file types.

Design Space does many amazing things, but it doesn't have the capability to let you make modifications to the design itself. For this reason, you might want to work with your own design software such as Photoshop or Illustrator.

When working with these programs, you can effectively use their tools to create your images and upload them to Design Space.

For those using art design software, this can be a relatively easy process. This section won't teach you how to use Photoshop, Illustrator, Paint or any of the design software, but it will help those who use these programs to modify their own images before uploading to Design Space. This is especially helpful if you want to use your own painting or drawing that you scanned into your computer. You can sharpen it to look like the original artwork before uploading to Design Space.

Preparing Artwork from Adobe Photoshop

There are two different types of images– Basic and Vector.

Adobe Photoshop is not a vector program, which means it cannot save vector files with the prefix ending with .svg and .dxf. There are conversion methods and I won't get into them here. Those looking to use their Design Space with Photoshop should know these skills enough to proceed accordingly.

How can you use the artwork you've created in Adobe Photoshop with your Cricut?

First, you can print the image on your home printer. You can cut it using your the "Print then Cut" feature in Design Space.

Or, you can cut or draw the outline of the image.

You can create a new image or modify one you already have using your Adobe Photoshop tools. You can use single or multiple layers, but the image will be flattened to a single layer when you save it.

When you've finished and the image is as you want it, under your file menu click "Save As." You'll name your file and save it as either a JPEG (.jpg), CompuServe GIF (.gif), PNG (.png), or BMP (.bmp). Any of these will work with your Cricut, however, if saving as a .jpg file, be sure to select "10" on the quality slider for the best results. With the other files, you can use the default setting.

Preparing Artwork from Adobe Illustrator

Adobe Illustrator will work almost the same as Photoshop. Illustrator also has an array of tools to create your design or upload and modify an existing design. Your image will easily upload to Design Space.

The difference between Photoshop and Adobe Illustrator is that Illustrator is a Vector file, and it saves vector files such as .svg and .dxf, but it can also be used to save .jpg, .png, and .bmp files.

Illustrator will let you do the following:

1. Print the image on your home printer and cut it out using your Cricut machine with the Print then Cut feature.

2. Cut or draw the outline of the image.

3. Create cuttable shapes and images. Multilayered images will be separated into layers on the Canvas.

4. Create or modify an image using any of the Adobe Illustrator tools. The file can be made of single or multiple layers.

Under the File Menu, you need to click "Export," then "Export As."

Name your file, then select AutoCAD Interchange File (.dxf). Accept the default settings if prompted with additional options.

Create or modify an image using any of the Adobe Illustrator tools. The file can be made of single or multiple layers.

Hey Let's Make Stuff suggests that "Shapes should be filled before saving for use in Cricut Design Space. Use the Outline Stroke tool found in the Object, then Path menus to convert strokes into shapes. Use the Create Outlines tool found in the Type Menu to outline text. Under the File Menu, click Save As. After naming your file select, AutoCAD Interchange File (.dxf). Accept the default settings if prompted with additional options.

"Create or modify an image using any of the Adobe Illustrator tools. The file can be made of single or multiple layers. Export as usual when you've completed your design."

Preparing artwork from CorelDRAW™

CorelDRAW™ is not as popular as Photoshop and Illustrator, but it is used by many artists and businesses.

CorelDRAW is a Vector program and is compatible with .svg and .dxf, files but it can also save .jpg, .png, and .bmp files.

You can create or modify an image using any of the CorelDRAW tools. The file can be made of single or multiple layers.

We will again use the step-by-step instructions provided by "Hey, Let's Make Stuff."

Under the File Menu, click Save As.

After naming your file select, DXF – AutoCAD (*.dxf) or SVG – Scalable Vector Graphics (*.svg). Accept the default settings if prompted with additional options.

Create or modify an image using any of the CorelDRAW tools. The file can be made of single or multiple layers.

Under the File Menu, click Export.

After naming your file, select one of the following file types: JPG – JPEG Bitmaps (*.jpg, *.jtf, *.jff, *.jpeg)

PNG – Portable Network Graphics (*.png)

BMP – Windows Bitmap (*.bmp, *.dib, *.rle)

GIF – CompuServe Bitmap (*.gif)

For .png and .gif files, accept the default settings if prompted with additional screens.

For best results with .jpg files, change the Quality setting to Highest.

For best results with .bmp files, change the Resolution to 300 dpi.

Cricut Keyboard Shortcut

Function	Windows	Mac
Select All	Ctrl A	CMD A
Group	Ctrl G	CMD G
Ungroup	Ctrl U	CMD U
Copy to clipboard	Ctrl C	CMD C
Paste from clipboard	Ctrl V	CMD V
Cut to clipboard	Ctrl X	CMD X
Print/Cut/Go		CMD P
Quit/Exit CCR	Ctrl E	CMD Q
Open & Close Menus and keypad drawer	Tab	Tab
Undo	Ctrl Z	CMD Z
Redo	Ctrl + Shift Z	CMD +Shift Z or CMD Y
New project	Ctrl N	CMD N
Open project	Ctrl O	CMD O
Save	Ctrl S	CMD S

Save As	Ctrl + Shift S	
Quick Type/Add Text Box	Ctrl T	CMD T
Send Front		open [
Send Back		close]
Send Forward	] or Ctrl up arrow	CMD Up arrow
Send Backward	[or Ctrl down arrow	CMD Down arrow
Exit Hide Contours and Edit Group modes	Esc	Esc
Nudge objects	Right/Left/Up/Down arrows	Right/Left/Up/Down arrows
Big Nudge objects	Shift Right/Left/Up/Down arrows	SHFT Right/Left/Up/Down arrows
Delete selected objects	Del	Del
Zoom in	Z + click on mat	Z + click on mat
Zoom out	Z + Alt + click on mat	Z + Alt + click on mat
Scale non proportionally	Alt + Click on height or width handle	CMD mouse down

by height or width		
Pan screen (mouse cursor changes to a hand)	Space bar and drag screen up or down	Space bar and drag screen up or down

New Features for Design Space

It would be remiss if it wasn't mentioned that as of August 2019, Design Space for Desktop Beta has been released for Windows and Mac OS software.

The announcement on the Cricut website reads, "In the coming weeks, our beta app will receive an update to support the ability to design offline. This means you can design and cut offline without an internet connection. To get to the front of the line for this feature, we recommend that you download Design Space for Desktop Beta by September 10th. Go download it now!"

This is good news for those thinking about purchasing Cricut Design Space, but who do not always have access to good, stable WiFi.

Having this ability is sure to make a lot of Design Space users very happy. Imagine being a passenger on a long car or bus trip and being able to design until you reach your destination.

It's also perfect for when your internet service goes out because of a storm or for repairs, or because you don't have reliable service.

What's Different About Design Space for Desktop Beta?

Let's read on to see what Cricut has to say about this news. "Many of you use the web version of Design Space to create and cut. Design Space for Desktop Beta is a version of Design Space that lives on your

Windows or Mac computer. You will launch the beta app right from your computer instead of going to design.cricut.com on the internet. The benefit of using the beta app is that we can give you features like offline (and seamlessly rollout future features) that will make Design Space an even better experience.

When you download Design Space for Desktop Beta, you'll sign in with your Cricut ID and access your projects as you typically do across your devices. All your content and favorite design features are in the same place.

Only soon, on top of the peace of mind you get from having your projects safe and sound in the cloud, you'll also have the choice to save them to your computer, too, so you can design with your saved project any time, even without an internet connection."

Typical with the manufacturer, they tease us with more.

"Because we are releasing Design Space for Desktop in beta first, there are certain features that will be available right away and others that will come in time. If you receive the offline feature during this first rollout, you can expect to:

● Save projects for offline use on your canvas

● Save images and fonts within a project for offline use

● Create new projects offline (if your internet goes down, you won't lose your project)

● Cut offline from anywhere

In the future, you'll also be able to:

● Download images for offline use

● Download fonts for offline use

If you have an iOS device, you can cut offline right now! For those of you designing on Android, we will plan to roll out the offline feature in the future."

How to Download Design Space Desktop Beta

Cricut's website provides a link for you to get started.

"Ready to get in on the action? Just download and install Design Space for Desktop Beta here. If you have more questions, check out this help article."

The release concludes, "We will roll out the offline feature to the beta app in phases over several weeks starting in September. This means some members may get the feature before others. We can't give you an exact date of when you'll get it, but the sooner you download the beta app, the better!"

This announcement is one of the most important examples of why you should check the Cricut website often and/or subscribe to their newsletter.

Their website also offers a plethora of project ideas, and you might want to try one, or many, out.

There are many project ideas on Pinterest and Etsy as well. If you're interested in selling your creations, you can browse Etsy shops to see what's hot and what's not.

Of course, the internet is filled with project ideas and that why I didn't get into detail with project instructions. They can be easily accessed by a simple search.

"Cricut projects" will give you 44.5 million results. That's surely a sign of the popularity of the machine and the countless creations you can make.

I will touch briefly on selling your creations for those looking to make a profit from their machine.

Selling for Profit

I've heard some people say they would like to sell what they make with their Cricut, but aren't sure how to or where to.

I recommend contacting your local Chamber of Commerce or local government to get a listing of upcoming craft fairs. These provide an excellent opportunity to showcase your creations and sell them or hand out business cards to potential customers. You should attend craft shows to see what's selling and what's not so you aren't stuck with a lot of product that isn't selling.

Signs, Signs, Everywhere a Sign

Right now, wooden and chalkboard signs are a hot commodity. There's no place like home, Christmas countdown, and any saying you think people will like will sell. You will have plenty of competition, but the better you make them, the better yours will sell.

Water Bottles

These are another hot commodity, and they sell well. Be sure if you are using a school logo that you get written permission. And, don't use licensed characters if you don't own the license.

Back to Selling

Don't be afraid to approach shops that sell country gifts and ask them to carry your creations. Many will do so on commission as they like to showcase local artists.

You may want to sell online from an Etsy store or your own website or blog. The advantage to this is that you don't need to stock a lot of inventory because you can make it as orders come in.

Don't limit yourself when selling. Try more than one venue and get your name out there. Some Cricut users make enough sales that they can quit their day jobs, and there's no end in sight to the popularity of Cricut-made merchandise.

Conclusion

I hope this book has helped you master the Cricut Design Space. It's a great little machine that can do so many different operations and allows you to make designs for inside and outside your home, to keep, to sell, and to give as gifts.

If you have yet to purchase your first machine, I hope this helps your decision. We want you to enjoy Cricut Design Space and much as thousands of users around the world.

Keep the tips and tricks provided close by as a reference guide so you aren't searching all over to find the answers to your questions.

Design Space makes Cricut a user-friendly die-cutter, and I can't stress enough how much you'll get out of the machine as you learn each process. If you're a newbie, as I said before, start slowly so you don't become overwhelmed and abandon your machine without giving it a chance.

Frustration is common with first-time users, so read through this book carefully before starting your first project.

As I said, if you're accustomed to MS Word, the Design Space toolbar will be easy for you to maneuver.

Thank you for selecting this book, and happy Cricuting!

CRICUT PROJECT IDEAS

A Step by Step Guide Book to Designing and Coming Up with Great and Amazing Project Ideas for Cricut Maker, Cricut Explore Air 2 and Cricut Design Space

Kimberly Johnson

Introduction

Cricut is the newest of a selection of private digital cutting machines specializing in die cutting items for home decoration, scrapbooking, paper cutting, card making, and much more. Everything you can do using a Cricut is only restricted by your creativity. These machines include Cricut cartridges for simple use. The cartridges consist of numerous amazing built-in templates for a variety of functions and dimensions.

This device is also very simple to take care of. The layouts can be selected from the cartridge or can be custom manufactured using the Cricut design studio to take your imagination to higher heights - but a computer is needed for this objective.

The Cricut package includes the following:
- Cricut machines: These are the resources which perform the real cutting because of your creative layouts.
- Gypsy: This is actually the total Cricut cartridge library at one go. It's a hand-held apparatus that features the entire Cricut design studio - so anytime we need to operate on a layout, the gypsy is conveniently available.
- Cricut Design Studio: It's the full-fledged program for creating any layout on a Cricut cutter. All you will need is a PC. One disappointment to your clients is the Cricut Design Studio isn't mac compatible. In addition, it can be used to readily Explore, cut and layout the whole cartridge library. The program also offers a choice to save the layout for future demands. Assessing a Cricut layout has never been simpler!
- Cuttlebug: It's the private die cutting and embossing system. It comprises various sizes and styles such as paper-crafting, home decoration, house jobs, events, and college projects. The plan is produced by top artists and provides sharp die cuts each and every time. Cuttlebug also includes professional

excellent embossing for connections using its different feel and measurements, which makes it an amazing system.

- Cricut cake: This is an optional piece of equipment used for creating designer confectioneries for cakes and other treats, in virtually no time.

- Cricut Expression: This is an advanced version that may be used for sheets as large as 24" x 12", so it can fit any aspect, be it professional or personal. Additionally, it boasts of several cartridges and innovative options, such as the adding of colours, printing, and much more, which makes it perfect for many projects.

Cricut is the handicraft enthusiast's best friend, or for anybody who likes to design and create. It provides over 250 different designs in various sizes. The layouts could be smaller than an inch or bigger up to one inch. The 8 different cutting angles provide precision reduction - all this together with appealing templates and stylized alphabets, offers much to pick from.

Before you buy your very first Cricut, it is important to consider all probable options to decide on the very best machine to match your crafting needs.

First, you must stock up on the fundamentals, such as Cricut ribbon and picture cartridges. These cartridges come in a variety of topics to showcase and commemorate any event, like vacations or forthcoming events. You'll also need a large quantity of coloured paper, along with a pad on which to cut that contrasts to the dimensions of your system.

If you are an avid scrapbooker, you ought to start looking into buying your first Cricut cutter or the Cricut Expression. This system will cut shapes, letters and themes to decorate your scrapbook pages. It is also possible to decorate bulletin boards, posters, party decorations, greeting cards or invitations of any sort. These cutters can also cut cloth. It's encouraged for you to starch the cloth first so as to make the job as simple as possible for your own system to finish. The gap between both is straightforward.

The Cricut Expression is a brand new, 12" x 24" version of the first Cricut. This system makes it easier to create large-scale jobs in a massive quantity – as long as you've got the right quantity of paper. Font and picture cartridges may be utilised in the two machines.

Have you heard of the Cricut Cake? This useful cutter is designed to cut nearly anything for baked products, such as frosting sheets, gum paste, fondant, cookie dough, tortillas, baking soda, gum and the majority of other soft food substances. Whatever material you choose to use must be between 1/6" and 1/8" thick. Keep the blade clean at all times so as to make sure you get the very best cut possible.

Another favourite Cricut option is the Cricut Cuttlebug. This system is small. It merely cuts paper that's 6 inches wide and weighs just 7 lbs. The Cuttlebug is mainly used for cutting and embossing specific crafts. This is the best way to decorate several greeting card type invitations. Once you include a range of coloured dies, the Cuttlebug is ready to emboss straight away. These dies are also harmonious with Sizzix, Big Shot and Thin Cuts machines, which serve a similar function.

Are you currently curious and are creating your personal t-shirts and cloth designs? Cricut also created the Yudu for all those crafters who love screen-printing and producing their own layouts. The Yudu enables its owners to attach it to a laser ink jet printer and make a layout to screen-print onto virtually anything! Yudus are used for straps, handbags, photograph frames, shoes - you name it.

Finally, if you would like to feed your newfound Cricut obsession, go right ahead and buy one of the newest Cricut Gypsys. This useful, hand-held apparatus will keep your font cartridges ready for simple portable use. It's possible to design from anyplace on the move, in the physician's office, even while on holiday, or merely sitting on your sofa. Anything you plan on the Gypsy is totally transferable to a Cricut device for die cutting. If you save your layout, it may be linked to one of your Cricut apparatus and published at a later moment.

This is a short overview of some of the cutting-edge machines Cricut sells. As you can see there's a fantastic assortment of machines for whichever specific kind of craft you wish to concentrate on. One thing is for certain. Whichever machine you select you will have many hours of inspiration and fun producing and creating your own crafting projects.

Cricut is your go-to brand for a selection of private digital cutting machines specializing in die cutting of items for home decoration, scrapbooking, paper cutting, card making, and much more. Everything you can do using a Cricut is only restricted by your creativity.

Complex Cricut suggestions for the craft project
Cricut private cutters are carrying handcrafts to a whole new level. People throughout the country are astonished at the amazing and advanced Cricut thoughts this machine may bring to your job listing. You can create almost anything amazing and one of a kind working with the Cricut cartridges.

How does a Cricut machine function? It is very straightforward. Simply load a Cricut cartridge to the machine, choose what colour card stock you would like to use for your individual layout and cut off. Each cartridge has different themed layouts from seasonal layouts to favourite cartoon characters. You can pick from the cut-out layouts to use for scrapbooks, picture frames, customized greeting cards, wall hangings, calendars and a lot more.

One of the amazing Cricut ideas it is possible to create as a craft is the Cricut calendar. Every month can be produced in another page and you'll be able to decorate these pages using various layouts. Wouldn't it be wonderful to make your February page employing the Love-struck Season cartridge? The Easter cartridge will supply you with endless layouts for the April page of the calendar. Your May calendar could be made with the Mother's Day cartridge. How interesting would it be to style your July page with trimmings made with the Independence Day season cartridge? December can be outfitted together with All the Joys of the Season cartridge and the Snow Friend's cartridge. You may select items to your heart's content.

Another fantastic idea you may make is a scrapbook. This well-loved craft job is why Cricut cutting machine were devised in the first place. Together with the Cricut die cutting machine, you can personalize scrapbooks for your kids, for mother-daughter or dad and son keepsakes. Cricut created cartridges that each little child would delight in using like the Once Upon a Princess cartridge or the Disney Tinker Bell and Friends' cartridge. Your small superhero would certainly love the Batman layout in the Batman: The Brave and the Bold or Robots cartridges. Cricut provides you lots of layouts to select from for scrapbooking ideas.

The Cricut layouts aren't only layout ideas, but additionally have fonts and alphabets in the Sesame Street font cartridge along with the Ashlyn's alphabet cartridge. Use these exciting tools when making your personalized gift like a wall-hanging picture frame for framing a photograph of an unforgettable occasion of the receiver of your gift. Embellish your wall hanging with pretty cut-outs produced by the Cricut cutter.

Your Cricut ideas are endless by means of this superb machine and also the Cricut cartridges to suit any event and job possible to consider. Creating a Cricut job with the entire family is a superb way to spend some time together and producing those gorgeous items can be a superb experience for everyone to achieve.

Ideas that could generate income
People really feel the Cricut machine is the one instrument that's responsible for the conceptualization of those layouts which we see in scrapbooks. In fact, the designs are derived in the brain of the consumer and are made concrete by the Cricut cutting machine.

In addition, there are other tools which help create the layouts such as cartridges and applications tools. The top software tool out there's is the Cricut Design Studio. With this application, you can create and edit your own designs and also edit current designs which are pre-packed.

Life is great indeed! People also believe the use of a Cricut cutting system is only restricted to the area of scrapbooking. Only a few men and women may know, but the Cricut machine in addition to the cartridges and the software tools may be used for a large number of things. There are a whole lot of Cricut projects which it is possible to use the Cricut cutting system for and only your mind can restrict what you could do.

Greeting cards are excellent Cricut projects for everyone to participate in. Together with the layouts you may receive from the Cricut cartridge along with the software tools you have set up; you can lay out covers that withstand the unconventional. The difficulty most men and women experience when they attempt to buy greeting cards is they can't find the type of card they're searching for. This may result in stress and a great deal of frustration on the purchaser's part. You're so much better off making your own personal greeting cards.

Cricut calendars are another fantastic reason to get a Cricut cutting device. A calendar is full of 12 months. You can get creative and search for layouts on your cartridge or software which could reflect the month that's inside your calendar. If we're at the month of December, then you can search for layouts that fit the mood and feeling of December. Start looking for snowmen, reindeers, and Christmas trees. I promise you that you have all of the layouts you will ever desire inside of your own software or cartridge.

Keep in mind, only your imagination can restrict what you do. These Cricut projects may be used either for individual satisfaction or revenue generating functions. Be imaginative with your Cricut machine. You never know what crazy thoughts can pop into your mind.

From the universe of record making, an individual may believe there are only hardware resources such as the Cricut cutting machine, as well as the Cricut Expression system. But there also are software tools which may help you create great Cricut ideas that could help you in the creation of your perfect scrapbook.

One of them is your Cricut Design Studio. This software tool is a fresh method for connecting your initial machine to your own computer and it may also works with the Cricut Expression. With the usage of an onscreen cutting mat, this program tool allows Explore, layout, and cutting from the whole Cricut cartridge library. The excellent thing about this is what you see is what you cut! Additionally, this application has an interface which is extremely user - friendly and has the capacity to store any of your own creations. This is a tool which any scrapbooker should get!

With this tool, it is possible to do anything and create countless Cricut ideas. The general rule here is to allow your creativity to know no limitations. When you make a scrapbook, the most important objective is to make layouts that jive with all the images you set in. Let us say for instance, you add some pictures of your wedding day.

You need to select or create a layout that will make an impression that could make anybody who looks at the images and the scrapbooks relive the memories. The exact same general rule will apply to anybody. You might even generate income out of this by helping people develop designs for their scrapbook.
The usage of the computer software isn't confined to only creating scrapbooks. As stated, earlier, let your creativity set the limitations and there should be no limitations. Besides scrapbooks, the next things you can make include: a. Wall hangings b. Image frames c. Greeting cards

Maybe the most frequent innovation of the Cricut machine aside from scrapbooks is Cricut calendars. The layouts which you receive from a Cricut system may be used to include spice and life to any calendar.

With the usage of a Cricut machine in addition to the software applications, you may produce layouts for every month in a calendar year. The trick is to pick any layout that could reflect exactly what that particular month is all about. October for instance where the very best layout is always a backdrop depicting Oktoberfest.

So, there you've got it, a few excellent Cricut ideas which could help you make money or just simply make you happier. Bear in mind, it's your own choice. Get ready to have a rocking good time!

Cricut cartridges are mainly the core of a Cricut cutting machine, which can be put within the cutter system to turn the layout just as the consumer wishes into a bit of paper.

A broad variety of cartridges can be found on the market, although not all these cartridges operate with all sorts of machines. As an example, the Cricut cartridge operates with Cricut machines only, and it's the vital element whereby crafters and artists can create many designs in wonderful colours and styles.

Together with the changes in printing technologies, a selection of cartridges was introduced recently with more packages to pick from compared to prior ones. The two main kinds of printer cartridges available are: the ink (used with an ink-jet printer), and laser cartridges, used in laser printers. In the case of all Cricut machines, they still use ink-jet printers easily.

All about Cricut ink cartridges:
At first, Cricut ink cartridges were only available in black, but after some time, a few different colours were introduced. Afterwards, together with advancements in printing technology, ink cartridges have been developed, and attempts were made to present different font styles, layout and colours for forming contours, too.
The key to the success of the Cricut system, is the use of distinct and special kinds of cartridges that enable users to obtain, cut and create in almost any font, layout, colour and design.
The general types of Cricut cartridges are:

* **Font cartridge:** It includes full alphabets, numbers and other symbols together with font styles and other font organizing shapes. Some of the favourite all-year seasonal and around cartridges comprise Forever Young, Jasmine, Teardrop, Lyrical Letters, Pumpkin carving for Halloween, Thanksgiving holiday, Winter Wonderland for the Christmas season, etc.
* **Shape cartridge:** It includes an assortment of shapes including boxes, tags, bags, animals, sports, paper dolls, etc.
* **Licensed cartridge**: It enables users to find the cut designed with favourite figures such as Disney's Micky Mouse, Hello Kitty, Pixar's Toy Story, etc.
* **Classmate cartridge**: As its name implies, is made specifically for classroom functions, which includes classroom fonts, shapes and classroom layout, visual analysis program, suggestions and representations of educators, etc.
* **Solutions cartridge**: It costs less than the rest. The shapes include welding, baseball, soccer, campout, etc.

The wide variety of Cricut cartridges, as mentioned above, provides crafters, particularly young customers, an opportunity to experiment with their artistic skills without the support of a computer, whereas the Cricut ink cartridge makes it a lot easier for them to create designs in a variety of shapes and colours.

Chapter 1 - What Is Cricut Design?

You have a Cricut cutting machine (the original Cricut, Cricut Expression, or even Cricut Create). After playing with it for a while, and even squandering a lot of paper with your errors, you know there's yet another item in the market called Cricut Design Studio. The Cricut Design studio software lets you learn what you are very likely to cut on your Cricut cutter before you cut the paper. It lets you connect letters together, alter shapes, etc.

The Cricut Design Studio program enables you to view before you cut, which is really a substantial paper saver. So, you should break down and purchase the Cricut Design Studio program. You start it up and there's a program disc, and a user guide about the very best way to set up the program along with a few basic conditions and applications, a USB cable plus a cunning mouse pad that is configured. You load the app onto your own computer and following that in the event that you are like me you say "what the hell do I do now?"

Cricut design studio from Provo Craft

Many crafting lovers have fallen in love with their die cutting system, "the Cricut." A brand-new addition to this popular product is the growth of a software program created just for Cricut users.
If you maybe you've found a passion for the Provo Craft Cricut cutting machines, then you are very likely to fall in love all over again as soon as you try the latest accession to the Cricut home - Cricut design studio program.
Cricut Design Studio is a computer program application produced by Provo Craft, the makers of the Cricut machine. Although the system itself empowers the user to cut unique fonts and shapes in a rage of measurements, the Cricut Design Studio takes it into an entirely new

level. Simply connect the Cricut to the computer with a USB port, install the program, and unleash a totally new measurement of crafting.

The Cricut design studio gives an entirely new dimension to your Cricut adventures, if you have the very first small Cricut or perhaps the larger Cricut Expression. One of the best components is this app is easy to use and understand. It's not vital to become a computer whiz to find it out and you may conduct an excellent number of imaginative effects together with the addition of this 1 slice of software.

The principal benefit of the Cricut Design Studio is your capacity for customers to weld, or perhaps link letters together with one another to form a single cutting edge. Gone are the cases of having to copy each letter at a time. Now letters, phrases, words and shapes can be plotted together before cutting making it faster and simpler than ever to add cuttings to jobs.

Another advantage of the Cricut Design Studio consists of that the shapes and letters that can be manipulated extensively before cutting. Users aren't restricted to only adjusting the measurements but may now change the shape attributes to better support their overall design. Each image may be elongated, reversed and made invisible to discover the particular look the crafter currently needs.

Even though the Cricut design studio includes benefit after benefit, my own personal favourite is the capability to incorporate pictures from a number of cartridges into one design. The user can design together with the cartridge options concurrently instead of being limited to cutting using one cartridge at a time.

Advanced along with ultra-creative users have created lots inspiring ideas by mixing many different cartridges to create unbelievable cutting-edge designs.

The Cricut Design Studio can also be in my own estimation, a necessity for each and every Cricut owner. Though there's a learning curve for it, after it is understood the creative options are totally infinite. The Cricut in addition to all the Design Studio has become a must-have resource for every scrapbooker and card maker today.

Here are just a few items that have helped me with all of the Cricut Design Studio software, and it will help you.

1. Loaded within this Cricut Design Studio software package is accessibility to all or any cartridges. Another wonderful element of this application is that with every new cartridge that is easily available that you purchase, you might just get on the Internet and update your software to the latest edition. Considering the Cricut Design Studio app has all the current cartridges, you are going to be able to list those that you need and then purchase them or put them on your want list. Notice: You are going to be able to use each cartridge that is in the Cricut Design Studio software, however you need to find that cartridge packaged in your Cricut cutter to actually use the image.

2. The manual describes welding. Welding is connecting letters or graphics together. Just remember if you want to combine it, you will need to look at the box to get the information onto your screen. The welding feature is excellent if analysing phrases or words. It will create the tradition of sticking it to your scrapbook page or greeting card super easy. When trimming letters that aren't welded together, you need to be cautious they're implemented directly as well as the spacing is good.

3. The Cricut Design studio app even has a feature that lets you use quite a few cartridges whenever you are creating a layout. For example: you're creating a birthday card that reads Happy Birthday Tapioca. You choose to use the tear drop cartridge for the words Happy Birthday and you would love to use the Jasmine cartridge to make the word Tapioca. This really isn't any trouble with this particular Cricut Design Studio program. The moment your Cricut is cutting it's likely to allow you to understand just what cartridge to load into your own Cricut cutter. How cool is that? The Cricut Design Studio program even allows you to create anything your imagination will allow. There are unlimited possibilities for your creativeness employing the Cricut Design Studio program.

Why get the design studio?

The Cricut Design Studio lets you combine images from a number of these cartridges you have and unite them into one design. It's possible to arrange your design before you set it to a cartridge. It's very easy to weld letters together, shrink or expand pictures, set a photo on a diagonal, and then stretch, rotate, or even use other images. You might even stop and save your design before it's completed, then return to finish it. At any time, you have the design just the way you want it, just slide in the first cartridge needed and push 1 button. The moment your Cricut reaches the stage where it needs another cartridge, then it will alert you so you might swap the cartridges. When you finish, it is possible to save your design into your computer or flash drive and you'll be able to share it with your friends.

Another benefit of Design Studio is it is possible to test every available design in the complete Cricut library, even if you've got the cartridge or not. Simply type in keywords to search for a particular image or word and you are in a position to determine exactly how it might look in your own ideas. This can let you decide on whether you'd like to get a particular cartridge or not. You could also preplant your design and save it until you get the crucial cartridge or borrow it from a friend.

Are there cons to the Cricut Design Studio?

The sole con is that you are restricted to using Design Studio at a spot where you've got access to a computer. In the event you've got a laptop, however, that is a non-issue.

In general, the Cricut Design Studio is a great addition to a Cricut collection. You are only limited by your own creativity.

One of the terrific benefits of possessing Cricut Design Studio is your capability to collaborate with others. Everyone who designs something can save it on their computer. Many elect to put the file online and allow other individuals to use their designs. The moment you get started browsing other people's work, you're going to be amazed at the incredible work of these generous and talented Cricut users. Following is a step-by-step manual to downloading and cutting along with other people's files.

You will discover different websites and sites that have work posted together with the design archives. Every person can shop and share their designs in a different way. Many use a third-party sharing site, although others keep the files hosted right there on their website. A range of the files on the Cricut.com message panel are saved as a text document and need to be changed before using them.

After you've discovered a file you want to use, you can begin the download process.

1. Click the link they have provided for you to the file. When it is hosted on their website, it will ask you if you'd love to begin, cancel or save. In the event the file is hosted on a file sharing site it will let you wait for the to "click here to download file." When you select that link it will take you into the display that asks if you want to begin, save or cancel.

2. Once you're on the open or shop display, you are going to need to choose save. Before you do it, make sure the file is showing the place where you want the file to be saved. You may opt to make a folder specifically for Cricut documents. If you'd like to change the document name, then take action at this phase. Click here to begin saving the file to your PC.

Now the file is on your computer, it's likely to start it within the Cricut Design Studio application. Stick to these easy activities to cut a layout that is stored.

1. Open the Cricut Design Studio app. Look on the "file" drop down menu in the top left corner and then choose "available."

2. After selecting "open" a screen will develop that shows cut files that were saved in the "my tasks" folder. These are files of your own you have made. To find the file that was downloaded and saved, find the folder where you saved it by picking it in the "look in" region.

3. Pick the document you will need to begin and click on the open button. This will bring up the file you downloaded and open it on your personal computer. To cut it, load the paper then click the scissors to cut it off. You might can also alter or boost the document in the event you need to, but be sure to always give credit where credit is expected instead of keeping a design as your own unless you created the entire file.

Spend some time browsing other people's designs and work and you will soon have more ideas and files than you can cut. Make sure you leave an opinion or a thank you after you use someone else's files and discuss exactly what you've created if at all possible. Start searching for an approaching article to show how to obtain files from the Cricut message boards and alter them in text files to create documents.

When you open your Cricut layout studio software, you will see 4 main elements: the electronic mat where your job is displayed, the Cricut cartridge library, the electronic key-pad overlay and the shape properties window.

The library includes posts of every Cricut cartridge printed. As more come out, you'll be able to improve your library so you can always get new tools into your creations. You're absolutely free to design with the cartridges in the plan studio library nonetheless, it's possible to simply cut using just the cartridges you have. The library can be used to provide you study content from the cartridges that you do not have, therefore use it like a tool that is going to support you to find precisely what you adore!

Searching through the library is straightforward. The Cricut cartridge library permits you to list a cartridge location in whatever arrangement you choose in the drop-down menu. You can organize your library list alphabetically by favourites by category or by the cartridges you have. It's also possible to browse through the library by using keywords (Tip: if you do a search by keyword, the simpler the search term, the greater!) Together with the auto-filler function anticipates what you might be looking for and provides you tips.

As you cycle during your Explore results, the electronic overlay alterations to show that cartridge location and feature your search outcome is situated in. This process makes it a whole lot simpler to get precisely what you want quickly. You can even customize exactly what screens in the electronic overlay if you happen to decide what it shows for your keyword isn't accurate.

The key-pad overlay is all but identical with the actual overlays that you set on your Cricut device. On the rear, you'll find the six feature buttons, both the "shift-lock" button, and the space/backspace buttons. Following the shift-lock buttons are engaged, they are highlighted like on the Cricut apparatus. When you set your mouse pointer on your image keys, then they are going to expand marginally to reveal the image key you will pick.

Working together with the virtual mat is just as natural as it gets. When you have chosen the contour which you want to use, it will appear on the electronic mat jointly with choice of controls. Selection choices are the 8 bands that show regarding the corners and sides of this shape. Virtually all of your image crafting will be carried out with these choices, as you execute them you will see the possibilities available to your creative ideas.

Welding basics

One of the easiest things you're likely to need to perform with the Cricut Design Studio is to put letters together to type a phrase. There are two approaches to link letters together. The first is to work along with the expression as one picture that may be manipulated together. The following method will be to make every individual letter as one picture that can be manipulated independently.

As you sort the letters into your own word, you will see they show up on the outside mat shortly one after another. When you decide on the pair of letters by clicking on a few of these lines, any alterations such as size will be applied to every one of those letters at the same time. Another strategy is to produce one letter, then hit enter prior to scanning the following. This creates each letter separately so you may control each letter individually.

To weld a word when the letters are just one group, adhere to the following steps:

Click on the word using the mouse so it is chosen.

Kerning is the space between letters. Put this in -.005 or leave at no cost. Reach applies.

The letters will go collectively, some may be touching while others may not. Decide on every letter in the word. It'll become a hurried line when that particular letter is selected. Transfer it together with all the nudge arrows until each connection is somewhat overlapping.

Opt for the whole word again and again analyze the welding box under shape properties.

The phrase will likely have dark lines showing where the clipping will be, whereas a lighter line will probably indicate where it has been welded together.

You will find times when you are going to need to use every single letter or graphic individually. This is quite helpful when you may need one letter dimension and then another letter or another dimension. To weld letters that are individual, follow these measures:

Pick the very first letter you're likely to need to use. Be sure to hit to deselect the connection prior to adding a new one.

Opt for another letter you will use. Notice that if you decide on each letter, it is its own letter. It could possibly be manipulated and not affect others at all.

Continue integrating letters and be sure to hit enter after each.

In this welding process the kerning feature is not employed. Simply select a letter, type in the measurements and appearance desired and examine the weld box.

Pick a different letter and control it as desired. Proceed into where it moves the first letter. You can choose how much it overlaps based on your layout. Look carefully at the welding box.

Continue until all letters have been manipulated along with the welding box being evaluated for each.

Preview the phrase. The finished letters will show in the welding box checked as a dark line cut with the lighter lines showing where they are welded. If any connection is a powerful filled letter instead, the welding box was not picked for that particular letter. Simply return and decide on the letter and check the welding box.

Welding is one of the most basic and popular jobs in the Cricut Design Studio. Practice the steps above and you will be on your way to using the Cricut in an entirely new way. If you are more of a visual learner, most step by step guides to welding between screenshots are available online.

Cricut machines help people a great deal with making scrapbooks. If it weren't for this particular instrument, folks would probably be cutting designs that they've assembled manually and that would require some rather careful hands. One mistake and that's likely to change the overall theme of your scrapbook. Furthermore, there are resources that you can use along with a few Cricut machines that may make the whole process a lot easier. One of them is the Cricut Design Studio software and Cricut mats.

Some people today confuse the Cricut method as the one directly accountable for creating the designs. That is a very major problem. The thing responsible for the designs are the software programs and that is the point at which the Cricut layout studio software comes into play.

This software tool includes lots and a lot of designs which are jazzy and could suit anyone's taste. The best thing about the app tool is the fact it grants the user rights to edit the designs it currently has and to create new ones.
It additionally has Internet service which permits Internet upgrades to your software. If you find new designs that are accessible on the Internet, you can add them to an app's library at the push of a button. The Cricut layout studio software is priced at $60. Search the Net with this program and it will provide you a few links where you can download the software from. And then, we have got Cricut mats.

The mat is responsible for holding the paper or vinyl you'll have the Cricut machine trimming your style on. This can be a very sticky piece of paper that is very like a ribbon pad. If you are not experienced in the process for applying this particular mat, then you're likely to end up buying more than you expect.

A fantastic approach to ensure the sturdiness of your mat is to cover it. Nearly all the time, the user fails to cover the mat after this and use lets lots of dust particles sit on the top layer of the mat. If you've got one pad, then use a translucent plastic to protect it. If you are using two, you might continue to keep both face to face. If your Cricut mats have lost their stickiness, you can use a decorative spray on to let it regain its adhesiveness. It's been tried and tested so you do not have to be concerned about doing this.

If you're a scrapbooker with a great deal of good ideas that you just don't necessarily know how to get out on paper, take into consideration the cost of Cricut Design Studio. This super software program can permit you to turn all of your fantastic ideas into magical creations right before your eyes.

You can find numerous top scrapbook designs and themes around.

You can find out about cartridges and also how to use these as well as how to use more than one cartridge on your design. Find out about the outside mat, as well as how to use it so as to generate the best designs for your scrapbook themes.

Organize everything in your own cartridge library and you can always get it if you desire it. You can add keywords to your library to make it a whole lot simpler to find just what you would like and a whole lot more. These are just a few examples of all of the things the Cricut Design Studio may do for you personally.

There is a small learning curve in regard to using the program, nevertheless, and additionally the manual it includes does not do an excellent job of describing things. Luckily there are a couple great, helpful tutorials and guides available on the market written by other people using the program that could aid you with creating a Cricut Design Studio job.

The minimum system requirements include:

OS = Windows 7

Processor rate = 1800 MHz

Ram = 512 MB

Free hard disk space = 100 MB
Topical media drive = CD/DVD-ROM

USB port = 1.1

Display resolution configurations = 1024x768 or higher

It is essential to be sure your computer meets these minimum requirements before investing in this application. When you know you meet the requirements and you get the program on your own, all you want to do is begin using it to make the best designs around for your own scrapbooks.

Cricut is the brand-new a choice of personal digital cutting machines specializing in the very cutting edge of things for home decoration, scrapbooking, paper cutting, card making, and much more. Whatever you might do with a Cricut is simply restricted by your own imagination. These machines include Cricut cartridges for easy use. The cartridges include numerous amazing built-in templates for many different uses and sizes. This gadget is also quite straightforward to maintain. The designs can be chosen from the cartridge or may be custom made using the Cricut Design Studio to take your creativity to great heights - but a computer is required for this particular purpose.

The Cricut bundle comprises these:

Cricut machines: All these are the sources which do the actual cutting based on your creative designs.

Gypsy: This really is really the total Cricut cartridge library in one go. It is a hand-held device that includes the total Cricut layout studio - to ensure anytime you want to run on a design the gypsy is handily offered.

Cricut Design Studio: It is the full-fledged program for producing any design on a Cricut cutter. All you'll need is a computer. Additionally, it may be used to easily investigate, cut and design from the entire cartridge library. The program also lets you save the design for future needs. Assessing a Cricut design has never been easier!

Cuttlebug: It is the personal die cutting and embossing system. It features different sizes and styles like paper-crafting, house decoration, home tasks, events, and faculty jobs. The program is designed by leading artists and offers sharp die cuts every time. Cuttlebug additionally includes professional exceptional embossing for connections with its various textures and sizes, making it a wonderful system.

Cricut Cake: This is an optional tool used for producing designer confectioneries for sandwiches and cakes and other snacks, in almost no time.

Cricut Expression: An advanced version called the Cricut Expression can be used for sheets as big as 24" x 12." Additionally, it includes cartridges and advanced possibilities, like the adding of colours, printing, plus far more, making it ideal for many jobs.

Cricut is the handicraft enthusiast's best buddy, or for anyone who wants to design and create. It supplies over 250 distinct designs in a variety of sizes. The designs can be bigger than an inch or larger than about 11 inches. The different cutting angles offer precision reduction - all of this together with templates that are appealing along with stylized alphabets, provides much to select from.

Knowing The Materials To Use With Cricut

The Cricut personal electronic cutter must be recognizable to anyone at anybody interested in home crafts, and especially scrapbooking. If you're a newcomer to the entire world, then suffice it to say the Cricut personal electronic cutter is a truly revolutionary cutting tool which can effortlessly cut any shape or design it is possible to consider. By the time you've read this guide, you should develop into someone who is much more knowledgeable on what this system (or more precisely, this variety of machines) can provide you.

The intention of the guide is to deliver an easy five-step procedure you can use so as to use a Cricut personal electronic cutter to make a visually stunning design. I will flesh out each of the steps with the thought processes you may encounter, and the choices you are going to need to make. After all, you are going to be able to go off and make something that's currently based on your own creativity.

Have an idea
The first step to creating your masterpiece is an idea. However, complicated by the technology you're using, it is useless if you don't have any inspiration to start with. It might possibly be that you understand exactly what it is you are trying to make - say a scrapbook page on your kid's college sports day or possibly a family reunion. You may not be so certain - in case, I urge a speedy look on Google for "scrapbooking websites" or something similar. Have a browse through a couple of those websites and you are likely to find almost endless inspiration extremely fast.

Which Cricut?
If you do not already have a Cricut personal electronic cutter - then you are going to need to decide at this stage which one fulfils your needs. Your choice will probably be based upon your budget, and if you are going to need anything more than fundamental cutting purposes. The precise information about what each version can do and the way they are purchased is beyond the scope of this guide, yet this info is publicly accessible online.

Select a cartridge
The following step is to choose an appropriate cartridge from the Cricut options. Again, going into detail concerning the Cricut cartridge procedure is out of scope for this specific post - the very best choice is to go and browse through the numerous accessible cartridges online at Amazon or somewhere similar. You're in a position to buy cartridges with designs and shapes for whatever you might think about. All cartridges are compatible with each Cricut personal electronic cutter variant model.

Customize your cut
With an idea, a system alongside a cartridge setup, you're nearly there. The prior decision-making point would be to choose how you want to

customize your design together with the further options available with the Cricut personal electronic cutter. This choice involves the dimensions of this app and works like a page, stretch-to-fit and lots of different men and women.

Hit a button

In the end, all of your job is completed - you should load your paper or card and hit the start button.

Should you abide by those five simple measures, you're in a position to go from a spark of inspiration for your professional jaw-dropping layout in super quick time. I expect you have gotten pleasure in the process and will get the outcome which you are looking for!

Tips To Help You Start

Capturing memories on a virtual camera, an HD camera, and a voice recorder make life more purposeful. Whenever there is a unique moment which you want to grab and maintain a place to return to at any given time, then you can accomplish this easily with the advice of these tools. But pictures are still the favourite medium by nearly all individuals. If you'd like to put together those pictures and compile them onto a distinguishing souvenir, you then can turn into scrapbooking.

Scrapbooking is a system of preserving ideas which has been in existence for quite some time, and it has evolved to be so much better. Years ago, the creation of one scrapbook was a monumentally crazy job. These days, however, with the introduction of apparatus such as the Cricut cutting machine, things are made much . If you are looking to make one, then this bad boy is the instrument for you. There are great Cricut ideas available on the marketplace that you might get the most out of.

Scrapbooks are only a few of the many Cricut ideas available on the marketplace. This instrument, if you know how to maximize it can assist you in generating items which go beyond scrapbooking such as calendars. If you buy a second-hand cartridge, then you are going to discover a lot of layouts uploaded in each and every one. These pre-generated themes may be used for a great deal of things such as picture frames, and greeting cards.

Only your creativity will limit your advancement using a Cricut device. Along with calendars, you're in a position to lay out every month to be a symbol of the weather, the mood, and special events which are connected with this. The Cricut machine will allow you to look for ideas, however, in the event one cartridge doesn't have the designs you want, you could always go and purchase a different one. It is that easy!
Cricut machines are marginally priced with the cost starting at $299. That's pretty hefty for anyone to begin with. Be a wise buyer. You may turn to the Internet to find good deals. Purchasing from eBay can likewise be a terrific move but can take a lot of risks if you're not experienced with eBay. In the event you're very concerned about that, you may always wait for a sale to occur at one of the regional cities and buy out there as that's going to most likely have a guarantee.

Those are simply some of the numerous amazing Cricut ideas that can be found on the market. Calendars alongside a whole lot of other things can be produced from the usage of this great machine. Bear in mind; only your creativity can limit what you can do.

Why should you get a personal Cricut cutter?

Are you into paper crafting? Can you really do a whole lot of scrapbooking? I have been that person for some time now, and I must say, one of the toughest components was cutting my shapes or letters. It takes forever. Lately, I'd been introduced to the Cricut personal cutter, which is an automatic cutting system which does all of this tedious job for you. I have done a bit of Explore with this specific solution and was eventually convinced I wanted to buy it. In this column, I shall show the top 5 reason I chose to purchase a Cricut personal cutter.

*Love the simplicity of clipping a range of sizes

Compared to other cutting-edge systems, with the Cricut personal cutter, it is possible to use the system to reduce any sizes of letters or shapes involving 1 to 2 5.5 inches. Formerly, to let me cut specific shapes using a standard die-cut platform I had to get different templates for every single letter and every single size of these letters. The superb thing about my choice to buy the Cricut personal cutter is that I did not need these various templates.

*It's light and easy to carry
The Cricut personal cutter is so easy to carry around, in contrast to other big and hefty die-cut machines. Moreover, you may also purchase a carrying bag for this. You can simply take it into a friends' home and have a scrapbooking party jointly. And if you ever have to move your own Cricut personal cutter, then it won't be an issue in any way.

*It's compact and conserves distance space
After you purchase a Cricut personal cutter, you do not have to prepare a lot of space to keep it in. It's fairly compact and doesn't occupy a significant quantity of space. Moreover, you do not have to experience the issue of keeping dividers for templates, such as with old designed die-cut machines. It is not hard to put your Cricut personal cutter on your desk without it taking up a lot of space.

*It works great for almost any sorts of jobs
Whether you're in the mood to do scrapbooking, or perhaps create a birthday celebration for a friend, or perhaps helping your child with a school job, you can pretty much use your Cricut personal cutter for whatever you would like. It has various shapes and attributes you may use. I must admit, when working together with all the Cricut personal cutters, the instant you get those creative juices flowing, then there are no limitations in what it is possible to create.

*It's automatic and great technology.

Instead of needing to manually cut every letter, the Cricut personal cutter does it automatically. All you have to do is put your paper on the mat, follow a few instructions, and press a couple buttons, together with the cutter can do all the challenging job for you. This truly is an excellent feature since it's likely to set up your personal Cricut personal cutter to start cutting something, and you're in a position to do anything else at the same time. This makes scrapbooking a breeze.

As it is possible for you to see from the high top five reasons I made a choice to purchase a Cricut personal cutter this is a very valuable tool that may allow you to cut a few distinct sizes, but additionally produce any job you want, using its high tech interface. So do not hesitate to take a peek at this superb tool and determine the way the Cricut personal cutter will help save you money and effort in your own papercraft projects like it has helped me.

Being a savvy person has never been easier when using the Cricut Expression 2. This handy-dandy item of gear has made it easy and enjoyable to make your own craft tasks personal and unique to your eyes. Since the Cricut Expression 2 is not the very first of its kind (hence the 2) the brand-new slick design together with the full colour LCD touch screen display with stylus shows its growth along with the times. Let's be fair; we do not need things to just work nicely, we additionally want it to look good too.

Scrapbooking could be of a creative outlet when compared with this hobby along with the many attributes the Cricut Expression 2 supplies you with. But do not make the mistake of thinking you're only limited to scrapbooking because it is possible to use this for almost any creative job you're doing or add to individual jobs that you've previously completed. Together with the Cricut can do, the possibilities are boundless!

Unlike the newest purchases, this tool includes two powerful cartridge's functions like the alphabet cartridge combined with another purpose like the frightening cartridge. The alphabet cartridge is precisely what you'll use for letters, numbers and layouts providing life to anything you write. No longer do you have to settle for plain Jane letters and figures considering that when using the Cricut Expression 2 plain is not ever an option.

Let us discuss the key cartridge. "Why?" you may inquire? Well, allow me to tell you this multi-purpose cartridge is where the imaginative pleasure starts! With this particular cartridge, you're likely to have the ability to acquire a great deal of designs, shapes and artwork that could open your mind and get the creative juices flowing so your jobs can develop into the masterpieces you planned them to become.

Characteristics like mat preview to allow you to see until you commit. Furthermore, there are material preferences, so you can get the job to perfection consequently. Furthermore, you will have a cutting place light to aid with the specific reductions you want done. There is definitely somebody at the Cricut development branch that is trying to please the client!

It consistently means more when you or someone you love makes something from scratch for you because they need to set a fantastic deal of energy and idea behind it to really sit down and create it. The Cricut Expression 2 allows everyone to start a brand-new process of production. In case you have not tapped into your inner craftiness, you have the ability to use the Expression 2 to expand your thoughts to what options you will find. Together with the beauty in this is the freedom you have obtained when using the decision to express yourself with no advice of hallmark or some other significant manufacturing.

Envision how refreshing it is to let yourself understand that you have the capability to show that self-in an artistic manner working together with the Cricut Expression 2. Occasionally we get wrapped up in our everyday lives. We do not take the chance to quantify this from the daily regimen and do something which we can genuinely appreciate. So, stop restricting yourself and start having fun.

Chapter 2 - Tools and Accessories

There are not many supplies you need to get started with your Cricut Explore, and they all arrive with the bundle when you purchase even the most fundamental Cricut Explore package--which means you do not need to purchase anything extra in the beginning! The two included Cricut accessories are a cutting mat and a carbide blade. Everything else is optional, but make it possible for you to do much more with this wonderful machine! Let us check these out!

Must-Have Cricut Explore Accessories

Cricut Explore blades

The Cricut Explore includes a super sharp German carbide fine-point blade so you may start cutting straight away. It's placed within the Cricut and can easily be changed when it dulls. I use the fine-point blade for nearly all my trimming, and it always lasts more than that I expect it to. If you're cutting tough substances, you might find you need to change it more frequently. The home with the blade is silver (old machines) or stone (newer machines).

There's also a deep cutting blade, which you will need for cutting heavier stuff, such as thin leather and wood. You will want to acquire the distinct home to it and then swap it from the machine. The home for the profound cut blade is shameful. It is also possible to purchase the blades separately as soon as you have the home.

Ultimately, there's a bonded fabric blade, that you will use to cut fabric that's been coated with heat n bond or another stabilizer.

Note that the Cricut Maker includes a knife blade, a rotary blade, a scoring wheel, a perforation blade, an engraving suggestion, a debossing tip, and a wavy tool--and not one of those tools are compatible with all the Cricut Explore. Have a look at my Cricut Maker accessories article to find out more.

Cutting mats

You will also receive a green 12″x12″ standard grip cutting mat in many Cricut Explore boxes. Some of the more recent machines have the light grip cutting mat. Both of the mats may be used for the majority of your crafting needs—card stock vinyl, etc. If you are using more delicate stuff, such as vellum or mild paper, then you may want to stay with all the light grip mat. If you are cutting heavier materials with an inclination to change, try out a purple strong grip cutting mat. I use my heavier cutting mat to cut chipboard and coated fabric. But the majority of the time I stick with all the green standard grip one.

If you are cutting bigger projects, Cricut additionally has 12 x 24 mats. I really like them for bigger vinyl jobs --I recently cut iron-on vinyl for 15 bags on a single sheet of vinyl with this bigger size, and it moved even quicker.

Regardless of what cutting mat you use; I suggest breaking it in a little bit prior to using it for the very first time. Take off the crystal-clear mat protector and adhere the mat into the very front of your top several times. It is going to pick up some of that lint and, believe it or not; this can help dramatically when removing your job from the mat after it has been cut. It is almost impossible to remove a job easily from a brand-spanking new mat.

Cricut toolset

Some time back, I wrote an in-depth post concerning the Cricut tool set. I will not go into much detail about the weeder, scraper, spatula, tweezers, scissors, trimmer, along with other resources except to state that every one of these tools are so helpful, and if you are likely to get any accessories to your device, I would get a tool collection. Be certain that you read that article about the best way best to use all of the tools! I also adore (such as love) my XL scraper. I basically do not use my little one --as the XL scraper is indeed much quicker and more successful.

Scoring stylus

If you would like to create cards, boxes, or anything else which needs precise folding, I suggest getting yourself a scoring stylus. This tool fits readily to the Cricut's carriage. The Cricut can hold a blade and scoring stylus at precisely the exact same time so you don't need to swap them out--you can score and cut at precisely the exact same moment! Scoring makes it effortless to fold your own projects. If you use jobs from the Cricut picture library, the grading layer is constructed into any document that has to be folded. Find out more about the scoring stylus.

Cricut pens

One of my absolute preferred accessories are Cricut pens. As soon as I received my own Cricut Explore, I did not realize that it could, besides scoring and cutting, also compose! My favourite use for this to tackle letters and cards. This past year I used my Cricut Explore for addressing Christmas cards, and it worked out great!

Where to buy affordable Cricut supplies

Among the questions I get most often is, "where do I purchase Cricut products cheap?"
The ideal thing to do would be to register to get emails from the Cricut store. They have sales going on all of the time. Vinyl could be 25 percent off for a week--stock up!
Obviously, most of us want to save cash, but a good deal of times shop coupons do not work on Cricut things on the Internet or in the local craft shop. However, be certain that you check the clearance department --you may also frequently find discontinued Cricut equipment available on clearance.
Amazon is always a fantastic spot to try for Cricut products in case you've got Amazon prime shipping (receive a free trial here!)) --it'll get to your home at no cost! Additionally, assess eBay--individuals frequently sell their equipment there.

How to produce a reverse canvas

Now let us do a job that looks a whole lot tougher than it really is--turning a plain, wrapped canvas into a piece of artwork using the opposite canvas technique! I am partnering with my favourite craft shop Joann with this enjoyable tutorial--you can get whatever you want (and more!) in-store or online!

I have made this adorable "eat, drink, and be merry" for the Christmas season, however this tutorial functions for almost any picture you may want! It is infinitely customizable. Here are only a couple of those things you can switch up when creating your personal reverse picture:

- Paint or stain the framework.
- Use a cut file picture with any sort of iron-on vinyl, such as sparkle, holographic, and much more.
- Use a print afterwards and cut the picture on iron-on vinyl.
- Hand-paint a picture on the canvas.
- Stencil a picture on the canvas.
- Use a "hot jumble canvas" technique.
- Use the framework as a shallow shadowbox for sentimental items such as movie tickets, infant wristbands from the hospital, or photographs.

Reverse Canvas Supplies

- Wrapped canvas
- Craft knife
- Acrylic ruler (optional)
- Iron-on vinyl (I used black, pink, and green)

- Easy press mini, easy press, or iron
- Pushpins
- Hot glue gun
- Cricut Design Space file

Reverse canvas instructions

Using the craft knife, carefully remove the canvas from the frame, cutting on the outside of the staples. I find an acrylic ruler makes this really easy.

Pull off the canvas and set the frame aside. If you want to paint or stain the frame, now is a good time to do that so it can dry while you do the rest of your project.

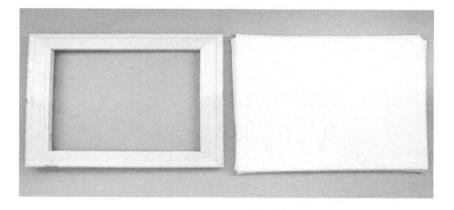

Cut your image using your Cricut. I decided on a cute "eat, drink, and be merry" file in Design Space (link in the supply list). Remember to reverse your iron-on vinyl before cutting and place the shiny side of the iron-on vinyl on the mat.

Centre your image on your canvas. It doesn't have to be perfectly centred—you'll have some wiggle room later in the process. Stick it using your preferred heat source. I'm using my easy press mini, which works perfectly for small projects like this.

Then repeat with the remaining two layers.

Center your canvas behind the frame. You'll see here that though I thought my canvas was straight, I ended up off-centering it a bit to get it squared up in the frame. Once centered, carefully flip the frame over.

Without shifting the canvas, pin the canvas to the back. This just helps you keep it lined up as you glue.

Starting in one corner, hot glue the canvas to the inner part of the frame, keeping the canvas taut.

Using the craft knife, trim off the extra canvas. I find the channel between the two parts of the frame makes a perfect guide for cutting off the back. If you want, you can cover the back with felt for a more finished look.

Flip it over and admire your handiwork! I love that this project looks much more complicated than it is. These reverse canvases are perfect for Christmas gifts for friends, family, and even neighbours!

Chapter 3 - Producing Cricut Stencil Using Stencil Blank

When it comes to particular craft classes, I get so many requests for earning home decor hints employing the Cricut. There are many methods to do so --now I am sharing the way to cut a stencil sterile and use paint. In the forthcoming weeks, I will also be discussing how to create a Cricut stencil together:

  Cricut stencil vinyl
  Cricut adhesive vinyl
  Freezer paper

You can also use iron-on vinyl on timber, which will be my taste --no mess!

But let's get cracking with this method--using stencil vinyl to create a stencil along with your Cricut Explore or Cricut Maker. You may find whatever you want to produce this job at the regional Joann or even online! I'm particular to purchasing online this season --I would rather have the wonderful email carrier deliver me my equipment compared to heading out in the rainy weather!

Cricut stencil supplies

  Green standard grip or purple strong grip mat
  Wood craft framework
  Stencil blank
  Roll of masking tape
  Craft paint in a number of colours such as white
  Sponge stipple brushes

Little, rigid paint brush
Paint tray
Merry & bright SVG

Mine arrived painted with a white backing board. If yours doesn't, you can hide the frame and paint the backing board white (or a different color if you want). You may stencil right on the raw timber, but you cannot actually fix jelqing in wood. It is possible, however, to use paint to touch up any bleeds on a painted sign. It is your choice!

Cricut Stencil Directions

Earning the stencil in Cricut Design Space

Create a new job in Cricut Design Space. On the left, click upload. Subsequently, navigate to this file you downloaded above.

Click Save.

Then choose the document you uploaded and then click on "insert images" to fetch it onto your own canvas.

I might have given you a real stencil record, but I needed to be sure you learned the procedure for turning a normal clip file into a stencil. Be aware you are going to want to use a stencil font, so the inside of your letters remain attached to a stencil.

Begin by clicking shapes from the left design panel and picking a square.

Then alter the dimensions of your square foot to match inside your framework. I love to make it around 1/2" smaller compared to my framework, so I have space to tape it into the backing board so it will not change. In this instance, I left my square 10" x 10" since my board is roughly 10.25" x 10.25."

So, you can line your square along with your picture correctly, pick the square foot by clicking on it and then send it using the arrange menu in the upper edit toolbar.

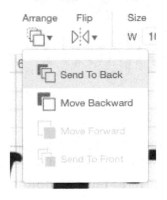

You can now line up your picture and the square foot. If you would like, use the align tools from the edit toolbar to be certain everything is recorded correctly.

Now we are going to slice! Slicing may be confusing to new Cricut users. There are two chief principles: 1) You can just cut two things at a time (in this instance, the picture and the square) and, 2) you will have plenty of leftover bits when you are done because you'll notice.

Click on either the square and the picture, then click slice in the base of the Layers panel to the right.

You will notice your layers panel currently includes three "slice results"--a shameful merry & bright, a grey merry & bright, plus a stencil piece. Delete the first two layers, so you're only left with your stencil piece.

Now you are prepared to cut your stencil! You will surely want to perform a little test cutting along with your blanks. I moved through three stencil blanks (folk art brand) until I got a feeling that really worked. You may test my placing, but certainly, make sure it's working before you cut your entire stencil!

Cutting the stencil
Click make it at the top right of your canvas.

There's nothing additional to do from the prepare screen, so click continue.

In case you've got a Cricut, place your dial to habit.

From the make screen, for the Explore or the Maker, click browse all materials and hunt for stencil.

In the bottom, you will see a green connection for material settings. This permits one to fine-tune all your settings. Scroll down to stencil film and switch it into the following settings: 350 strain and 3x multi-cut.

Click Save. You'll need to go back to browse all materials and select stencil film as the material.

All Materials   Favorites

stencil

3 results

Sandblast Stencil

✓ Stencil Film – 0.4 mm

Stencil Vinyl

c

Material settings

Done

Set your stencil picture onto your own mat. Put your mat beneath the guides and press the blinking arrow to fit your mat in your machine.

Press the blinkings along with your Cricut to cut your stencil film. Important: once you turn the mat from your system following the cut, try to be certain it's cut all of the way through. Otherwise, press on the "c" one longer, and it'll cut again. You cannot do so if you choose the mat from this machine, however, so be certain that you inspect the cut together with the mat still in the Cricut.

We can stencil our sign! Begin by taping your stencil into the interior of your framework. You do not need it changing around!

There are a few options here; however, I haven't found either of them work for me personally.

You can dab on a coating of white paint on your stencil. The concept is that the white paint will bleed providing you a crisper line. That is true, except I've discovered that using two coats of paint (the white and the color) can occasionally make my stencil peel once I pull this up. Not necessarily, but it is a risk.

The next is dabbing a layer of mod podge in your stencil. Same concept, but I frequently observe the exact same result, together with my paint really pulling as I lift the stencil. It is possible to play around and see whether one of these choices work for you!

For me personally, I love to go right to the paint. Using sponge daubers, get a small quantity of paint onto the sponge, then dab it on a scratch paper, then paint the stencil. You want to use hardly any paint and use a dabbing motion rather than brushing. This can assist in preventing bleeding.

Continue with this technique for the remaining part of the sign with all the other colors.

Before the paint is actually set, peel back the tape and then carefully lift the stencil (this can keep your paint from sticking and pulling upward).

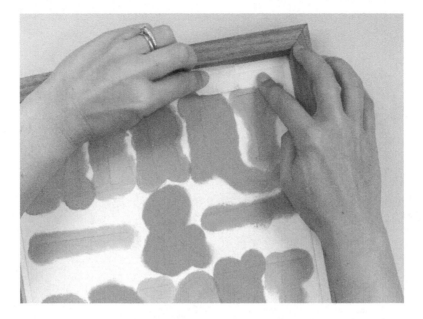

There is a good chance you are still going to have a little bit of bleeding. You can see a little in mine at the underside "r" below.

If you use a small quantity of paint and use a dabbing motion, it ought to be kept to a minimal. Use white paint along with a tiny stiff paintbrush to touch up any areas that require it.

Once dry, it is possible to seal the art with a little poly coating if you would like --but when it is for indoor use, I usually skip this step.

You may use this method to generate all kinds of stencilled signs! This merry & bright sign could be so adorable in a conventional palette of greens and reds, or in place of white chalk on a chalkboard!

Chapter 4 - How to Make Personalized Plates And Mugs

Create your own mug with vinyl
    10 minutes (time spent performing things)
    5 minutes (time spent around)
    15 minutes (total project time)

Tools
    Cricut Explore air and fundamental tools
    Scissors

Materials
    Exterior glue vinyl in whatever colors you would like (I used silver, slate grey, and dark blue)
    Transport tape
    "Baby it's cold outside" layout (you can find my Cricut layout here)
    Rubbing alcohol
    Cotton balls

This Valentine's Day cocktail job is ideal for a "first time" plastic undertaking. Therefore, if you got a Cricut device for Christmas, now's the time to get it from the box and begin creating!

Here is what you will have to create these cute mugs.

- Cricut system (I used my Cricut Explore Air Two; however, you could use any Explore device or the Maker. -- do not stress silhouette users, I still have not forgotten about you! You might even use the SVG document)
- Heat transport plastic -- yes, I will place HTV onto a ceramic mug! What??? Stick around -- you will see!
- Better collectively SVG document (you can find this here)
- Mini handheld iron or heat media using a mug attachment

Here are the ways for the best way to decorate mugs with iron-on vinyl along with a Cricut.

DIRECTIONS

Begin with opening Cricut Design space on your browser and begin a fresh project. Click on the "insert text" button on the left and right type your text to the new text box. On the right, below the "edit" tab, you can change the font and size and orientation of your text if you want. I changed the font to wildflower.

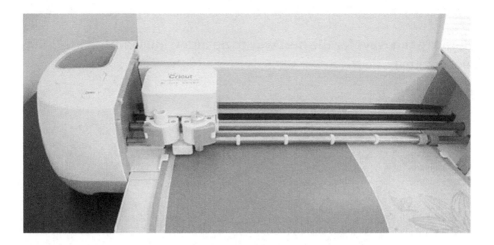

I then clicked "insert images" and discovered a cute snowflake I enjoyed and added it. I resized the picture so it would match on the mug and put it under my text.

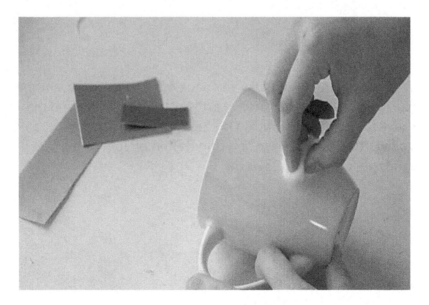

That was it; it is ready to cutback! Just click on the go button, placing the dial in your Cricut device to vinyl, along with the program, will help you through the remaining steps for cutting and loading every distinct layer of vinyl.

While your vinyl is cutting, use a cotton ball soaked in rubbing alcohol to wash your mug in which you intend to set your vinyl. The rubbing alcohol will remove any grease and grime from your fingers so the plastic sticks.

Once your vinyl is cut, weed off any desktop vinyl using the weeding tool, leaving the letters and layout on the backing paper.

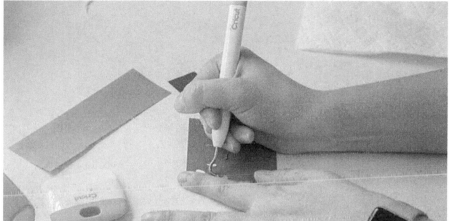

Then trim a slice of tape to exactly the identical dimensions as your vinyl layout. Remove the backing paper in the transport tape and stick the tape onto your vinyl layout. Use the scraper tool to actually press the tape onto the vinyl, so it sticks.

Gently peel the tape; it must follow the vinyl nicely enough to lift up the letters off the backing paper. Then place the vinyl layout on your mug, using the scraper tool to actually stick the vinyl letters onto the mug.

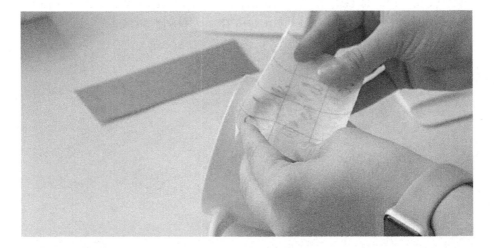

When the vinyl is actually stuck onto the mug, then gently peel back the tape, leaving the vinyl letters onto the mug. And you are done!

Fill it with your favourite hot drink and revel in it!

I propose hand-washing your mug; the dishwasher can be really tough on your dishes and also the vinyl letters might begin to peel off after repeated washing.

Chapter 5 - More Cricut Machine Activities

Crafting Hobbyists

Crafting is just among those most famous hobbies in the world today. You can find a lot of men, women and even kids who like crafting and a few who make a professional living from it. You'll discover a great deal of special tools, software and supplies programs accessible to assist these crafting fans make the most of the moment.

The Cricut system is just that. It's a digital cutter which aids with papercrafts. With only a small button, you'll be able to create lovely designs and receive help with crafts like home decor, artwork, paper crafting and much more. This system is quite simple to navigate and use so that the one thing you really must be concerned about is being imaginative and empowering your imagination to run rampant.

There's no need to get a PC to use the Cricut device. All you will need is a typical electrical outlet to plug it into, and you're prepared to proceed. Before you begin, it's beneficial to take a little time and get more comfortable with this particular machine. Have a peek in the paper feed to comprehend how everything functions.

The on button, clip button and stop button will be grouped together on the right of this device, the newspaper feed is in the back.

To begin, first find the crafts you want to work on. Put a Cricut cartridge into the device, and you also get to select from several layouts, measurements and find each detail of the fashion. You will find countless hundreds of ideas, so the layouts you're ready to create with your crafting are going to be unlimited.

There's a user manual that includes the machine you can look through if you're experiencing any issues. The Cricut method is actually a priceless investment for any crafter who chooses takes their particular hobby seriously.

Using Cricut cutting machines on craft projects

A growing number of people are choosing to create their very own scrapbooking materials, cards and invitations. These do-it-yourself choices allow a fantastic deal and give you more room for customization compared to their own mass-produced options. Not only are homemade invitations a good deal more customizable, but they also cost less than shop-bought options. Cricut private cutting machines also make it possible for those who have minimal time and much less expertise to create professional-looking craft jobs anytime.

Cricut cutting machines are available anyplace in craft shops alongside department stores which contain artwork and art segments. On the other hand, the absolute best bargains are usually found on the Internet. For your occasional do-it-yourself, the entrance level variant, together with easily available sale costs of approximately $100 is more than adequate. It's more than capable of developing a huge variety of distinct shape mixes and needs hardly any maintenance. More seasoned crafters, or people who handle home companies that create customized paper goods, may discover that bigger models are somewhat more depending on their own requirements.

These machines are automatic, and also a good deal easier to use than manual paper cutters. Normally, they can cut quite heavy paper stock, allowing scrapbookers to create layouts that have several different colors and textures. For advice about the best approach to use a system, you will find a choice of websites offering information from frequent amateur customers.

They're a substantial source for inspiration and information, demonstrating the way the system may be best employed. Those websites are a terrific destination for the ones just beginning, the best feature of a house Cricut machine is it has the capacity to make completely one-of-a-kind pages. Experiment with new forms and color combinations to make something distinctive and memorable.

Cricut cutting machines are adaptable and can be used for just about any type of craft project.

Make professional hunting scrapbooks using Cricut personal cutting machines

A Cricut cutting machine can be a vital requirement for any scrapbooker. These machines also make it possible for clients to cut paper to a variety of intriguing shapes, making personalizing each page in a scrapbook simple and pleasurable. Made to be small enough to go with you when you travel, they'll occupy little space in your house and may be carried out with you for virtually any scrapbooking celebrations you may attend. They're the ideal tool for everybody who's searching for a user-friendly way of producing specific borders, sew or other page designs.

Cricut machines can make shapes which are anywhere from 1" to over 5" tall. Simple to alter metal cutting patterns are used to make uniform shapes on several kinds of artwork paper. These include custom decoration, joyous shapes or intriguing borders that could reflect the content of every page. As many identifying thicknesses of card stock may be used, scrapbookers must take note that paper in a lower grade might cause the blades to dull faster. This typically implies you want to always keep a tab on the sharpness of the blade and then replace them if needed to maintain results which are exceptional.

A Cricut machine isn't a small investment. Prices start at roughly $100 online, which might put this cutting-edge device from reach to get a couple of. However, once taking under consideration the price of buying packs of pre-cut shapes and letters, most dedicated scrapbook fans do find the apparatus will eventually pay for itself. It could also be used for additional paper crafts, like making custom invitations, gift tags and cards. The Cricut firm has a fantastic standing in the business world, and their goods are certainly likely to last a long time; therefore, no replacement ought to be required, despite heavy usage.

Scrapbooking is getting more popular than ever with the use of Cricut cartridges. Creating a scrapbook might be enjoyable for the whole family. It's an innovative means to keep family history with photos, journal entries, in addition to memorabilia. Implementing a Cricut expression cutting machine with its massive library of Cricut cartridges makes past images come home to a future generation!

Soon agreeing to the production of photos, people began producing ideas of this way kind to keep the photographs. From the 15th century as when cheap newspaper became accessible to the average citizen in England, scrapbooks known as scrapbooks were kept to put quotations, poetry, correspondence, together with recipes.

Afterwards as now, each scrapbook was unique to the writer's specific theme. From the 16th century, friendship documents were the rage. These records were like modern-day yearbooks, where buddies sign each other's yearbook at the end of the college year.

All those virulent outlets afforded girls in succeeding generations with chances to develop their literacy skills by reproducing their own personal history. It may be difficult for people to imagine now, but women living prior to the 18th and 19th centuries normally didn't possess the ability to read and write made easily available for them.

The producers of Provo craft certainly don't want to have these days return when girls were kept in the dark! In reality, they churn out inventions annually with each passing year to bring our creativity to light. As an example, the handy Cricut Jukebox was created for scrapbookers to conveniently preserve nearly all those Cricut cartridges effortlessly. Implementing the jukeboxes, there's not any need to prevent your creative stream if you would really like to change cartridges out.

Besides the recently published Old West and Hannah Montana, you'll find wonderful classics like a Disney Mickey font cartridge alongside Christmas Solutions cartridge. Two of my favourites, which I've been astounded at the activities results, would be the Home Accents solutions cartridge along with also the Home Decor solutions cartridge. In case you've ever wondered exactly what Provo craft indicates by boundless chances within their motto have a look at these impressive cartridges!

Use your Cricut machine to make money scrapbooking

If you are into scrapbooking at all then no doubt you've learned about Provocraft's Cricut cutting machines. They're amazing machines which take an excellent deal of effort out of plenty of jobs, do not take a computer to use, and they're so straightforward and intuitive to understand how to use! In the event you've ever used one, then you probably have noticed precisely just how much fun they are, but have you thought about how to earn money doing what you really love?

Earning money out of this passion is really a fantasy of all; however, they generally think that it is too hard and give up. The easy truth is that doing so is not really that hard! The only limitation is the creativity and what it is likely to create. Here's a few suggestions to get you started with the process to make additional money with your hobby:

Decorate Themed Parties

Children like to have themed celebrations. When it's a Pokémon celebration, a Bakugan birthday celebration or a Disney character costume party, children just love them. You may easily make some money by creating decoration packs for these sorts of events. Print and cut out a great deal of different sized decorations, and create customized title tags which the children can adhere, produce playing cards in addition to character cards that the youngsters can collect and swap together.

Custom Made Cards and Invitations
Who does not love a personalized thank you card or invitation? It reveals a whole lot of love and thought has gone into them. If you love doing so, why don't you market some of those creations to earn a little cash at precisely the same moment? It's actually surprising how a great deal of individuals want to acquire a custom-made card or invitations created for birthdays, anniversaries, birthdays, anniversaries, get-togethers, and other occasions. Fairly often your local arts and crafts shop are prone to place your creations for sale and show them to their

clientele. Apparently, they frequently take a cut, but additionally it saves you the time of needing to go out and find people yourself.

Custom made scrapbook layouts

Scrapbooking can lead to an obsession collectively. We are always trying to create this fantastic page design, or find that perfect touch which may make our scrapbooks that much better. You can use this Cricut method to create die cuts of listing page designs and market them to other fans all on your own. If it is your passion, then it won't be any trouble thinking up a few to-die-for layouts!

Create a site

You may consistently promote your goods online. Nowadays it's fairly straightforward to make an online website. Go to blogger.com and register to get a completely free site, then with just a little practice you'll be able to yield a superb little site featuring each of the fantastic products which you supply. Put it onto a business card (also free using tons of these online offers from the market) and send it out to anyone that you match. They easily have the ability to how off everything you provide in one location and make a buy.

All these are only a few ideas you can use to get started making cash with your hobbies. Do not be intimidated and believe you're not good enough or it's too hard. Just begin trying, and you might end up amazed at exactly how great your attempts turn out.

Cricut scrapbook number one idea

The number one greatest idea to use your Cricut on would be to make something for your little ones!

Children like to follow all types of tales. Yet one story they likely would love to listen to over and over again could be the story of their birth. That is why, many may prefer creating baby scrapbook to show in a more concrete fashion how they were born. However, it doesn't imply that baby scrapbooks are restricted to the "how" of giving birth. Some

197

small details are critical to generate a far more striking baby scrapbook your kid will like and be extremely proud of as they grow. And because a baby scrapbook is a very small child's bibliography, your children are going to love precisely how much they mean to you personally.

Having a newborn infant in the household is pleasurable. Each day the infant will look marginally different from the preceding day as it grows so quickly. One way to keep these intriguing memories alive is to make a baby scrapbook. Along with the scrapbook you're likely to have the ability to examine it in case you need to and can share it with your family and friends.

If you're planning to use your Cricut device to create a scrapbook for the baby ahead, then here are a couple of things that you've got to consider so you won't confine yourself by developing a baby scrapbook which merely tells the time of birth, measurements and weight of your infant.

To make a baby scrapbook, you need to specify your beginning point. It could be the baby shower or possibly the day of the baby's birth. Moreover, you need to set when to finish the scrapbook. Normally, a baby scrapbook will show the child's first year however, you could go longer in the event you'd really like to. In the process, you want to accumulate things that may be contained in the scrapbook such as the presents you get at your baby shower. Some can even include the infant's first haircut along with various events which the child did for the very first time.

Elect to use a color that may establish the topic of this scrapbook. The standard colour of a baby boy's album is powder blue, while the infant girl's album is pink. You may or might not use these colors and could use another.
You request: "What picture should I include from the listing?"

Many baby scrapbooks could include the facts about the infant upon arrival. All these are the time of birth, weight, time of arrival, the length of labor, the colour of their hair and eyes, and physician's name and the titles of the group who helped the physician at the birth. And naturally, the images of you and your kid in the hospital once you gave birth.

Some contain images of you because you're pregnant. Moments like this can help keep your kid learn how you personally, as a mom cared for him before he was born.

Additional things you want to include are the photographs of the infant's development month by month using a dimension reference (normally a stuffed toy), photographs of the home you reside in and also the nursery, photographs of their family members enjoying the infant, photographs of the infant sleeping, photographs taken while the infant is bathing, photographs with their favourite toys, and extra joyous moments that include them.

As was mentioned earlier, many baby scrapbooks could incorporate the baby's firsts. All these would be your baby's first smile, first bathroom crawl, first roll over, first sat up, first steps, etc. Baby scrapbooks may include their favourites such as their favourite tune, toys, bedtime stories, etc.

The nice thing about this is that you may always add whatever is connected to your child as he or she's growing up.

Added vital events which may or might not be captured by memorabilia may be written in the book.

You may write about the significance and value of this title, your length of stay in the hospital, additional men and women who were current in the hospital, their particular response when you gave birth, and their own feelings the minute they delivered your baby, and also the way in which they amuse the infant. Perhaps you will write about stories that may further exemplify these occasions which are recorded in photos. Stories such as the infant's very first moments, babysitting, together with mannerisms (did he or she suck their thumb... And things such as individuals in their life).

You have obtained the photographs, what items to write about and also the scrapbook to put it together; what is next?

Well, creating baby scrapbook is genuinely a personal thing. It is your decision what other items that you would like to integrate so your kid will know precisely how he or she developed.

Some of the benefits of owning the Cricut machine is the fact that it was created for in home use. It's somewhat expensive but worth the cost. My partner was fortunate enough to find it available for $179.99. Provocraft provides a storage bag that's on wheels so you may take it to scrapbook cropping courses or scrapbook celebrations. Its cartridge based and contains a huge variety of styles of letters, phrases and shapes to choose from. The Cricut cartridges marketplace costs approximately $90.00. The cartridges feature an overlay that's set onto the Cricut apparatus. These overlays provide you a number of 3-D effects. A number of them are proof, tags, charms, shadowing, positive and negative imaging. Everything is done right from the touch of a button. It is only restricted to one's creativity.

You can cut the picture as little as 1" or as big as 5 ½." It is likely to use many different thicknesses of paper, but I have a propensity to use more of a moderate card stock. The cutting knife is much more elastic. There's an anxiety setting for thicker papers. Additionally, a rate setting for how quickly you'd like it to cut back. There's an expansion port for future updates. The replacement components for the body are rather pricey. As an instance the cutting mats can be purchased 2 in a bundle for $10.00.

The die cutting machine will not feature everything you want to start. I would have to play with it a little because there is a learning curve. By way of example, for thinner paper you should use the lower rate or it will tear the paper. Another instance, for thicker paper you are most likely to have to fix the blade and place the rate button on a cut.

Whenever you're accustomed to it, then it gives you plenty of enjoyment to use it. I especially adore the fact you're all set to rate the expired discounts for simple paper piecing methods. The ideas you are in a position to get for fresh scrapbook page designs are infinite.

Some of the drawbacks are you can't personalize your own die cuts. You may just use what's on the cartridges. The mat that communicates with the die cutting equipment is sticky. I discovered the stickiness wears off immediately. For the mat I use a repositionable spray adhesive. You're restricted to using only real card stock paper. Whatever brand you choose. The blade can't cut any additional substances. I truly like to create chipboard monograms and I'm unable to this using this method.

No wonder they predict it gives Christmas cheer. This cartridge has many intriguing shapes which allow you to truly feel airy and joyful. If you aren't in the Christmas spirit yet, this cartridge certainly offers you the jump start you need. From a grinning reindeer to bits of candy, you will have the ability to decorate your scrapbook pages and you also can't overlook Santa and his sleigh.

All the Cricut cartridges have work keys nevertheless, the one I enjoy the most with this particular cartridge is your position card feature. Every one of the shapes which are on the cartridge are easily accessible to place on a place card, making it ideal for an adult dinner party to your kid's play bash. Whatever celebration you are having, you can make place cards for your guests that will ensure they feel unique.

There's also a label feature. It is not crucial to go and buy gift tags this season for your presents. Just take out this cartridge, your favourite paper, some ribbon and create your own. Now that is going to be a saver for a single pocket simply by producing them yourself. If you are like me you would not even have to buy the equipment, then they are based alongside your "crafting stash of bits."

I just thought of a very adorable idea. If you're creating a scrapbook and possess a border of Christmas lights which are united with slender decoration. (I'd need to do this properly now) it's possible to have a glance at my website in order to see how adorable it was and it just took me around 10 minutes from start to finish.

Additionally, I made Santa a location card to depart with his cookies on Christmas Eve. You may find dozens and dozens of items you will have the ability to produce with this Cricut cartridge. You merely need some imagination and some Christmas cheer to get you crafting.

Scrapbooking is straightforward and just about anybody can get it done. There are essentially 3 jobs and if you do them well you will have the ability to generate a superb scrapbook. These three jobs include organizing photographs, devising designs, and prep workspace. Here are some steps to generate your own scrapbook.

First you need to determine the subject you may use. You'll come across a great deal of potential topics it's possible to pick from. A fast-online study gets your creative juice flowing. What I typically like to do would be go to images.google.com and hunt for scrapbooking topics to find out what other individuals do. And do not neglect to get ideas from other household members. By considering all the ideas from several people you will run into a few wise insights regarding the best approach to make the entire scrapbook look great.

One thing you may find hard in case you haven't done any scrapbooking would be to find pictures. If you're into scrapbooking and are likely to make a great deal of scrapbooks, then you might elect to invest in a digital cutter such as the Cricut personal cutting machine. With help from a computer you will be able to produce all types of shapes and contours. But to start with you can simply use oblong or circle sized templates and subsequently cut the pictures by hand so they are prepared for the scrapbook. It is easy to find these templates in the regional craft shops. Be certain you do a few practice cuts on scrap papers before doing it on the real image. This may be one thing which you don't wish to hurry, as a wrong cut will harm the image and it might be permanent. Also be sure you use a sharp blade so you get a clean edge with a single fold.

Scrapbooking is no doubt among the most interesting things you can do. It will bring back all of the intriguing memories the moment you look at it decades later. These memories are priceless and can't be traded for anything else. A well-done scrapbook may be rewarding enough to be passed down for centuries.

The best way to remove vinyl decals

Decals have become a fairly common attachment for houses, vehicles, and a great deal more. With machines such as Silhouette and Cricut which can be found on the current market, it's simple for everybody to create and design their very own stickers. While we are busy sticking and putting our stickers onto things, many don't think about what they will do after the decal has worn out and they no longer desire it. So, while some are providing the best way how to produce and install stickers, we believed it may be an excellent concept to explain out how to eliminate them this time around.

Heat:

Much like most sticky stuff, heating up the outside can let you remove the decal considerably simpler. When working on a car, you may set it in the sunlight to get a bit hot, and that should be sufficient to get the process moving. Many installers choose to use hairdryers or heating guns, and these certainly are a simpler option if working inside. Just make certain not to make the things too hot with the heating since you do not need to get the scraping. Constantly work in segments, as heating up the whole surface at once will probably be a significant waste of time because the minute you enter another segment, it's very likely to get chilled.

Scrape:

When you have implemented the warmth, you have to be to start scraping the plastic. With this specific component I use a plastic razor blade or credit card. Do not use metal! This is merely very likely to cause harm to anything your decal is on (especially vehicles). You do not have to scratch the whole decal back, only enough to have the ability to get a good grip onto it and peel it off.

Peel:

When you have the boundaries peeled up, you have the capacity to start peeling off the material. You should really get this done slowly, as fast motions will probably make the substance tear or leave extra glue behind. I also advise you to get this done at about a 120-degree angle to start ripping and this can ensure you remove the entire decal simultaneously.

Remove the goo:

Once you are finished removing the decal, you're probably going to see a dirty/sticky outline of where your decal was. You will find an assortment of special products you might use to eliminate this, but I'm a lover of Goo Be Gone. Make sure you read the back of the bottle prior to use to be certain it won't result in certain discolouration or damage to some stage you're working on till you begin. I use the liquid with a terry cloth since it's harder and will work better to remove any grime. You might choose to wipe down the surface a few times, but in the very long run you want to get a new and pleasant surface ready for an upcoming decal project!

Chapter 6 - Editing Cricut Projects

Cricut Design Space doesn't autosave your endeavours, therefore (as a wonderful practice), I advise you to save your project after you place the exact first piece, shape, or image on the canvas area.

Sometimes, tasks can take some time, and if you do not save your job while you can, your valuable time and precious work will pay a visit to the trash if Design Space crashes.

I've lost a few minutes before studying my lesson, so, please save as you go. Notice: "I save modifications in my job every five minutes or so. When you start on a brand-new canvas, then the save option (found in the upper right-hand corner of the window) will probably be greyed out, however whenever you put in a picture, it's likely to activate.

To save your project, put the very first thing (text, picture, contours, etc.) You can use it on your own canvas.

When you click save, a little window will pop up asking you to name your job. If you are just using Cricut pictures or fonts, then you are going to have the option to discuss your work on Facebook or perhaps Pinterest.

But if you use your own pictures, subsequently the "public" option will not appear. Don't worry though; you are still able to see your creations in the "my tasks" window which will I show you later on.

After naming your project, click on save. A blue banner advertisement will appear with this window, notifying you that the job is saved.

Now, you can start altering your design by integrating text, or changing colors. In this circumstance, I just altered the color of the file. Nothing complicated.

Just remember to store your work every three to five minutes; believe me, you don't want to waste time in the event the app crashes.

If at any period you would like to produce a new job, make sure your job is saved. No worries, however.

If for any reason you still have unsaved modifications, Design Space may deliver a warning.

Don't take this warning lightly; in the event you click on "replace" instead of "save" you will lose your hard work. It happened to me personally, and it might happen to you!

Openwork at Cricut Design Space desktop

To start a project, you've established, you want a clean and fresh new canvas.

Currently, there's not a method for you to mix jobs. Let's hope Cricut adds this functionality soon.

It is likely to discover your designs in two different manners. The first and fastest one is by simply clicking on the "my projects" shortcut found in the right corner of the window.

The next method is by clicking the projects option on the left of the image and see the drop-down menu and then choose the option "my projects" (read the several options of the drop-down menu to find prepared cut jobs).

As you can see on the screenshot above, the job I created is right there. The arrangement of those jobs is predicated on the previous date.

From the "my projects" view, you can edit, delete, customize, and reduce your previously established tasks.

There are different areas when you can click on a particular job; if you click on the "share" choice, you will be motivated to devote a description, photos, etc. And if you click on the 3 dots (bottom-right of each task), then you are going to be able to delete it manually.

If you want to personalize your job or delete it at once, then you'll have to click on the featured image of your design.

Upon clicking a tiny window will open, and you'll have the ability to talk about and see all of the information concerning the task, like the fonts, shapes, and images you have used.

First and foremost, from this window, you have the ability to personalize your work or send it to cut. The "make it" shortcut is great as though your project has been created, it's possible to bypass all the Design Space process and see the mat preview right away.

However, in the event that you want to edit the appearance of your design, click personalize.

Now let's find out how to edit your own undertaking!

Edit projects in the Cricut Design Space desktop

Once you click customize for any job, you have the ability to edit and change things around.

Take a peek at the following screenshot to see the alterations I made to the original design.

Insert form: Add a circle to the image and change color.

Weld: Select the first image and click on the weld tool (bottom of the layers panel) to acquire all our design in 1 layer.

Twist: Place the plotted image in the middle of the ring then pick either ring and then click on the slice tool (together with the weld tool).

Keep the purple ring with a cut-out picture.

This editing is simple. I'm confident you can do it, but just what I wanted to show is the best way to proceed after editing work.

Here's the product, if you click rescue you will revaluate your primary design and if this is what you need, great. However, if you still want to keep the job you started with, click on save and select the choice "save."

Once you click "save" you're going to be motivated to modify the name of your primary project; in this scenario, I just added a "2" to the title.

Easy, right?

But should you decide to use either design again, return to your own jobs and you'll see some are easily available.

Save, open & edit projects out of the Cricut Design Space app (iPad, phone).

The steps you need to store, edit it, and then begin work in Cricut's app are incredibly similar to those that you would make from the PC.

You can find it out fairly quickly, but I want to inform you I grew several white hairs searching for each among the options, so here I am to make it easy for you.

Let us find out together!

Save project in the Cricut Design Space program

The Cricut Design Space app contains three particular viewpoints: home, canvas, and produce.
Ordinarily, when you start the app, the option is going to be placed on "home." To start focusing on a brand-new job, click on the blue square with and sign then tap "canvas."
To be able to save your job, you need to place at least 1 item (kind, text, image). For purposes of this tutorial, I used the image #m44919.
After placing a product, then tap the save icon found on the upper-left corner of this plan and select the choice "save."
When you tap save a little window will pop up in which you'll be able to enter the name of your work, and where you'd love to conserve your own endeavour.
Choose "save to the Cloud" if you want to enter your jobs from the computer, and you have got a reliable online connection. Choose "save iPad/iPhone" in the event that you don't have reliable Internet and appreciate having the capacity to work offline.

When choosing "save iPad," then you won't have the capability to find individual's jobs on your PC. However, you are likely to be able to use that job again and again without access to the Web.

I select "save to the Cloud" because I love having accessibility to my tasks on my personal PC. But by all means, pick whichever matches your needs the best.

Save changes as you operate on your style sense in the event the app crashes, or you might lose all of your hard work.

One thing to consider is the way to start a new job when you have something on your canvas. (it took me a while to figure it out).

Visit the "home" view and tap "new project." If you have unsaved modifications, the application provides a warning. Select previews and save each one of the alterations and repeat precisely the same method to remove any hints.

Don't take this warning lightly; in the event that you don't save, your job will probably be missing.

Openwork in Cricut Design Space program

To begin an already established project, first, make certain your canvas is sterile (no extra jobs, text, design, or shapes) and move into the "house" standpoint of this plan.

With this view, and below your profile picture, there's a drop-down menu, then click and select where your project is (Cloud or iPad/iPhone).

Notice: by that drop-down (additionally if you are connected to the Internet) menu, then you may even find prepared to cut jobs, no current tasks in your system, etc.

As most of my tasks are on the Cloud, so I chose "my jobs on the Cloud." As you can see in the screenshot down below, I'll find the tasks I have been working on throughout this tutorial.

Outstanding!

From that standpoint, "home/my jobs in the Cloud," you can carry out a couple of things on each undertaking.

Should you tap the "chat" alternative, you will be motivated to create a description, photos, etc. Your own endeavour. And, in the event you click on the 3 dots (bottom-right of each job), then you are going to be able to delete it manually.

If you'd love to personalize your job or delete it at once, then you'll have to tap on the featured image of your design.

Upon tapping the view your phone will change, and you'll be in a position to see all of the information concerning the job, like the fonts, shapes, and images you have got.

First and foremost, from this window, you can personalize your work or send it to cut. The "make it" shortcut is great because when your project has been created, it's possible to bypass all the Design Space process and see the mat preview right away.

However, in the event that you'd love to edit the appearance of your design, click personalize.

Now let's find out how to edit your undertaking!

Edit projects in Cricut Design Space program

If you tap customize for almost any job, you will be able to edit and change things around.

Take a peek at the following screenshot to observe the alterations I made in the original design.

Select all of the letters inside this "daydream outline."

Weld each of the inner letters.

Twist the outline of the coating together with the letters that are welded.

Notice: Slice and weld are inside the action menu.

This editing is very simple, I'm sure you could do considerably better, but precisely what I wanted to show is the best way to proceed after seeing an already recognized undertaking.

In case you tap rescue, then you will revaluate your primary design and if this is what you require great. However, if you still want to keep up the job you started with, click on save and select the choice "save."

Once you click "save" you're going to be motivated to modify the name of your primary project; in this scenario, I just added a "2" to the title.

Easy, right?

Best Strategies For Picking The Ideal Cricut Personal Electronic Cutter

The assortment of Cricut personal digital cutter machines was created to automate lots of those tricky crafting jobs. If you have not heard of these earlier, then keep reading in the event you would like to know how to take your house crafts to the next level. If you're conscious of these, you might be asking yourself how to select which of these cutting machines is suitable for you. Within another guide, I'll be helping you select which one of the four Cricut versions is the best fit for your needs. In the process, you are very likely to comprehend the benefits and pitfalls of each machine, which usually means you are in a position to make an educated choice.

The four models we are most likely to be considering are th standard Cricut personal electronic cutter, the Cricut Create, the Cricut Expression and the Cricut Cake.

The easiest version to try in the start is the Cricut Cake. This was created with a single goal in mind- to create professional-looking decorations. It can cut shapes from bread, fondant, gum paste and other raw materials. It's very much like the Cricut Expression system, but the working parts are changed to make them appropriate for foods. That means parts which have to be cleaned can be readily eliminated. If you are looking to create edible decorations, then that is the only option from the scope. This variant retails from approximately $270.

The other three Cricut personal electronic cutter versions are acceptable for printing. They cut from the exact same substances, such as paper, card, vinyl and vellum. Which version you choose will depend upon your budget and requirements.

Budget

The standard Cricut personal digital cutter is the cheapest priced in the range, costing roughly $100.

Next up is your Cricut Create, starting from $160 and upwards.

The very best of the range of versions is your Cricut Expression, that will set you back about $225.

Prerequisites

All models are compatible with the whole selection of Cricut cartridges. This typically means you've got an almost infinite supply of die cutting layouts, as you can always purchase more cartridges. Therefore, there are two major aspects on your needs to make your pick. These can be the measurements of machine and cuts, in addition to the assortment of die cutting options.
The standard personal electronics cutter and Create machines are small and portable. They will cut contours about 11.5 inches. The Create has a considerably wider variety of capacities.

The Expression is a larger machine, made to get a permanent place in a desk or workbench. It is going to cut up shapes to approximately 23.5 inches, and also employs a huge variety of functions.

By taking into account these factors, you'll have to have the ability to choose the Cricut personal electronic cutter that's best for you.

Individuals really think the Cricut system is one tool that's responsible for the conceptualization of those designs that we find in scrapbooks. In fact, the layouts come from the brain of the consumer and then are made concrete with the Cricut cutting system.
Additionally, there are other tools that make the layouts such as cartridges and software programs. The best software program out there is the Cricut Design Studio. With this system, you can edit and

produce your personal designs and edit existing designs which are pre-packaged.

Life is great really! People also feel the use of a Cricut cutting process is only restricted to the topic of scrapbooking. Only a couple people understand that the Cricut machine along with the cartridges and the software tools may possibly be used to make a substantial variety of things. You'll come across a good deal of Cricut projects it is likely to use the Cricut cutting platform for many things and only your mind can restrict what you can do.

Greeting cards are outstanding Cricut jobs for anyone to take part in. With all the layouts you'll have the ability to get in the Cricut cartridge along with the software applications that you've set up, and your layout covers that defy the unconventional. The difficulty that lots of individuals experience when they try to purchase greeting cards is that they cannot track down the kind of the card they're searching for. This may result in anxiety and a fantastic deal of frustration regarding the purchaser's part. You're a whole lot better off creating your own greeting cards.

Cricut calendars are just another great idea to use a Cricut cutting device. A calendar is filled with 12 months. You may get creative and hunt for designs on your cartridge or software that may reflect the whole month that's on your calendar. If we are in the month of December, you may seek out layouts which fit the mood and sense of December. Start searching for snowmen, reindeers, and Christmas trees. I promise you that you have got all the layouts you will ever want inside your applications or cartridge.

Remember, only your creativity can limit what you do. These Cricut jobs could possibly be used either for personal satisfaction or revenue generating purposes. Be creative with your preferred machine. You never know what kind of thoughts can pop into your mind.

This report clarifies the numerous uses of the Cricut Jukebox system, however, a justification for your Cricut system, called the private electronics monitoring system will be in order. The Cricut personal cutter is an entire cutting platform employed for crafting. It is lightweight and designed to help with your home, office or faculty scrapbooking and other jobs. It's fairly user friendly and exceptionally convenient. As a plug in, cut and design machine, it is completely beneficial for individuals focusing on card making, scrapbook construction and perhaps even paper crafting.

However, the Cricut cutter system needs cartridges to get the job done. It has lots of cartridges to cut layouts of any kind and any dimension, determined by the selection of the consumer. People can shell out a great deal of time loading and reloading individual cartridges they work with. To be in a position to make unique layouts and cut them out, you need to go from one cartridge to another, which might be quite time consuming. But there is a machine designed to lower the issue of loading and reloading, or changing of cartridges - voila! - the revolutionary Cricut Jukebox machine.

What's this Cricut Jukebox apparatus? It is an extremely valuable machine, valuable to anyone who participates in the art of crafting. Cricut Jukebox, which looks like a simple cartridge, isn't just a box. It is a system or tool that, when plugged into the Cricut cutter system, can supply six (6) cartridges of special layouts and measurements. Apparently, the wide variety of those 6 cartridges should be up to your liking and wants. This application will surely provide you a hand in your cutting and designing tasks. The Jukebox eases and eliminates the trouble of shifting the cartridges in and out of your Cricut machine.

There are more attributes of this machine you need to find out about. This Cricut Jukebox system is searchable. Which means you can operate with more than one jukebox whilst working with your Cricut machine. Considering the jukebox system gives a unique quality that enables three jukeboxes to be used at the same time, you've got the means of using more cartridges when you have the need to. One jukebox holds 6 cartridges, so therefore, in case you simultaneously use 3 jukeboxes in one time, you will have 18 cartridges prepared to use. How can that? Each Cricut jukebox is equipped with cable wires - a very simple procedure to follow. Just plug in one jukebox on your Cricut device and plug in a different jukebox to the first one which you attached into the primary Cricut apparatus, which you can then proceed to plug them one after another. In other words, connect one with a different one- easy!

Another fantastic feature of the Jukebox, is that you can stack them to minimize space in your office, allowing you to run them safely in minimal space - and far more, it provides a compartment where you might safely stack your own cartridges. The Cricut Jukebox is portable and simple to use, thus, you've got benefit as well as simplicity of use. It isn't necessary to depend on a person changing cartridges, as soon as you're in a position to take advantage of just pushing buttons, and keeping cartridges of your choice at the tip of your fingers!

Although, all the variations of Cricut cutting machines function in a similar technique to some extent using only a lot of variation to the specific same layout and attributes, the Cricut Design has emerged as a versatile system which has changed the crafting industry by introducing a couple of new features that improved its functionality.

The Cricut machine lets users cut many letters, shapes and words for classroom décor, signage, scrapbooks, and a whole lot more.

Chapter 7 - How to Create Personalized Pillows

Among my favourite characteristics of Cricut Design Space is your capability to use system fonts. As a consequence, you may download fonts from the Web and use them in your regular crafting world! I really like it. Whenever you have the liberty to use any font you would like, the alternatives for typography projects explode!

For my initial typography job, I made a pillow with one of my own favourite quotations on it- "At the touch of love, everyone becomes a poet," by Plato.

There are a lot of sites where you can download fonts at no cost, but my favorite is dafont.com. Dafont.com permits users to upload fonts they've designed. Be aware that most of the fonts have special instructions and asks that you use them for individual use only.

Want to make this pillow? It is ready-to-make!

Materials needed:

    Cricut Explorer® or Maker machine

    Cricut® 12" x 12" standard grip mat

    Cricut weeder tool

    Purple iron-on

    Gold iron-on

    20" x 20" pillow shape and protect

    Easy press or iron

    Press fabric or clean cotton fabric

1: Download your favourite

The fonts you will need to make this job are: Mastoc, Bream Catcher, and Authentic Hilton. Click the hyperlinks to be taken to www.dafont.com.

****Please be aware that Mastoc and Authentic Hilton should be used for individual use only. ****

You have to download and install these fonts for the job to get the job done.
To install, start the downloaded font (tagged .ttf) and put in it to your PC.
It works better if you download the fonts prior to launching Cricut Design Space. Otherwise, you will want to close the browser and then reopen it after installing the fonts to automatically refresh your font file.

2: Produce design

Insert text on your canvas. The fonts will be automatically a part of this system fonts as soon as you've installed them. You can filter fonts in Design Space by clicking system fonts from the top window.

Once I have determined which words I need in each font, then I begin placing them in a design. The very first step would be to weld the script fonts collectively. Choose the words and ungroup the letters.

Transfer the letters next to each other before you are happy with how they look. Then pick each the letters and weld them together.

Organize all the words on your layout, pick all the words, and weld them together so that the words will cut as one whole design.

3: Cut out design

In Cricut Design Space, cut pictures from the iron-on. Make sure to check the "mirror pictures (for iron-on)" box in the mat preview before you cut. (if cutting numerous mats, make certain to check that box to get every mat which has iron-on.)

4: Put iron-on

Weed excess iron-on round the picture.

5: Use iron-on on pillow

Follow the program directions for Cricut iron-on to stick the cut phrases onto the front of the pillow.

Use our easypress or an iron on the purple picture first, then do the gold image.

Supplies you'll need:

   Cricut Explore or maker machine
   Cricut® 12" x 24" standard grip cutting mat
   Cricut® tools, weeder
   Cricut® iron-on lite in gray
   Cricut® iron-on lite in black
   Cricut® iron-on lite in red
   Cricut® iron-on lite in cyan
   Cricut® iron-on lite in maize
   White canvas cloth
   Red cotton cloth
   Blue cotton cloth
   Literary cotton cloth

Dark cotton cloth
Dark and white cotton cloth
Iron or easypress
Press fabric or clean cotton fabric
Scissors
Sewing machine and thread
Needle
Polyester fiberfill (not pictured)

1: Cut your pictures

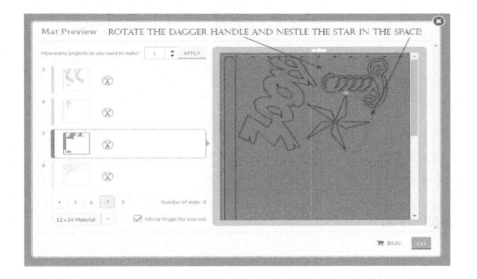

Open the pillow job in Cricut Design Space™ and click on create it. The project file contains the pictures for thirteen cushions: (two) swords, (1) dagger, (1) grenade, (3) ninja stars, (1)"flourish" term, (2) hitting fists, (1) bomb and (2) knives. Bear in mind that if you merely wish to cut some of the cushions or more of a single kind of cushion, you could always click on customize rather than make it and change the document to satisfy your requirements.

Some important tips for this job:

-Make certain to click on the "mirror picture (for iron-on)" button for each mat in the job on the mat preview display. Considering that every one of the mats includes iron-on, you'll have to click onto each mat and select to mirror the picture.

-The program determines where the cuts will happen on the mat. For this job, I needed to save my iron-on material, and so I moved the pictures around on the mat to make the best use of the leading area. Additionally, this is performed in the mat preview display.

-Simply click on each picture and move them around until they are tucked right into each other. This ninja star would not have cut since the iron-on substance is 19" long and the star was set lower than that on the mat.

-Assess each mat. I transferred pictures around on all them.

2: Iron images onto canvas

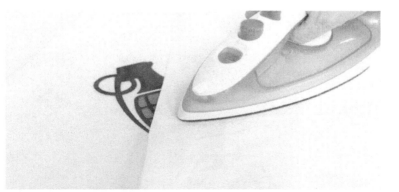

Iron the pictures onto white canvas leaving approximately 5-6" of distance between pictures for cutting and stitching. It is possible to accelerate the process using our easypress as it's a larger surface compared to a conventional iron and much more consistent heating throughout the plate.

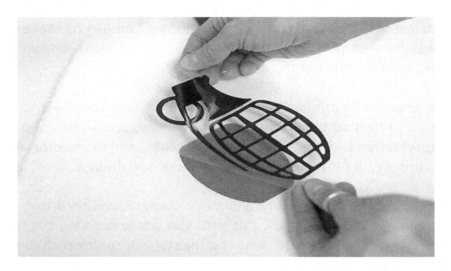

For the layered images, begin with ironing the base layer set up. Eliminate the liner.

Twist the top picture over the base image and iron in place. You can find more directions about the best way best to use Cricut® iron-on here.

3: Cut fabric shapes

Use scissors to cut each picture. Make sure to leave at least 2-3" of space around the pictures for stitching seam, trimming and cutting.

You do not need to be perfect! The attractiveness of these interesting cushions is their wonky shape that really adds to their appeal.

4: **Cut out sourcing**

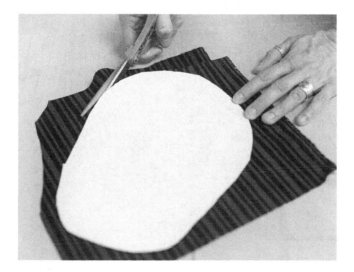

Set the cut canvas pictures face down on the backing cloth (right sides together). Use scissors to cut the backing to coordinate with the front part.

5: Stitch fabric together

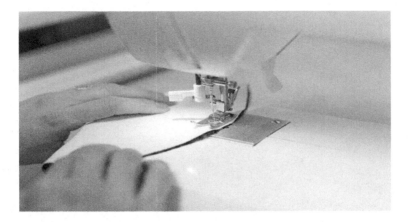

Use a sewing machine to sew around the borders of every cushion. Leave about two 1/2" open (unstitched) for turning and stuffing. I used 1/4" seams.

6: Switch pillows and materials

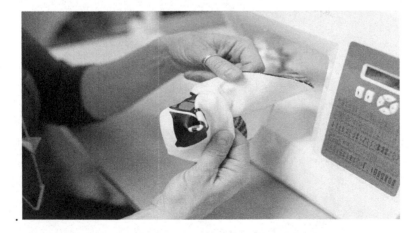

Turn the cushions inside out and stuff them with fiberfill.

7: Hand-stitch the openings

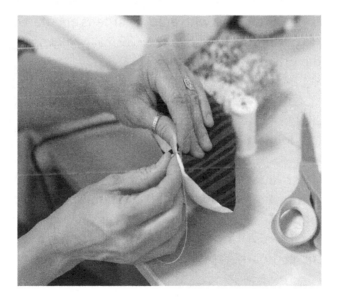

Use a needle and thread to hand-stitch the openings shut.

227

Chapter Eight - The Way To Make Personalized Totes And Decorations

In case you have tried painting or stencilling cloths, then you know it could be rather hard to obtain a quite clean and consistent outcome. Prepared to meet a new love?

Iron-on vinyl! Now I'm going to discuss with you the way to use Cricut iron-on vinyl along with the Cricut Easy press two to make a gorgeous floral canvas bag really fast and readily. Wouldn't this tote be a fantastic present for a friend who enjoys gardens and flowers? Oh, also do not forget your mother!
Step 1: Cut the Cricut iron-on vinyl

If you're just getting started on Cricut projects, assess outside this comprehensive Cricut beginner's tutorial about how I generated my very first Cricut job (a gorgeous card!) in only 20 minutes.

Significant: After launching the floral design in Cricut Design Space, resize it to match your job. Next, you'll be prompted to select materials. If you're using Cricut glitter iron on vinyl, be certain you click on the "browse all materials" tab to obtain the "glitter iron-on," since it's thicker to cut compared to the normal iron-on vinyl. (See picture below.)

Click "mirror picture (for iron-on)" accordingly as it flips your picture. This isn't too crucial here but it's great to form a custom for iron-on projects so once you produce something with numbers or letters, it is going to go on properly.

Put your iron vinyl glistening plastic-side down on your standard grip cutting mat. Insert the mat into the Cricut, press clip, and see the magic happen.

Do not peel off the Cricut vinyl sheet off the mat however. We will eliminate the excess vinyl that is part of your layout.

Use the Cricut weeding tool to prop up a tiny corner, then peel off the piece. This Cricut tools fundamental place is amazing: it comprises the weeder, scraper, and spatula that I love, and much more! As you go, you'll see a small bit of glitter staying on the sheet. This is no issue.

The weeding tool made the process so much simpler. As soon as you finish weeding, peel the plastic sheet using the plastic layout attached onto it. We're now prepared to iron it onto our canvas tote bag!
Step 2: Move vinyl layout onto clean canvas tote bag.

You can use an iron to do iron-on plastic jobs, but an iron may have very irregular temperatures in the center to the outer borders. The heating on the Cricut Easypress is totally across its surface just like a conventional heat press. It's super-fast to warm up and as simple to use as an iron.

Set the Cricut Easypress to 315°. It will heat up in about 2-3 minutes. Put the bag on an even surface like an ironing board. I used the Cricut Easypress mat that's created for using together with the Easypress heat press machine. The mat provides a smooth and even surface on front of the canvas bag, and is super simple to store when not being used.

Put the design together with the glistening plastic side on the canvas tote bag. The plastic protects the Cricut vinyl. Never allow the vinyl to touch the iron directly!

Put the layout in the specific place you need on the canvas bag and put the Easypress at the top for 30 minutes.

My layout is somewhat larger than the 9"x9" region of the Easypress, therefore I transferred the Easypress to distinct locations and replicated the 30 second procedure.

Allow the vinyl to cool, and then peel the plastic back from your picture. Such an exciting moment!

The vinyl should adhere. If you discover it begins to pull up, put the vinyl down and use more heat on your area.

Our new canvas tote bag is ideal for all of the overflowing prosperity from our backyard!

Personalized Home Décor

The Cricut machine is an excellent tool. The world of scrapbooking hasn't been the exact same ever since the debut of the Cricut cutting machine. This instrument has revolutionized how we cut designs from paper, vinyl and cloth.

Back in the times of metal and wood, the craft of maintaining memories was crude. Man used nothing but paintings, portraits and writing as tools for capturing memories and making certain future generations could see them. There was not any way of recording voice and movement back then. As the years progressed, things changed.

Tech experienced a massive boom as a result of the fantastic minds that inhabited the late 18th and 19 century. You look around you and that which was once a dream is currently possible. A method or procedure that was introduced in the 19th century that was regarded as a distinctive method of preserving memories has been the method of scrapbooking. This procedure involved the introduction of a publication which would house images that shared a frequent theme.

When scrapbooking was comparatively fresh, things were hard as it came to the real process of producing them. The conceptualization was simple, but the cutting stage was what challenged scrapbookers far and close as the procedure alone demanded the most stable hands on Earth. However, with the debut of the Cricut cutting machine, the cutting-edge stage has been quite simple. There's really a whole lot of Cricut jobs out there which it is possible to participate in by means of your Cricut machine. Let us talk a little about a few of them, shall we?

You will find Cricut jobs which may enable you to attain personal satisfaction or assist you in making money. For many people the Cricut system is simply confined to simply being an instrument for scrapbooking. In fact, the Cricut cutting machine may be used for a whole lot of things. Keep in mind, the layouts which are observed on your applications tool or cartridges may be used for a great deal of things.

For starters, it is possible to make greeting cards. I am pretty much convinced that most people have had horrible experiences before which are connected without finding the ideal gift card. Using a Cricut machine and application or a cartridge, you may make your very own personalized gift cards. You may either sell them in case you would like to or simply continue making cards for your personal satisfaction.

You will find so many Cricut projects which you can participate in using all the Cricut machines. The rule of thumb would be to be imaginative and never allow your mind to set limitations.

Cricut Suggestions For Promoting Your Greeting Card Projects

You've just bought a Cricut private cutting machine together with its collection of cartridges you can use to begin a wonderful job. This revolutionary machine has revolutionized the arts and crafts hobby all around the world. Using its popularity increasing, you also need to think of great Cricut tips which you can begin promoting in local craft displays, on the Internet or in the regional specialty shops near you.

To get started with your Cricut jobs, allow me to assist you with some good Cricut ideas that you can start with. With these terrific ideas, now you can produce your initial line-up of innovative craft layouts and

231

individuals can search for your services or purchase your creations. Isn't it a superb idea to do what you really love and in precisely the exact same time earn a little excess money?

You can start your initial Cricut job by producing a range of cards. Be innovative and creative with your card undertaking. Come up with a number of greeting cards. Include birthday cards for many ages and sexes, a few thank you cards, anniversary, sympathy and blank cards for use for almost any events. Embellish you cards with blossoms or phrases adorned with unique shapes and colors produced from the Cricut cutting machine. You may pack them in sets up to 6 cards a box, as well as make customized envelopes t you may create using your system.
Bundle your created cards nicely for shops owners to become interested in selling your merchandise. It may be a very professional business person and not only a crafter attempting to sell your hobbies. Together with your Cricut system you can also produce your cards. Apart from promoting your greeting cards from craft shops, you can take orders for events like baby showers, baby christenings, birthday parties and a lot more.

There's a site named shop handmade at which you can sell your things. The best part is this website needs no monthly membership fee. Additionally, there are craft displays or trade fairs where you set up a booth to exhibit your crafted cards and collections.
Cricut includes a succession of cartridges you may use with topics for Christmas, Valentine's Day, Easter, Mother's Day or Father's Day. With these cartridges you can produce a lot of ideas for your greeting cards for each event.

Another card job you could do is to make custom made wedding favours, wedding shower and a lot more. From the Cricut solution series there's a cartridge known as wedding for all of the fantastic wedding motifs you may consider. The home accent cartridge includes amazing flowers and designs you may use for your wedding gown.

Your Cricut suggestions for promoting your craft layout are endless and the possibilities are infinite. The best part is that you can earn additional money while doing what you love best! Have fun with your endeavours!

Cricut suggestions for scrapbooking

Scrapbooking is the most recent craft craze. With the invention of digital cameras, picture albums are left behind. At this time, you have a much better way to maintain your photographs. With the improvement of technologies, Cricut suggestions for making scrapbooks are as simple as a touch of button. Cricut private cutter came up with the Cricut Expression as the reply to your scrapbooking needs. This permits you to create a number of the most intriguing and appealing contours to decorate your most straightforward paper craft projects.

The Cricut is a lightweight machine and could be carried anywhere like an arts and crafts celebration. After traveling, the machine includes a carrying case made for traveling and features padding, handle and wheels. With electric power and enthusiasm for scrapbooking, you may start creating exquisite crafts.

The Cricut looks like a photo printer that lets you to cut and design unique layouts to use on your scrapbooking projects. It has the capability to make several shapes and dimensions up to 24 inches. The Cricut will cut any paper such as card stock, vellum and chipboard.

The Cricut Expression machine is a fantastic tool which can help make your jobs enjoyable to perform. It's a simple to use cutting platform which does require a computer to operate. It cuts letters, shapes and phrases in little or large sizes. Not only does it cut paper goods, in addition, it can cut thin magnets along with some cloth and etch eyeglasses. This enhanced machine will be able to help you conserve paper and also make many copies of your chosen design or shape. It may definitely take your scrapbooking job to another level of different Cricut ideas.

It may cost you $350 to have a Cricut Expression machine should you purchase it from a retail shops. But you can buy a cheaper priced machine via the Web for as low as $150. Cricut cartridges may cost you around $80, but it is possible to discover online bargains under $30. Each cartridge has over 2,000 pictures you can use broadly.
Produce beautiful scrapbooks, greeting cards, calendars, posters, signage, house decor, teaching tools, company promotional products, and statements in only moments.

Using its multi-function capacity, crafters like you may turn your imaginative ideas into unique works of art. Together with the Cricut machine, it is possible to set you standing as a skilled crafter. Now you can unleash your initial creations for others to respect as well as buy.

Your great Cricut ideas could be made by the Cricut Expression machine. With its varied functions and the capacity to make myriad of jobs, investing in this Cricut system lets you express yourself and do what is important for you personally. Creative scrapbook ideas are now able to be turned into an art.

Five easy Cricut vinyl projects which you must try

Have you heard of Cricut plastic? If you have the personal electronic cutter the Circuit Expression die cut machine from Provocraft, then there's a great likelihood you know of it. But if you are like many crafters, then you might end up reluctant to use your device for cutting plastic, not understanding the numerous prospective jobs this useful product can create.

To get you started, here are five simple projects to attempt:

1. Wall lettering

Wall letters are likely among the most well-known applications for Cricut vinyl. Before die cuts, homeowners would need to employ an artist or muralist whenever they desired favourite phrases or get phrases hand painted on their own walls. Either that, or they'd need a great deal of patience and a reasonable amount of ability to perform it themselves. But plastic die cuts generate a similar appearance, with a fraction of the hassle and price.

2. Storage containers

Should you be a company freak (or for those who have ambitions to become one!), then you are going to love this thought. Cricut vinyl may be used to cut decorative tags, which could then be affixed to the exterior of assorted forms of storage containers. As an instance, consider your scrapbooking place. It's possible to sort out different ribbons, buttons, beads, and other embellishments that you use for your designs into different glass jars, then use your die cut machine to cut tags identifying the contents of each jar. The identical concept applies to a kid's playroom. It's possible to cut out words (or graphics - based on the age of your child), which you could then stick to your children's plastic storage containers and containers, to assist your child in keeping her or his toys sorted and keep the place clean.

3. Yard signs

Should you have something to sell or a company to market, then you might wish to think about using Cricut vinyl to make custom cheap yard signs. Want an example? Garage sale signs will look amazing if made using this procedure, and they'll really be fun to create! The same is true when you operate a house childcare center or other home-based small businesses. You may use vinyl to generate custom signs for your lawn to get the word out to prospective clients.

4. Vehicle signs

The good thing about vinyl is that it's very durable. This makes it ideal if you would like to produce your personal "bumper sticker" or other sign for your car or truck. It is possible to use these car decals as an enjoyable expression of your identity or to market your company. As mentioned previously in this guide, producing your own customized signs is a fantastic way to inexpensively market your business.

5. House numbers

So that visitors in addition to emergency personnel can find their houses, many people prefer to place their own sign on the outside of the property. This is still another project which it is possible to produce using Cricut vinyl.

Tags, bags, boxes, and much more Cricut cartridge - 7 tips you can use now

Go above and beyond and learn exactly how much it is possible to produce using the tags, bags, boxes, and much more Cricut cartridge- 7 tips you can use now. Hailed for its innovative design, flexibility and concentration on utility instead of mere ribbon, the tags, bags, boxes, and much more Cricut cartridge is a must-have thing for any do-it-yourself ace.

1. First things first, Explore every bit of the exceptionally diverse and flexible Cricut cartridge.
Shoppers who haven't yet undergone the gloriousness that's this cartridge might believe it's only a one-note cartridge for all those random occasions when you want tags, boxes, bags, and even more. To the contrary, this cartridge is made for these pragmatic applications, but also for all those random moments of absolute craftiness.

2. Make tags!

The cartridge features tags within a vast array of designs, shapes and dimensions. Users may pick and choose as they please. Make customized tags for everything in gifts, garage sales, auctions, keepsakes and mementos, title tags and much more with the support of this unique Cricut cartridge.

3. Make bags!

For all those unfamiliar with the tags, bags, boxes, and much more Cricut cartridge, users may select a bag and along with the Cricut machine can cut it. The bag, however, isn't fully constructed. All it takes is the smallest bit of adhesive, coordination and voila- you have a bag. Bags vary from purse-type satchels to baskets to cosmetic bags.

4. Make boxes!

Boxes can be particularly helpful for present giving, including keepsakes and for compartmentalizing the remainder of your life. Box designs vary, but like the bags, they do need a little bit of folding and building after the whole piece is cut out.

5. Use the whole cartridge to throw a lavish party complete with party favours!

Ideas include expanding the tags to make personalized, casual invitations, together with the tags as title tags for guests, together with the bags to keep party favours and last but not least, using boxes to carry snacks, candy or individual products.

6. Get the advantage of the distinctive capabilities.

Particular features make it possible for users to choose the tags, boxes and bags template and put in their own spin on matters. These choices include: window, mirror, mirror/window, mirror/windows, shadow, and blackout imaginative capabilities. Personalize each product even more by adding your own personal touch and distinctive effect with these attributes.

7. Produce jobs for your children or for your inner child.
Organize and spend some time on jobs including personalized jewellery boxes, colourful crayon boxes, matching purses for children and their dolls or possibly a cake shaped box to get a piece of birthday cake to go.

Quick and easy handmade Easter greeting card suggestions

Are you currently on the lookout for some fast, simple and very affordable handmade Easter greeting card ideas? If this is so, I've got two greeting card layouts I would like to discuss with you now. This undertaking could be great to create with older kids, scouting troops, church youth groups, paper craft classes as well as college classes.

We left those cards with 10-14-year-old girls for them to give to their parents for Easter. After they were done making them, they were rather pleased with their creations. If you do not have a Cricut die cutting machine (used to cut the ovals and lettering) you can hand draw and then cut out different sized oval shapes and you can buy letter stickers in the regional arts and crafts shop. We used the Cricut George and basic shapes cartridge for all these endeavours.

Items needed:
4" by 5" blank cardstock note cards with envelopes
Various scrapbooking newspapers (hooks and prints)
Decorative edge scissors and normal edge scissors

Adhesives - glue dots, glue sticks and glue pens
Various colored scrapbooking fine tip pens and markers

*optional ink pads and Easter sentiments rubber stamps

For all these 2 layouts we used self-stick plastic scrapbooking net from mint green and 4 mm round self-stick purple rhinestones.

For card number one:

Cover the front of the card with pink scrapbooking paper which has been cut to match. Employing the Cricut set on the amount one size placing and using the Cricut Georges basic shapes cartridge we cut eight ovals from various colored papers. Using the identical cartridge turn your dial to the shadow option and cut four ovals (we used dark blue paper) as those will function as the foundation for the eggs.

With your glue stick, paste a bigger oval on top of each bigger oval to function as your Easter egg. Using decorative scissors, cut part the remaining smaller ovals into different widths. With a glue pencil, glue up the cut bits onto the eggs and then let dry. (approximately 5-10 minutes). If wanted. . .use different colored markers to include polka dots and squiggles for your own eggs to decorate them further. Applying glue dots, then attach each egg onto the greeting card close to the top and moving across the front. Using the Cricut Georges basic shapes cartridge place your dial into the number two dimensions setting. Cut the letters out of moderate blue scrapbooking paper. Cut a strip out of white scrapbooking paper which measures 2" by 5" in size and then glue it to some dark blue scrapbooking paper that's cut slightly bigger than your strip. We used decorative edge scissors to add interest to the design. Glue this strip on the lower half of the card. With a glue pen glue every letter onto the snowy foundation strip to define the word Easter. If wanted. . .use an ink pad and rubber stamp to stamp a belief inside or compose your own personal message.

For card number 2:
Cover the front of your card with pink scrapbooking newspaper. With a part of self-adhesive plastic mesh in a mint green colour, attach this to the centre front. Use blue self-stick letters (in this instance we spelled out the word Easter) and put people right over the net strip. Employing the Cricut die cutting machine and the Georges basic shapes cartridge, then cut two purple ovals on the 2 1/2 size placing and onto the shadow impact, cut one moderate blue oval on precisely the exact same setting. These 3 ovals will function as your foundation for those eggs.

Employing the exact same 2 1/2 size placing cut six to eight more ovals from different coloured scrapbooking papers. Glue these ovals on every one of the larger ovals which you cut out. Employing wavy border decorative scissors, cut a part the rest of the ovals. Use a glue pen or a glue stick and use those bits to decorate your egg foundations. Once done, use adhesive dots to attach your eggs in addition to the vinyl mesh strip. We chose to decorate the egg at the centre with small purple self-stick rhinestones to add decorative attention to it. With an ink pad and rubber stamp, stamp your opinion inside or handwrite your message.

There you have it.
Two fast and effortless handmade Easter themes for greeting cards which you may make with older kids or make them yourself. Happy crafting!

Conclusion

Cricut is your new a conclusion of personal digital cutting machines focusing on the maximum advantage of things for home decoration, scrap booking, paper trimming, card making, and much more. Whatever you might do with a Cricut is only limited by your own imagination. These machines include Cricut cartridges for easy use. The cartridges comprise numerous amazing built in templates for a variety of dimensions and applications. This gadget can also be quite straightforward to watch over. The designs can be chosen from the cartridge or may be custom made using the Cricut Design Studio to take originality to elevated heights - but a computer is vital for this particular function.

The Cricut bundle comprises these:

Cricut machines: These will function as tools which perform the die cutting owing to some creative designs.

Gypsy: This is in fact really the entire Cricut cartridge library in one go. It is a hand-held device that comprises the complete Cricut Design Studio - to ensure any time we'll need to produce a design the Gypsy is conveniently supplied.

Cricut design studio: It is the full-fledged app for producing just about any design on a Cricut cutter. All you'll need is a computer. Not only that, but may be used to easily explore, cut and design the entire cartridge library. The program also gives a decision to conserve the design to potential requirements. Assessing a Cricut design has never been easier!

Cuttlebug: It is the personal die cutting and embossing system. It features different sizes and styles such as paper-crafting, house decoration, house tasks, events, and faculty tasks. The program is created by leading artists that offers sharp die cuts every time. Cuttlebug also comprises professional exceptional embossing for connections with its different feel and measurements, making it an outstanding system.

Cricut cake: This is an optional tool used for producing designer confectioneries for sandwiches and cakes and other snacks, in almost no time.

An advanced version called the Cricut Expression could be used for sheets as large as 24" x 12," therefore fitting into a measurement, be it personal or professional. Not only that, but it features cartridges and advanced possibilities, like the adding of colors, printing, and much more, making it ideal for many jobs.

Cricut is the handicraft enthusiast's best buddy, or for anyone who'd love to design and create. It supplies over 250 distinct designs in many of sizes. The designs could be up to compared an inch or larger. The different cutting angles offer precision cutting - all of this together with templates that are attractive collectively with interlocking alphabets, provide lots to select from.

Now that you've got your own Cricut machine, why don't you start making great jobs like handmade greeting cards? Start selling them in local craft exhibits, online, or at specialty shops in town.

Now everybody can use a little additional money. Your first of many Cricut jobs will be to produce an assortment of about 10 to 12 cards. Be creative, you are going to find a good deal of ideas it is possible to take into account. Contained inside this variety you've got to get a couple greeting cards (make sure you make cards for women, men and also cards for children), make sure you include thank you, anniversary, get well and a sympathy card.

Some more tasks that you're in a place to make on your Cricut cutting machine is going to be to make blank inside note cards for nearly any purpose. You will have many card ideas such as blossoms that could be layered over the cover by way of a rhinestone centre, or maybe just the expression "hi" adorned with a couple unique shapes. You're ready to package them up in sets of 4-6 cards. With your Cricut cutting tool that does a variety of tasks with the push of a little button. All types of ideas will start flowing from your creative mind. You can also produce decorated boxes to place your cards into.

Now you need to take your Cricut jobs with lots of your suggestions and take them into a shop (florists, bakery, salons, along with small gift shops) and also talk to the proprietor. Have a look at the pricing available for each and every shop proprietor. Make sure you customize the price sheet with the name of the company that you're extremely likely to furnish them. You'll look like a very professional businessman instead of merely a crafter expecting to provide your personal card ideas.

Some owners may even permit you to leave your cards at their shop on consignment and merely keep a percentage when you sell them. (I have done consignment earlier at a local florist and at a luxurious nail salon additionally and really did great. What a great spot to display your Cricut cards compared to in a place that is 95 percent women, who would be the very best shoppers. Besides the cards that I provided in these shops, I got special buys for baby showers and birth announcements) just be sure that you leave your business cards at these shops.

Clients might wish to get you for specific orders. It's likewise possible to market online at a wonderful location on the Internet called shop handmade, it's great since it's free. Or it's also possible to advertise your Cricut tasks at local craft displays. While creating your cards remember Christmas as well as other big holidays which people send cards such as Christmas Day, Easter, Mother's Day, or Father's Day!

Another of many jobs it's very likely to create together with your Cricut cutting machine will be to create a custom baby shower or marriage or maybe wedding invitation. There are lots of ideas for these sorts of cards. You will encounter a great deal of Cricut cartridges that are made specifically for these jobs. In the Cricut choice collection there is a cartridge called wedding to get all those wonderful wedding contours it is possible to envision, and they have a home accent cartridge that has amazing swirly flowers and shapes it is also feasible to use for a wedding theme. In case you choose to proceed into the baby shower or birth announcement training course, you'll see fantastic cartridges such as New Arrival and soon to be printed A Youngster's Year.

Whichever path you require be certain that you create several samples in several distinct fashions. Take them to shows, go to wedding retreats in the region, bakeries, florists and baby boutiques. I can't stop thinking of ideas. I just had another one to find a superb job. See I told you that your ideas will start to stream after you start with your Cricut cutting device.

In the event you have any party centers for children's birthday parties locally it's extremely likely you could supply, customize and create goodie bags, and title tags. Show them samples of numerous topics which you've got (formed from the Cricut cartridges that you have). Maybe you will compose a catalogue to leave there so customers will be able to discover the choice that you'd love to supply them.

Cricut is a well-known manufacturer of equipment everywhere in the country. It is an exciting and one of a kind gadget used by most women and guys who would like to do exceptional and innovative jobs. At this moment, there are just three different versions of Cricut: the Cricut Create machine, the luxury Cricut Expression and of course, the standard Cricut personal electronic cutter machine.

Before improving on how Cricut can raise the society, let's have a peek at its start. Cricut was initially made using a massive firm called Provocraft which was a tiny store. Approximately forty years before, the company of Provocraft started as a retail store in the tiny town of Provo, Utah. With their resourcefulness and creativity, the company eventually grew over the years. They finally had a total of ten stores with an approximately 200,000 feet distribution centre.

If you examine the standard Cricut machine, it looks like an inkjet printer. But it doesn't need a computer to be used at all. An ordinary person has the capacity to use its function since you do not need programming skills too. Among with its advantages includes being lightweight. Its blade even cuts thin and thick papers that vary from one inch to 5.5 inches in size.

Cricut just weighs a half lb and this includes the power connector. What's more, it's extremely easy to take it any place like parties or event demonstrations since it's a portable product. Using its distinctive and sleek design, it's suitable for almost any crafting workplace.

As stated earlier, it may cut to 5.5 inches but that's just one attribute that it has. It cuts borders and names to around twenty-five inches, so therefore, making it an ideal match to a paper functioning with a dimension of 12 x 12 inches. Unlike other manufacturers, Cricut's most important facet is it has the capability to cut a great deal of things. Cricut can also cut a paper which has an extensive variety of roughly 0.5 mm thick. Luckily, Provocraft has supplied additional materials such as designer paper pads together with cardstock pads which may be used together with Cricut cartridges. In reality, these two different sorts of papers are made to match perfectly with Cricut.

If you ask many Cricut customers, then they'd undoubtedly say that the Cricut digital die cutter is the best one of the best cutters. This is only because Cricut cartridges have a massive set of choices with respect to fonts, colours, styles and designs, therefore, fostering the most level of imagination without the necessity of a PC.

If you don't know, using Cricut cartridges can produce miniature folds which you set inside the Cricut for you to set the form of shape, layout, font or layout that you would like to cut on. The cartridge has distinct types. It includes: ribbon cartridges, licensed cartridges, kind cartridges, choices cartridges and classmate cartridges.

In the end, you are very lucky since buying a Cricut cutter also enables one to get a free cartridge! This totally free cartridge includes several basic shapes that might now provide you with the opportunity to create a few decorations and shapes. Otherwise joyful, you can purchase additional Cricut cartridges to add to your collection. The more cartridges you have, the increased likelihood of creating exceptional artwork.

Generally speaking, serious scrapbookers invest a great deal of money in their hobby. But there are numerous frugal scrapbooking ideas that could readily be integrated into your endeavours and designs to help cut down those expenses. Standard household products, and yes, even things which would ordinarily end up in the garbage, can be used. Listed below are a couple suggestions that will save cash in your pocketbook, in addition to help you recycle items which would otherwise wind up in the landfill.

1. Cereal boxes
Should you possess a die cut machine capable of cutting chipboard, like the Cricut Expression, do not buy chipboard in the craft shop. Rather, use cereal boxes. When you stick vibrant paper into the cereal box die cuts, nobody could possibly guess it came out of your pantry! You might even use inexpensive cookie cutters as designs for your cereal box chipboard shapes.

2. Wallpaper remnants
Many wallpaper remnants are as amazing as the expensive papers in the scrapbooking shops. Paint and wallcovering stores normally have a library of background sample books. After the background is stopped, these novels are lost. Ask the employees if they'd give the publications to you rather than throwing them out. Regrettably, there's a great possibility that these samples aren't acid-free. Even though they might

not be acceptable for your scrapbook pages, they're the perfect touch for handmade cards and other paper crafting projects.

3. Gift wrap

Think of all the gorgeous gift wrap that winds up in the landfill. Rather than throwing it away, recycle it. At birthday parties and other special events, consult with the guest of honour to learn whether or not she has some plans to use the gift wrapping after unwrapping gifts. Should they intend to throw it away, then you can amass a fantastic range of gift-wrapping paper which may be used for your own chosen paper crafting projects.

4. Fabric and ribbon scraps

If sewing is just another one of your hobbies, you know that cloth and ribbon bits are the ideal match for your paper crafting projects. A number of these cloth and decoration scraps are too little for stitching, yet will be the ideal size for accenting handmade cards and much more. Request your family and friends that sew to keep a Ziploc to accumulate their bits. Rather than throwing them out they could give them to you!

5. Office goods

Lots of the goods in the scrapbooking aisle are just adorned office equipment. Office goods, however, are substantially more economical, and may be jazzed up with hardly any work. By way of instance, paper attachments are essentially the exact same thing as the vibrant braids which are used for scrapbooking. Paint them with cheap acrylic paints to coincide with your designs.

Using a little creativity and innovative thinking, you're surely going to find even more prevalent household products which you can use for frugal scrapbooking ideas. Keep an inexpensive container useful nearby, and because you run across odds and ends that may find another life in one of your endeavours, put it in the container before you find a use for it.

247

CRICUT MAKER

A Beginner's Guide to Start Using your Cricut Maker. Learn How to Set Up your Machine and Start Creating Amazing Projects. Master All the Tips and Tricks to Become an Expert

Kimberly Johnson

Introduction to Cricut Maker

Cricut is a brand of cutting plotters, or computer-controlled cutting machines, designed for home crafters. Consumers often use the machines for cutting paper, felt, vinyl, fabric, and other materials such as leather, matboard, and even wood.

❖ Models

The original Cricut machine has cutting mats of 6 by 12 inches (150 mm × 300 mm), the larger Cricut Explore allows mats of 12 × 12 and 12 × 24. The largest machine will produce letters from a half-inch to 231⁄2 inches high. Both the Cricut and Cricut Explore Air 2 require mats and blades which can be adjusted to cut through various types of paper, vinyl, and other sheet products. The Cricut operates as a paper cutter based upon cutting parameters programmed into the machine and resembles a desktop printer. Cricut Cake produces stylized edible fondants cut into various shapes from fondant sheets, and is used by chefs in the preparation and ornamentation of cakes.

Current Models

❖ Cricut Explore One

The Explore One is a wired die-cutting machine that can cut a variety of materials from paper to fabric and more. This machine has 1 tool slot, compared to all other currently supported models which have two. Note: there is a wireless Bluetooth adapter available for purchase separately.

❖ Cricut Explore Air

The Explore Air is a wireless die-cutting machine that can cut a variety of materials from paper to bonded fabric. This machine is essentially the same as its second iteration, besides the housing and slower cutting abilities. This model has two slots, one for your pens then the second one for your blade.

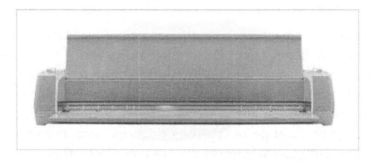

❖ Cricut Explore Air 2

The Explore Air 2 is a minor refresh of the Explore Airline which added three colors (Mint Blue, Rose Anna, Giffin Lilac). It also added a Fast Mode to cut vinyl, iron-on heat transfer vinyl, and card stock at "up to 2x speeds.

❖ Cricut Maker

The Cricut Maker is a new line released on August 20, 2017, designed to cut thicker materials such as balsa wood, basswood, non-bonded fabric, leather, and felt. The Maker is the only Cricut machine that supports the use of a Rotary Blade for cutting fabric directly and a single or double scoring wheel with variable pressure to score thicker papers than the original scoring stylus that uses the QuickSwap housing.

❖ Cricut Joy

Introduced Feb. 12, 2020, the Cricut Joy is a smaller, more light-weight version at 5" x 8" and less than 4 lb. The Cricut Joy is aimed at the casual crafter market. The Joy introduces two new features not elsewhere available in the Cricut product portfolio. With specialty accessories and materials (labeled Smart Materials), the Joy can cut single designs up to four feet long and repeated cuts up to 20 feet. "With its precision blade, Cricut Joy cuts lots of materials in any shape you say – everything from vinyl and iron-on to cardstock, peel-and-stick label paper, and even that construction paper you already have at home.

❖ **Cricut EasyPress 2**

A square surface device for heat transfer designs and Infusible Ink materials, offered in 6" x 7", 9" x 9", and 12" x 10" sizes. The press provides constant heat and pressure over materials. Power, temperature, timer, increase, decrease, and start buttons are located at the top for various project settings and needs.

❖ **Cricut EasyPress Mini**

A miniature heat press/ iron. Approximately 4 inches long and 2.5 inches wide of heating surface. Equipped with three heat settings. Low for sensitive base material heat transfer 255°F (125°C) – 295°F (145°C), medium for more basic material heat transfer 300°F (150°C) – 355°F (180°C), and high for heavy-duty material heat transfer and specifically Infusible Ink materials 360°F (185°C) – 400°F (205°C).[8] The temperature button and indicator are located on the point side of the handle, when the indicator is glowing yellow then the device is heating to the desired temperature, when green the device has reached temperature and ready for use. To adjust the heat press button until cycles to needed level 1-low, 2-medium, and three-high.

❖ **Original Cricut**

The original Cricut comes with a 6" x 12" cutting mat and images can be cut in a range from 1" to 5 1/2" tall. The original Cricut is compatible with all original Cricut cartridges. The original Cricut cannot cut as many different types of materials that the newer Cricut machines can. However, Cricut does make a Deep Cut Blade & Housing that can allow original Cricut owners to cut material up to 1.55mm thick, such as magnet, chipboard, and stamp materials. The original Cricut is also compatible with the Cricut Design Craft Room.

❖ **Cricut Expression**

The Cricut Expression offers several advantages over the previous model. First, it allows users to cut shapes and fonts in a range from 1/4" to 231/2", and comes with a 12" x 12" cutting matting with adjustable slides so that users no longer need to trim their media down to 6" x 12". It cuts a wider range of materials, including vellum, fabric, chipboard, vinyl, and thin foils. It also features an LCD screen to preview the work and has featured such Quantity and Auto-Fill. A "Paper Saver" mode and choice of Portrait or Landscape Orientation have also been added. The basic model has two cartridges included in the purchase, Plantin School Book and Accent Essentials.

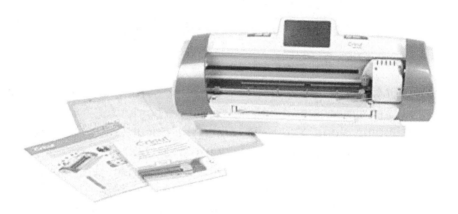

❖ **Cricut Imagine**

This machine was unique in that it had an HP 97 inkjet printer built into it so that it could both cut and print images. This machine also had a revamped touch screen interface and was extremely large and heavy. The machine had an extremely short life span of almost one year.

❖ **Cricut Expression 2**

The Cricut Expression 2 has an updated exterior from the Cricut Expression. It comes with a 12" x 12" cutting mat. This machine does not have the keyboard that the original Cricut and the Cricut expression have. Instead, it features a new full-color LCD touch screen. The LCD touch screen displays the keyboard on the screen and allows you to see where your images will be on the mat before cutting. It also has the new feature of independent image sizing and image rotation directly on the LCD screen.

❖ **Cricut Mini**

The Cricut Mini is a small personal electronic cutting machine. Unlike the other Cricut machines it only works with a computer, it can not cut images standing alone. You have to use the Cricut Craft Room design software. The Cricut Mini comes with over 500 images that are automatically unlocked when you connect your Cricut with the Cricut Craft Room design software or the Cricut Gypsy device. The machine does have a cartridge port that is compatible with all Cricut cartridges except the Cricut imagine cartridges. The Cricut Mini also features a unique mat size of 8.5" x 12". The Cricut Mini can cut images in a range of 1/4" to 11 1/2". The Cricut Mini relied exclusively on using Cricut Craft Room, a computer program that no longer functions. Of all the Legacy Cricut machines, the Mini is the only one that is now obsolete and not usable in any way.

❖ **Cricut Cake**

The Cricut Cake was one of the first vinyl cutters that you could cut edible vinyl. This was only for cakes. You can still cut your normal Vinyl, Iron-on, and other materials.

Chapter 1: What is s Cricut Maker

So What Is A Cricut Maker?

The Cricut Maker is the latest and most advanced machine in the Cricut product line. It can cut through (and deboss, score and engrave) a vast array of flat materials under 2.4 mm thickness; from delicate items like paper through to cardstock, fabrics (from denim to chiffon) and vinyl, to heavier and tougher materials like leather; even some woods and metals! These materials are prepared for cutting by laying on 12" x 12" (or 12" x 24") sticky mats (which range from 'Light Grip' to 'Heavy Grip', depending on the material you are using at the time) which then feed through the cutting machine.

This Maker is Cricut's top-of-the-line cutting machine. It can be used for craft & hobby applications, as well as small business applications. Hundreds, if not thousands of people, are making an income with the Cricut Maker, selling products on Etsy or FB Marketplace. The Cricut Maker was released in late 2017 and was an immediate hit with crafters, bloggers, and creative folk all around the world.

Pros:

- ❖ Best craft cutting machine
- ❖ Beautiful design
- ❖ Quality components
- ❖ Works smoothly
- ❖ Quiet
- ❖ Cuts hundreds of materials
- ❖ Good for business
- ❖ Easy to learn how to use
- ❖ Great support & community
- ❖ Create amazing projects

Cons:

- ❖ Pricey if only for occasional use
- ❖ Design Space Software can be slow
- ❖ Only comes in 12 inches wide

What Can The Cricut Maker Cut

Here's an idea of some of the more unusual materials which can be cut with the Cricut Maker.

Fabrics like:

- ❖ Sailcloth
- ❖ Terry cloth
- ❖ Light cotton
- ❖ Velveteen
- ❖ Garment leather
- ❖ Tooling leather
- ❖ Nylon
- ❖ Bonded polyester
- ❖ Muslin
- ❖ Interesting materials:
- ❖ Washi sheet
- ❖ Shrinky dink
- ❖ Acetate
- ❖ 2.4mm basswood
- ❖ Chiffon
- ❖ Damask chipboard
- ❖ Rice paper
- ❖ Moleskin
- ❖ Tulle

There are so many craft projects that can be done with the Maker. Other popular things people make include:

- ❖ Intricate paper flowers
- ❖ quilts

- ❖ Soft toys
- ❖ Wood model animals
- ❖ Scrapbooking decals
- ❖ Stencils
- ❖ Complex cards & boxes

I'm sure there are a few materials that the Cricut Maker can cut in that list that you've never even heard of! I had to look up Shrinky Dink – it's a type of polystyrene that does some amazing things when heated. But I'm sure you can see that the Maker is capable of cutting a huge range of fabrics, vinyl, craft boards, papers, and more. In the Maker box comes a set of standard tools and blades with others available for separate purchase as you start designing and crafting more advanced projects.

It's a sleek-looking machine which comes in a few colorways; I've got the classic 'champagne' model. It has built-in storage for your tools and a really useful docking slot for your tablet, 'phone, or, in my case, a BrightPad (again, this is a really useful tool for 'weeding', which simply means to remove the 'negative' / unwanted bits from your cut design) – there's a USB port to the side which lets you charge your devices whilst you work. The Cricut pairs with your device (via Bluetooth or cable) so that you can access its companion software.

Cricut Design Space And Cricut Access

Design Space is a user-friendly / shockingly easy-to-learn, software design package and digital resource library which is compatible with a range of devices – I primarily use my laptop (Windows) but I also have the App on my Android (it works on iOS and Mac too!) 'Cricut Access' is the optional subscription element of Design Space which allows you to, well, access additional predesigned projects and images, etc. (You absolutely can use one without the other). You can also upload a variety of files including your jpeg and SVG files and fonts (my goodness, I've spent hours and hours, doing just that!) Design Space converts them to either .svg ('cut') images or 'print and cuts images').

So What Projects Can You Make?

The list is nigh on endless; with my Maker I've discovered, I can create anything from customized clothing, wall graphics, decals to jazz up my home decor, wall art, papercrafts, quilts, 3D projects to name but a few and, yes, a whole range of sewing and clothing projects!

Cricut Maker Changes Everything.

It handles fabrics, leather, paper, and balsa wood with effortless precision. Cuts sewing patterns in just a few clicks. And places more creative possibilities than ever at your fingertips. Meet Cricut Maker – the ultimate smart cutting machine.

A Whole New Material World.

Cricut Maker quickly and accurately cuts 300+ materials, from the most delicate paper and fabric to the tough stuff like matboard, leather, and basswood. Now your creative potential is exponential.

More Tools. More Materials. More Possibilities.

Cricut Maker offers the widest range of tools for cutting, scoring, writing, and adding decorative effects all so you can take on virtually any project you can imagine. Plus, with more tools coming, Cricut Maker grows with you as you master each new craft. Let's start with the biggest difference between the machines, Cricut Maker's Adaptive Tool System. Cricut Maker has a completely different technology built into the machine, that we call the Adaptive Tool System, which allows for us to expand the suite of tools you can use for several cutting and scoring applications.

The Adaptive Tool System can control your tools to cut from side-to-side, move up and down, and lift and turn, so you can cut more materials with more pressure than ever before. This is what makes it easy to cut through the fabric without a backer (right off of the bolt) using the all-new Rotary Blade. We'll talk more about the Rotary Blade below. Cricut Maker can cut hundreds of materials from delicate papers and fabrics to denser materials like leather, chipboard, balsa wood, and more.

Little Things That Add Up To Something Big.

Cricut Maker is full of thoughtful touches to make your DIY experience easier. Extra built-in storage keeps your tools organized and within reach. A helpful docking slot holds your tablet or smartphone. And the convenient USB port lets you charge your device in a flash.

Cricut Maker Tools

Now that we've explained the technology differences between the Cricut machine lines, we want you to know what tools you can use with what machine. To cut all these wonderful materials, 6 blades can be used with the Maker. The first 3 blades listed below can also be used with the Explore Air 2, while the last 5 blades are exclusively Cricut Maker tools. All of the tools you love and use with your Cricut Explore family of machines also work with the Cricut Maker. This includes the Fine Point Blade, Deep Point Blade, Bonded Fabric Blade, Scoring Stylus, and Cricut Pens.

The new tools that were designed specifically to work with Cricut Maker, because of the Adaptive Tool System, include the Rotary Blade, Knife Blade, and Single and Double Scoring Wheels, Wavy Blade, Perforation Blade, Fine Debossing Tip, and Engraving Tip.

1. The Premium Fine Point Blade: Is used for standard materials like HTV and adhesive vinyl

2. The Deep Point Blade: Is used for thicker materials like corrugated paper and thin leather

3. The Bonded Fabric Blade: Is used for cutting bonded fabrics like bonded denim and bonded felt

4. The Rotary Blade: Is best for flexible or soft materials like oilcloth and organza. Rotary Blade brings infinitely customizable, precision fabric cutting to the home for the very first time. Use it to cut cotton, fleece, denim, and more. With its gliding, rolling action, it cuts virtually any fabric quickly and accurately without backing material. Rotary Blade comes in the box with Cricut Maker.

5. The Knife Blade: Is for cutting even thicker materials like 7-ounce tooling leather or 2.4 mm balsa wood. The extra-deep Knife Blade cuts through dense materials up to 2.4 mm (3/32") thick with unprecedented ease and safety, almost like an automated X-ACTO blade. It's ideal for thicker materials like balsa wood, matboard, and heavy leather.

6. The Scoring Wheel: Single wheel is for thinner materials, double wheel for thicker materials. Scoring Wheel tools for Cricut Maker create crisp creases in a variety of materials for perfect, effortless folds and a flawless finish. We've rigorously tested a wide range of materials so you'll always know which tool to use to get the best result.

7. The Engraving Tool: Can be used to engrave a variety of surfaces. Make a lasting impression with Cricut Engraving Tip. To get professional-looking results, just snap this tip onto the QuickSwap Housing and tell your Cricut Maker to "Go!" Watch with awe as you write personalized text or create monograms, draw decorative flourishes and embellishments, or inscribe your favorite quotes on a keepsake. For an eye-catching effect, engrave Cricut Aluminum Sheets or anodized aluminum to reveal the silver beneath.

8. The Wavy Blade: Cuts with a wavy line. The Wavy Blade adds a whimsical wavy edge to any design in half the time of a drag blade. This specially sculpted stainless steel blade is great for original decals, envelopes, cards, gift tags, and collage projects, or anytime you need fabulously finished edges and stylish design accents.

9. The Debossing Tool: Does the opposite of embossing, pressing down into your cardstock. Add professional polish and elevated elegance to papercrafts. To create crisp, detailed debossed designs, just snap this tip onto the QuickSwap Housing (sold separately) and tell your Cricut Maker to "Go!" Unlike embossing folders, which lock you into a specific design, this rolling debossing ball, powered by your Cricut Maker, gives you free rein to customize, personalize, and design with incredible intricacy. Make a dimensional wedding card, thank you card with your monogram, or add a flourish to gift boxes, tags, and more. Creates a stunning effect on foil cardstock, coated paper, shimmer and glitter paper, foil cardstock, and much more.

10. The Perforation Blade: Is used to semi-cut a line. It allows you to create a line that can be cleanly torn or folded. Get the perfect tear quickly and effortlessly with precise perforation cuts on a variety of projects. Evenly spaced perforation lines allow for clean, even tearing without the need to fold beforehand – especially great for shapes with curves! We love these projects in Design Space that use the Perforation Blade to create unique punch outs that allow you to interact with your project long after it's complete!

Cricut Maker Vs Explore Air 2

The Cricut Maker is the better machine when compared with the Explore Air 2. The Maker is for those who want and need the best machine possible. The differences between the Air 2 and the Cricut Maker include:

- ❖ Cut hundreds of more materials
- ❖ Ipad or tablet stand
- ❖ Commercial grade cutting power
- ❖ Controlled completely through the computer (no setting dials)
- ❖ Takes a rotary blade, knife blade, and scoring wheel to achieve a much greater range of projects

The Power Of A Professional Machine. The Simplicity Of Cricut.

1. Cuts The Most Materials: Cricut Maker cuts hundreds of materials quickly and accurately, from the most delicate paper and fabric to matboard and leather.

2. Expandable Suite Of Tools: With a wide range of tools for cutting, scoring, writing, and adding decorative effects, Cricut Maker grows with you as you learn each new craft.

3. Rotary Blade: With its gliding, rolling action, this blade cuts through virtually any fabric quickly and accurately – without backing material.

4. Knife Blade: This extra-deep blade slices through heavier materials like 2.4 mm (3/32") balsa wood and matboard with ease.

5. QuickSwap Tools: Effortlessly switch between tools for pro-level scoring, engraving, debossing, perforation, and other decorative effects.

6. Adaptive Tool System: This professional cutting technology intelligently controls the direction of the blade and adds up to 10X more cutting force.

7. Digital Sewing Pattern Library: Access hundreds of patterns from brands like Riley Blake. Pick a project, and the machine cuts all the pieces you need.

8. Easy-To-Learn Design Space Software: Fully loaded with advanced features including Offline Mode, Print Then Cut, and SnapMat™. For iOS, Android™, Windows, and Mac.

9. Flexibility To Upload Your Designs: Use your images and fonts for free in a variety of standard file formats.

10. 50 Ready-To-Make Projects: Includes 25 digital sewing patterns plus more projects that demonstrate what Cricut Maker can do.

Common Questions About The Cricut Maker

Well, first things first...here's a little background on the Cricut Maker. The Cricut Maker is an electronic cutting machine (also called a craft plotter or die-cutting machine). You can think of it like a printer; you create an image or design on your computer, smartphone, or tablet, and then send it to the machine. Except that instead of printing your design, the Maker cuts it out of whatever material you want!

The Cricut Maker is great for crafters, quilters, sewers, DIYers, and anyone else with a creative streak! It has an adaptive tool system that allows you to switch between blades and accessories so you can do any type of project. Want to cut sewing patterns and fabric? Switch to the rotary blade. Want to cut balsa wood or leather? Switch to the knife blade. Want to draw something, or add scoring lines to your project? The Cricut pen and scoring wheel are perfect! No matter what type of project you want to do, the Cricut Maker can handle it!

Will It Be Easy For Me To Learn The Software And Use It To Design My Project Or Make Ready-To-Make Projects?

Yep, I think so! I think that Cricut Design Space is pretty intuitive, even if you're not tech-savvy. Cricut has a little walkthrough tutorial that you go through when you first set up your machine, and it does a pretty good job of showing you the basics of Design Space (at least, enough to make any of the ready-to-make projects in the Cricut library)

What Kinds Of Crafts And DIY Projects Can I Make?

The only limit here is your imagination! You can make pretty much anything from greeting cards and paper projects to home decor to wedding/party/event decorations to clothing and quilts.

Can I Use My Old Cartridges?

The original Cricut machines used physical plastic cartridges that you could insert into the machine itself to access image content. The physical cartridges have been retired and now Cricut has digital cartridges (basically an "image set" of related images available in the Cricut library). But don't worry! If you have physical cartridges from a previous Cricut machine, you can still use those images! You can link your physical cartridge to the digital version in Cricut Design Space, and then you can use the digital version of all of your images whenever you want.

Can I Upload My Images?

Yep! Here is a step by step tutorial showing you how to upload your images to Cricut Design Space. You can upload basic images like a jpeg or png, or you can upload a vector file if you have an image that has multiple layers. Design Space supports upload of the following file types:

❖ jpg , gif , png , BMP , SVG , pdf

Chapter 2 : What Is a Cricut Machine

What In The World Is A Cricut Machine?

A Cricut is a cutting machine – that's the short answer – that allows you to cut and create beautiful and magnificent crafts with materials you didn't even know existed. Depending on the model you have you can also draw, emboss, and create folding lines to make 3D projects, greeting cards, boxes, etc. The Cricut is a great machine for people that love crafting, and for or people that need to cut a lot of things and different types of materials. A Cricut is a cutting machine that can cut several different materials for your craft projects like paper, vinyl, and cardstock. Some Cricut machines can even cut thin wood, leather, fabric, and more.

What Is A Cricut Machine?

The Cricut Explore Air is a die-cutting machine (aka craft plotter or cutting machine). You can think of it like a printer; you create an image or design on your computer and then send it to the machine. Except that instead of printing your design, the Cricut machine cuts it out of whatever material you want! The Cricut Explore Air can cut paper, vinyl, fabric, craft foam, sticker paper, faux leather, and more!

What Can I Do With A Cricut Machine?

There are TONS of things you can do with a Cricut machine! There's no way I could even list all the possibilities, but here are a few popular types of projects to give you an idea of what the machine can do.

- ❖ Cut out fun shapes and letters for scrapbooking
- ❖ Make custom, handmade cards for any special occasion

- ❖ Design an onesie or a t-shirt
- ❖ Make a leather bracelet
- ❖ Make buntings and other party decorations
- ❖ Create your stencils for painting
- ❖ Make a vinyl sticker for your car window
- ❖ Label stuff in your pantry, or a playroom
- ❖ Make monogram pillows
- ❖ Create your own Christmas ornaments
- ❖ Address an envelope
- ❖ Decorate a mug, cup, or tumbler
- ❖ Etch glass at home
- ❖ Create your wall decals
- ❖ Make a painted wooden sign
- ❖ Make your window clings
- ❖ Cut appliqués or quilt squares
- ❖ Create decals for a stand mixer

Cricut machines are so useful as they can work on various materials, such as felt, paper, and vinyl. There are many things that you could do with Cricut machines. Outlined below are the kinds of projects in which the Cricut machines can help:

- ❖ Come up with a sticker made of vinyl for your car's window
- ❖ Label your things in the playroom or pantry
- ❖ Design a t-shirt or onesie
- ❖ Make a trendy leather bracelet
- ❖ Cut out letters and fun shapes for scrapbooking
- ❖ Create custom and handmade cards for all special occasions
- ❖ Create party decorations like buntings
- ❖ Create stencils necessary for painting
- ❖ Create monogram pillows
- ❖ Make ornaments for Christmas
- ❖ Address the envelopes
- ❖ Decorate mugs, cups, or tumblers
- ❖ Engrave glass
- ❖ Create personalized wall decals

- ❖ Make painted wooden signs
- ❖ Make window clings
- ❖ Cut quilt squares or appliques
- ❖ Make decals for your stand mixer

Every Cricut machine comes with a special set of thin and thick materials the unit can cut. On the other hand, most of the cutting machines made by Cricut can cut thin materials like paper, vellum, vinyl, and many more. Other models out there can work on hundreds of materials such as faux leather, chipboard, felt, and fabric (check out fabric cutters). This incredible cutting function of these units made them worth the money, and they can be so advantageous, especially for experienced crafters.

What Is The Cricut Compatible With?

For your machine to work, you need to be connected to the Cricut Design Space. The Cricut Design Space is only compatible with Windows and Mac operating systems. In other words; you need a desktop computer for you to use the Cricut Machines. If you want to use your machine without the internet you need to download the Cricut Design Space app. This app is extremely useful and it connects via Bluetooth. This app is available only for iOS a.k.a iPhone and Apple users. However, if you are an Android user don't lose hope! Cricut just released a beta option and although It doesn't have all the capabilities you would have on an iPhone. I am pretty sure one day it will get there.

Can I Connect My Cricut Via Bluetooth To My Phone Or Computer?

It depends on the machine you have. The Explore Air 2, and Maker, and Joy have built-in Bluetooth technology so they can connect with your desktop or phone.

Do I Need To Have Internet For Me To Use The Cricut?

No, to work on your projects you don't need an ongoing online connection. However, you need to be connected to the Internet to get your machine up and running you need to install Cricut Design Space.

Keep in mind that If you want to use Cricut images and fonts you need to download them (while you're online) for future offline use. Also, if you an iOS (iPhone – iPad) you can cut and create projects offline, but you can't download images and fonts for future use. If you have an Android device, Cricut is still working on an offline feature.

How Does The Cricut Work?

So far you've learned about the Cricut itself. Things like the mats, blades, materials, and what the machines are compatible with. But how does the Cricut work? For the Cricut Machine to cut, you need to use it along with the Cricut Design Space. This is the area where you'll lay and organize your design to be cut. You can connect a Cricut to your computer wirelessly, create or download designs onto your computer, and then send them to your Cricut for cutting. Cricut has software called Design Space (available for Windows, MAC & smartphones) that allows you to create and import designs to cut with your machine. The Cricut houses a tiny blade (or rotary cutter, or pen, or scoring tool) inside. Once you have a design ready to cut in Design Space, you can fasten your desired material onto a 12 inch wide cutting mat, send your design from your computer to your Cricut wirelessly, and then load your material into your machine. With the press of a button, your project will begin cutting

What Is Cricut Design Space?

The Cricut Design Space is the software that allows you to organize, create, and finally cut your projects. Without Design Space, you can't work your machine. That's why is very important for you to learn how to use it. The Cricut Machine is great but if you don't learn how to use the Design Space, it's like buying a camera and not taking photos. Or buying a Smart Phone and not making a phone or video call.

What Is Cricut Access?

Cricut Access is a giant library that will allow you to select and create already designed projects. This is very useful if you are just getting started. When you have Cricut Access and depending on the plan you have you can select unique fonts, graphics, 3D Projects, and if you can think it, they have it. They have projects for any occasion and any materials you like to work with. It's quite impressive.

Where Can I Find Free Cut Files For The Cricut?

There are many places where you can find FREE cut files. I am creating a HUGE LIBRARY full of them and other things like patterns and images for you to cut. Here's a list of some places to find SVG files as well

- ❖ **Daydream Into Reality Library:** These goodies are only available to my subscribers. And trust me. This library is growing a lot. Not only you can get Cut files, but also other sorts of amazing printables for any occasion.
- ❖ **Cricut Design Space:** Cut the free images of the week.
- ❖ **Jennifer Maker:** She also has an amazing library, you also need to subscribe.
- ❖ **SVG & ME:** Amazing and beautiful library
- ❖ **Pixabay:** They have tons of SVG files that you can download for free and even use for commercial purposes!

What Materials Can I Cut With The Cricut?

There are hundreds literally of materials you can cut with these amazing machine these are some of them:

- ❖ Plan Paper
- ❖ All kinds of cardstock
- ❖ Metallic Paper
- ❖ Vinyl (Iron on, glitter, permanent, removable)
- ❖ Fabric and textiles
- ❖ Faux Leather
- ❖ Corrugated Paper
- ❖ Thin Woods (Cricut Maker only)
- ❖ Sticker Paper
- ❖ Parchment Paper
- ❖ And more!

What Is The Cricut Adaptive Tool System?

The Cricut Adaptive System is an extremely and powerful feature that only the Cricut Maker has. This feature controls the direction and of the blade at all times. This tool is so amazing that it can adjust the pressure of the blade to match the materials you are working with!. This technology is what allows the Cricut Maker to cut with 10X more force than any of the other Cricut Explore Family machines.

What Are Some Of The Projects I Can Do With A Cricut Machine?

There are many projects you can create with a Cricut machine! This is just a tiny list of some of the things you can accomplish.

- ❖ **Home Decoration:** Decals for your windows, walls. Or something that I like a lot is to personalize things like baskets, or even your cooking spices.
- ❖ **Stickers:** For planning, journaling, and more
- ❖ **Greeting Cards:** You can create high-end greeting cards. Like those, you see in the store!
- ❖ **Clothing Items:** Cut and iron on beautiful and personalized designs on your T-Shirts.
- ❖ **3D Projects:** like gift boxes and even paper toys!

With the Cricut Maker, you can cut wood and create 3D and sturdy projects. Cut fabric and create fashion items for your clothing and more. Your imagination is the limit!

What Is A Cricut Blade And Which One Do I Need?

The blade is what cuts the materials. lol Right?. However, there's something very important for you to know before you get started and if you are planning on cutting thicker materials. Right now, there are seven types of blades and three other crafting tools available for the bigger machines (Explore and Maker).

- ❖ **Fine Point Blade:** Ideal for light and medium materials like paper, vinyl, and cardstock. It comes now in gold color.

- ❖ **Deep Point Blade:** Great for thick materials like chipboard, thick cardstock, foam sheets, etc.
- ❖ **Bonded Fabric Blade:** Ideal for cutting a wide variety of fabrics! The fabric needs to be bonded with a backing material.
- ❖ **Rotary Blade (Only For The Cricut Maker):** Cuts pretty much any type of fabric and the fabric can be just placed on the mat. It comes with the Maker.
- ❖ **Knife Blade (Only For The Cricut Maker):** This impressive little blade can cut very thick materials like basswood!
- ❖ **Quick Swap Perforation Blade:** This particular blade will allow you to create projects with a tear finish. With this tool, a new world of possibilities has open. It only works with the Cricut Maker.
- ❖ **Quick Swap Wavy blade:** Instead of cutting straight lines like the rotary or fine point blade, this tool will create wavy effects on your final cuts. It only works with the Cricut Maker.
- ❖ **Quick Swap Debossing Tip:** This tip will push the material in, and it will create beautiful and detailed designs. The debossing will bring your projects to a whole new level because of the detail you can now add to your designs. It only works with the Cricut Maker.
- ❖ **Quick Swap Engraving Tip:** The Engraving Tip is something that many crafters have been waiting for! With this tool, you'll be able to engrave a wide variety of materials. It only works with the Cricut Maker.
- ❖ **Quick Swap Scoring Wheel Tips:** The Scoring Wheel is a tool that allows you to create beautiful, edgy, and crispy folds on your materials. It only works with the Cricut Maker.
- ❖ **Foil Transfer Kit:** The "Foil Transfer Kit" allows you to create beautiful and crisp foil effects on your projects. It's compatible with the Cricut Maker and any of the Explore family machines. This kit is 3 tools in 1; to best suit your project, Cricut has fine, medium, and bold tips. The Cricut Joy only has a "Fine Point Blade" as well, but it only works with that particular device.

What Blades Come With Each Cricut Machine?

When you buy just a machine (No bundle) they usually come with a blade. Let's see what blade comes with each machine!

- ❖ **Cricut Explore Air 2:** Fine point blade
- ❖ **Cricut Maker:** Rotary blade, fine point blade
- ❖ **Cricut Joy:** Fine point blade

What In The World Is A Cricut Easy Press?

A Cricut Easy Press is a very cool device that allows you to transfer your Iron-On vinyl to T-shirts, sweaters, quilts, and more! It comes in 3 different sizes and you can get the one that meets your needs. The sizes are:

- ❖ **9×9 Inches:** This size is great to transfer designs to Adult size T-Shirts
- ❖ **6×7 Inches:** Ideal to iron on small pieces of clothing like onesies and other baby clothes.
- ❖ **10×12 Inches:** Perfect to Iron on in big surfaces like quilts and blankets.
- ❖ **Easy Press Mini:** Idea to press HTV on small areas like pockets, hats, etc.

How Long Does The Cricut Blade Last?

Cricut Blades last depending on the material and the frequency you use them. There's not a specific time for it. If you see your materials aren't being cut with the same crispiness and ease that they used to. Then it's time for you to replace it.

What Other Cricut Accessories Do I Need?

This is a tricky question and It depends on the kind of materials you want to work with and cut. Although the Cricut machines are capable of many things, you need to use it with the right tools to truly make it work. For instance, if you have any of the Explore Family Machines and want to cut fabric, you need to make sure that you have:

- ❖ Backing Material

- ❖ Fabric Bonded Blade
- ❖ Standard Grip Mat

On the other hand, if you want to cut fabric with the maker you can also use the above tool, or you can opt for a rotary blade plus a Fabric Grip Mat. Most common and lightweight materials can be cut with the Fine Point Blade (The blade that comes with each machine) and the Standard grip Mat. But as you explore and become more aware of your machine and the materials you are using, things will become so much easier. I know it's tricky but once you get the hang of it you will be an expert. The good thing about this machine is that when you are going to cut a certain material, the program will tell you exactly what materials you need!

COOL RIGHT?

Another important thing here and something that I consider extremely important is to get is some of their great tools. There are many different sets for you to choose from. However, the most common are the Basic and the Essential Toolset.

Basic Tool Set + Scoring Stylus

The Basic Tool Set comes with (This is the one I got):

- ❖ **Tweezers:** Great to manipulate delicate materials
- ❖ **Weeder:** Helps you separate and remove negative cuts
- ❖ **Scissors:** With a blade cover
- ❖ **Spatula:** For you to take your cut from the Mat
- ❖ **Scraper:** Cleans your mat and also helps transfer designs from one surface to another.

The Essential Tool Set Comes With:

- ❖ **Scoring Stylus:** Great to add folding lines for 3D projects, cards, etc.
- ❖ **Trimmer + Replacement Blade:** For you to cut materials that are **wider than 12 inches**

274

❖ **Scoring Blade (For The Trimmer):** To add folding lines to your project.

Can Cricut Cut Fabric, Wood, And Leather?

Yes, along with paper, vinyl & cardstock some Cricut machines can cut materials like fabric, leather, and even wood! Read on to see which machines can cut thicker or more delicate materials.

Which Cricut Should I Buy?

There are currently three types of Cricut machines on the market: Cricut Explore Air 2, Cricut Maker, and Cricut Joy (this one just came out). Choosing which machine to buy will depend on what types of project you'd like to make. All machines come with Cricut's free Design Space software.

❖ **Cricut Explore Air 2**

This is the machine that I'd recommend purchasing for most projects. It's Cricut's most popular machine, and it will cover most materials you'll use for a wide variety of DIY projects like vinyl, paper, cardstock, and chipboard. You can cut over 100 materials with this machine, and you can use 4 tools for cutting, writing, and scoring.

❖ **Cricut Maker**

This machine does everything the Cricut Explore Air 2 does, with the addition of being able to cut thicker or more delicate materials like leather, thin woods, and fabrics. You can cut over 300 materials with this machine, and you can use over 12 tools for cutting, writing, scoring, and other pro-level effects. I'd recommend this machine if you want to venture into more complicated projects and experiment with a wider range of materials.

❖ **Cricut Joy**

The newest Cricut machine, Cricut Joy, is a more compact machine than the other two for quick, everyday DIY projects. It can only cut materials up to 5.5 inches wide, but you can purchase material that is very long (up to 20 feet). It cuts over 50 materials and can use 2 tools for cutting and writing. I'd recommend this machine if you want to spend less and create simple projects like vinyl signs, cards, and small iron-on designs.

Are Cricut Machines Hard To Use?

Cricut machines come with a thorough online manual and there are a lot of other Cricut resources online, so they are fairly easy to learn how to use. Design Space and the Cricut machine itself are both designed to be very user-friendly, and you don't need lots of graphic design experience to use them (though it does help if you want to create your designs from scratch). There's a library of images and designs in Cricut's Design Space that are simple to import as a new project. Some are free, and some can be purchased at a low cost.

Are Cricut Machines Worth It?

If you love to craft – especially with paper and vinyl – a Cricut machine is a good investment. It will make your cut projects look crisp and professional, and once you are confident using it, your crafts will be much quicker to create. There are also many ways you can make money with your Cricut, like selling custom t-shirts, mugs, decals, etc. online or at craft fairs.

What Can I Do With A Cricut?

Wow! Listing everything would be a long list! But, here's a shortlist of Cricut project ideas.

1. School Projects: My elementary-aged daughter can use my Cricut machine. She has used it on several projects this year already!

2. Card Stock Projects: Crafters and party planners can make greeting cards, party invitations, party decorations, costume pieces, Bible journaling embellishments, and more!

3. Vinyl Projects: Use permanent vinyl for outdoor projects (update a mailbox maybe) and kitchen items (like mugs) that can be hand washed. Use removable vinyl for wall projects.

4. Iron-On Projects: One of the most popular uses for the Cricut, iron-on vinyl (also known as heat transfer vinyl) is used to make custom shirts, bags, hats, and more!

5. Craft Foam Projects: Craft foam projects are fun for kid crafts, wreaths, and more.

6. Window Cling Projects: Imagine making your window clings for holidays! With the Cricut, easily cut window cling material into different shapes and decor, like these Preschool Shape ideas.

7. Print And Cut Projects: Working in conjunction with your home printer, the Cricut allows crafters to print photos or images out on their computer and then cut them with the Cricut. From printable magnets to sticker paper, there are so many options for customized gifts or favors for weddings, etc.

8. Faux Leather Projects: One of my favorite mediums, create lovely jewelry items or fashion accessories with faux leather or add a leather look to cards, pillows, and more.

9. Adhesive Foil And Washi Sheet Projects: Would you like to add a custom look to a photo frame or your phone case? Adhesive foil and washi sheets are excellent for these projects! The adhesive foil adds a shiny, metallic look to any project, like these pretty Family Ornaments that I made last year.

10. Stenciled Wood Projects: I discovered stencil vinyl this year, and I love it! Create your adhesive stencil with stencil vinyl, adhere it to wood, and then paint. Remove the stencil vinyl after the paint has dried, and, there you go! Create custom wood signs and more with stencil vinyl.

Are Cricut Machines Worth It?

If you love to craft especially with paper and vinyl a Cricut machine is a good investment. It will make your cut projects look crisp and professional, and once you are confident using it, your crafts will be much quicker to create. There are also many ways you can make money with your Cricut, like selling custom t-shirts, mugs, decals, etc. online or at craft fairs. I have used my Cricut machines a lot, and continue to get more and more ideas on things I could create with them!

Chapter 3 : Maker Vs Explore Air 2

Cricut Maker Vs Cricut Explore Air 2: What To Know Before You Buy?

What Cricut machine should you buy? Is the Cricut Maker the best machine? There are many types of cutting machines and one of the most famous brands is Cricut. Of course, Cricut didn't just make one cutting machine. So what machine should you get? Read on to help you decide.

The Cricut Machine:

If you're new to the arts and crafts hobby, you've probably heard of the importance of a Cricut machine. It's your primary cutting machine that easily cuts your designs and fonts. It uses Design Space as its main designing software, and it cuts on command. Cricut has several machines available in the market. After all, it caters to different customers with different materials to use. So far, the most famous one is the Cricut Maker, but this isn't their first model. Cricut's first model is the Cricut Explore One. The Explore series has three models, but the latest one is Explore Air 2. For this article, you're going to be reading about both the Cricut Maker and the Cricut Explore Air 2. Why? They're the newest and most versatile machines so the two should go head-to-head. What are you waiting for?

The Cricut Explore Air 2

Explore Air 2 is the newest version of the Explore series of Cricut. This means that if you're comparing the Air 2 to the other Explore cutting machines, then you would find the former to be much stronger and faster. For starters, the Explore Air 2 uses a Smart Set Dial for its technology. In other words, it can cut more accurately and it makes use of a Bluetooth connection.

Now, this is a big deal because back when Bluetooth connection wasn't found everywhere, the Explore Air 2 already had it. It was advanced for its series, yet it retained the simplicity of the Cricut machines.

Today, the connectivity features of the Explore Air 2 is nothing new. However, it still manages to stand out because of its ability to cut up to 100 materials. If you plan on cutting vinyl, different types of paper, and other medium-weight fabrics, then look no further because the Explore Air 2 is perfect for you. Known as a mid-range cutting machine, the Explore Air 2 is ideal for those who want to cut different materials, but do not necessarily need a heavy-duty device.

Tools And Blades Of The Explore Air 2

Aside from the materials, what are other tools and blades that you can use with the Explore Air 2?

1. Fine Point Blade

The fine point blade is not unique to the Explore Air 2 because all Cricut machines have this. Nonetheless, it's right to mention it so you know that you have a go-to blade to use for several materials. If you don't know what blade to use, this will usually be your first choice.

2. Deep Point Blade

If there's a fine point blade, there's also a deep point blade. This blade is great for cutting thicker materials like boards and thick fabrics. What makes this possible is the angle of the blade. If the fine blade has 45 degrees, this one has 60 degrees. The steeper angle helps to cut through thick materials.

3. Bonded Fabric Blade

Another blade that you can use with the Explore Air 2 is the bonded fabric blade. This is specifically for fabrics only. If you use it on other materials, you're just going to ruin the blade and you don't want that. Before you cut, though, don't forget to bond the fabric.

4. Cricut Pens

Other than blades, the Explore Air 2 also has Cricut pens that come with it. These pens are great for making your crafts more personalized. Did you know that these pens can cut and write?

5. Scoring Stylus

This stylus is used for materials that you plan on folding. So if you're into creating cards and boxes, then you'll find the scoring stylus very useful.

The Cricut Maker

By now, you've been hearing a lot about the Cricut Maker. What makes it so special? Among all the other Cricut machines, the Cricut Maker is the only machine that can cut through several materials. No, you don't need to bond your fabric for the Cricut Maker. It can cut through unbonded fabric, denim, and tissue paper. How's that for a heavy-duty machine?

The Cricut Maker uses Adaptive Tool System, a technology used in cutting different materials. This technology makes this machine adaptable to different blades. This means that if you use different tools, the pressure will adapt to make the cuts precise no matter what the tool is.

Tools And Blades Of The Cricut Maker

Speaking of tools, here are additional blades and tools that the Cricut Maker has that the Explore Air 2 doesn't (take note that all of Explore Air 2's tools and blades are also compatible with the Cricut Maker).

1. Rotary Blade

Do you ever struggle to cut into the fabric when it's not placed in a backing material? With the rotary blade, you don't have to worry about that anymore. This blade comes with every purchase of the Cricut Maker so you don't have to pay extra for a new tool.

2. Knife Blade

Another tool that you can have with your Cricut Maker is the knife blade. You're probably familiar with this and know that this is the strongest among all blades you'll find on a cutting machine. If you have to cut through thick and tough materials, this is the blade to use. It's perfect for cutting wood and leather.

3. Quick Swap Tools

How do you change tools easily? It's with the help of the QuickSwap system that only the Cricut Maker has. This system includes five tools that use the same housing so you don't need to change housings every single time you use a different material. What are the five tools? It's the scoring tip, engraving tip, debossing tip, wavy blade, and perforation blade. If you have no idea how to use them yet, you're going to find out as you try different materials and designs in the Cricut Maker.

What Does The Explore Air 2 And The Cricut Maker Have In Common?

These two cutting machines have a lot of differences, but since they're both Cricut machines, they still have some things in common. One of their similarities is the software that they use for designing projects to cut. They both use Design Space, which is given for free whenever you purchase a Cricut cutting machine. Unfortunately, this software is the only program you can use if you want to load your designs to the cutting machine. Other software will not have the same compatibility.

Another similarity is the number of materials each cutting machine can cut through. If you thought the Explore Air 2 was no match for the Maker, think again. It can also cut through 100 different materials. The two Cricut machines also come with 50 free projects. These projects usually don't come for free, but since Cricut has pre-designed templates, you can load them and see them being cut right away. If you want more projects you can also subscribe to Cricut Access which is available for buyers of the Cricut Explorer Air 2

Cricut Maker Or The Explore Air.

And the best part? Both have a starter project that acts as your guide to using the Cricut machines. Even if you're already familiar with how cutting machines work, having this first Project is a thoughtful gesture from Cricut.

Which One Is Better?

The real question here is – which model to get. If the Cricut Maker has all the features of the Explore Air 2, then why not get it? Not so fast. The Cricut Maker comes with its own set of flaws, so you have to compare these two before deciding. Here are some factors you can consider.

1. Materials

Both the Cricut Maker and the Explore Air 2 cut through 100 different materials. The main difference is that the latter can cut through the 100 most popular materials. This means that if there's a certain wood you want to try but it's not often used in crafts, chances are that the Explore Air 2 won't be able to cut it. If you're into more unique materials, then the Cricut Maker has the better edge on this one. The only catch with the Cricut Maker is that it can only cut a depth of 2.4 mm which is not as different from the 2 mm depth of the Explore Air 2.

2. Compatible Tools

Based on the specs mentioned a while ago, the Cricut Maker is compatible with more tools and blades. This means that if you will use different materials, there's a higher chance that you will be able to use the right blade to cut through it neatly. The rotary blade and the knife blade are two great additions to the Cricut Maker that make people want to buy it. Couple that with the quick swap tools that come with two other blades.

3. Technology

And then you have the technology. As a newer model, the Cricut Maker has more advanced technology in its cutting system. The Adaptive Tool System is great for adjusting the pressure the blades put on the material. Why is pressure important? Without the right pressure, the accuracy of the cut won't be spot on. This is something the Cricut Maker has mastered. However, the Explore Air 2 's Smart Set Dial technology is not so bad itself. It's not as accurate, but it can do detailed cuts on a wide range of designs. If you're worried that the Explore Air 2 is not the best in cutting, don't be. All of Cricut's cutting machines are done in high-quality anyway.

4. Price

Which is more expensive? For obvious reasons, the Cricut Maker is the more expensive machine given that it has more features and compatibilities with other blades. It also uses a newer technology that goes beyond "smart' cutting machines. However, just because it's more expensive doesn't mean that it's better. For some people, the features of the Explore Air 2 are enough that they don't need to buy a pricier cutting machine. Besides, if the Explore Air 2 cuts through the materials you want to use, why to waste money on a more expensive device, right?. But if you plan on upgrading in a few months or years, then you might want to buy the Cricut Maker instead so you don't have to end up with two cutting machines.

5. Design

Last but not least is the design. For some, since they're all cutting machines, it doesn't matter. But if you're the type that takes into account what their crafting tools look like, then you might want to know this. Explore Air 2 has a lot of colors in pastel shades. On the other hand, the Cricut Maker only has three – green, rose, and blue. When it

284

comes to storage space, the holders for your tools and blades are more spacious in the Cricut Maker than those in the Explore Air 2. In fact, in the Explore Air 2, you only have one holder for your blades and tools. In the Cricut Maker, you have two.

Chapter 4 : Tools and Accessories to Work for Circuit

What Cricut Accessories Do I Need?

What tools and gadgets you need will vary wildly depending on what you want to do with your Cricut. If you are cutting lots of vinyl then you need a wedding toolset and a scraper as well as a heat source. If you are cutting fabric then you'll want some pink mats and a brayer. No matter what you are cutting I have put together a huge list of useful and fun accessories.

Cricut Weeding Tool

This Cricut Weeding Tool which looks a bit like something you'd find in the dentist's office is ideal for poking out tiny pieces of cut-out paper (or other substances). It's also helpful for picking up items with adhesive on it (so they don't stick to your fingers). And take advantage of the curved section of the hook to hold down pieces when you're making complicated projects. You'll appreciate this tool when your nail or the pointy end of a scissor is too big for the task.

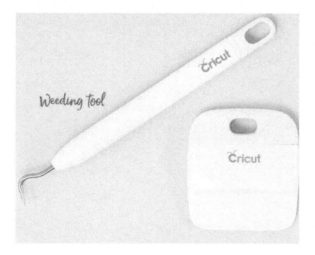

Cricut Infusible Ink Pens

Use these markers to create transfers that can then be used on Cricut blank products such as t-shirts, tote bags, coasters, and more. These heat-transfer inks adhere to the end product completely which means you'll never have a stiff line or fraying edge around a transfer, as you would with an iron-on transfer. The colors are rich and vibrant.

Cricut StandardGrip Cutting 12x12 3-Pack

Hear us out: Yes, your Cricut comes with a mat. But once you're cranking on a project, you'll appreciate the convenience of having several available. As one reviewer notes, it's not uncommon for projects to call for upwards of 15 mats. And while you can pull the paper off after it runs through the Cricut machine, then reuse the mat, that's a slow process having more mats available is a huge time-saver. These mats can be used with the Cricut Maker and Cricut Explore machines. Make sure to pick the mat that's right for your needs each three-pack is intended for different usages, such as with fabric or cardstock.

Cricut Tools Scoring Stylus

Use this stylus in your Cricut Explore machine to score lines it's perfect if you're making things that you want to fold up, like a greeting card or anything three-dimensional. If you're making many cards (hello, winter holidays or wedding invites!) you'll appreciate this time-saving device, and that it will prevent you from frustratingly uneven folds. Just note that some reviewers felt that the stylus did not score deeply enough.

Cricut Tools, XL Scraper

Make clean-up a breeze with help from this scraper, which scoops up tiny scraps of paper with ease. Plus, you can also use it to smooth out vinyl (bubble-free!). It's significantly larger than the scraper that comes in starter packs or that may have accompanied your machine. It especially comes in handy when it's time for bigger projects with lots of little pieces floating around.

Cricut Brayer

Before you get started on a project with a soft material, like vinyl or fabric, you want to make sure it is laying completely flat on the mat to avoid puckers and bubbles from ruining your designs. Press the Cricut Brayer along on top of the materials on your cutting mat to smooth lines and move air bubbles after you lay your material down. Reviewers note that it has a nice weight in the hand and is super simple to use.

Cricut Bright Pad

Do your eyes ache while weeding as you struggle to figure out what to remove? The Cricut Bright Pad is a major convenience. This illuminated pad has an adjustable LED light so that you can weed and trace with ease the backlight makes it easier to spot the scores in the paper, so you can easily take your weeding tool and get to work.

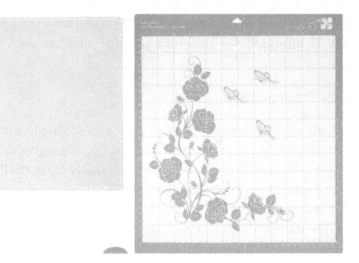

Cricut Ultimate Fine Point Pen Set

This set of 30 pens works in all Cricut Explore machines, including the Cricut Joy. (Note: With the Cricut Explore One machine, an adapter is required, per the manufacturer.) Use these pens to transfer drawn designs onto paper via your Cricut's design software or just use them to freestyle draw without the machine. Reviewers appreciate the pens' vibrant colors other packs are available with different color palettes and finished. According to Cricut, these pens are nontoxic, and after drying, the ink will stay in place permanently.

All Purpose Mat Set

Cricut has 4 different colors of mats right now. The pink mat (not listed or pictured) is designed for cutting fabric. The blue mat is the light grip mat that you will use with paper and other lightweight materials like crepe paper.

This mat has less adhesive and allows you to cut materials that previously would have stuck to a traditional mat. The trick for using the blue mat is to turn the mat over and peel the mat away from the paper rather than peeling the paper away from the mat. The green mat is your standard mat that works well with vinyl, iron-on, and I also use it for felt. The purple mat is the heavy-duty mat that you will use for thicker items like wood veneer and other heavy-duty materials. The extra ling mats are great for making multiples or larger designs. This bundle is a great deal and a great way to stock up on mats.

- ❖ LightGrip Mat – Blue: Thin materials like paper
- ❖ Standard Mat – Green: Medium Weight Materials like cardstock
- ❖ StrongGrip Mat – Purple: Thick materials like poster board and wood

❖ FabricGrip Mat – Pink: Designed for fabric only.

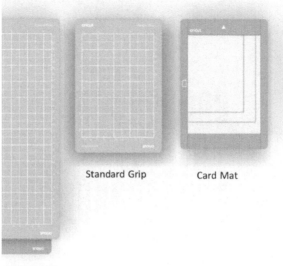

Standard Grip   Card Mat

& Light Grip

Rolling Craft Tote

If you don't have a table or counter space for your machine then you must have a great place to store it. Grab this tote to store all of your Cricut accessories. It rolls so you can roll it right into your storage closet or roll it out the door to a friend's house for a day of cutting and crafting. The fabric is beautiful and it just screams for some customization with iron-on! Right? Then pair it with this machine tote. These used to come as a set, but now you can easily get them separately and set the machine tote right on top of the craft tote. Use a cute belt or a bungee cord to hold the machine tote on top when you are headed out for a day of crafting!

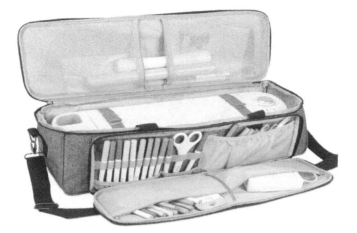

Wavy Blade

The wavy blade is amazing for use with fabric and felt. The wavy blade adds a curved edge to any project. It is also great for use with paper and would be an amazing addition to your tool kit if you are creating flowers with your machine. The wavy blade is one of the newest blades for the Cricut Maker and cannot be used with the Explore line of machines.

Blades

- ❖ **Fine Point Blade:** Medium Weight Materials
- ❖ **Deep Point Blade:** Thick Materials (2 mm)
- ❖ **Bonded Fabric Blade:** Only to use with fabric and backing material
- ❖ **Rotary Blade (Cricut Maker only):** Fabric, not backing needed
- ❖ **Knife Blade (Cricut Maker only):** Thick and dense materials like basswood .

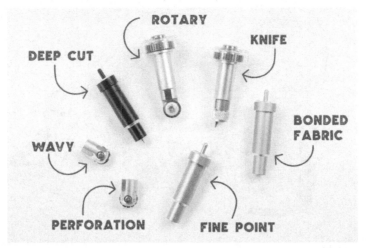

Once you get your Cricut, it can be easy to get overwhelmed with everything there is to learn. There are so many materials and tools out there to work with! How do you know what to buy? How do you know which tools are most helpful for you and your crafting? We've been there and we want to help you out! In this article today, we're going to show you ten Cricut tools that we faithfully use in our crafting. These essential tools are everything you need for a Cricut crafting session.

Scissors

Cricut Scissors have hardened stainless steel blades for durability and smooth, even cuts. The micro-tip blade gives you greater precision on all materials. A removable cover protects the blades.

Tweezers

Cricut Tweezers lift and secure in one step with their reverse grip design - squeeze the handle together to open, and release pressure to clamp together. Smooth interior points help prevent tearing or marring your materials.

Weeder

Cricut Weeder is for "weeding," or removing negative pieces around a cut image. When working with iron-on or vinyl images, it helps you precisely remove everything that isn't part of your design from the carrier sheet. It's also great for poking out tiny negative pieces from a cut cardstock image. This tool truly is a must-have when it comes to Cricut crafting! If you aren't familiar with weeding yet, you will be soon. When your Cricut cuts materials like vinyl or iron-on, you'll need to remove the excess material from around your design and also inside of the design. You're removing negative space so you can get to your design.

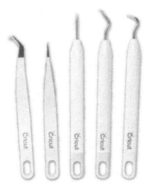

Spatula

Cricut Spatula precisely lifts images from the Cricut cutting mat, preventing intricate images from tearing or curling. The angled head of the spatula allows it to slide underneath the material with ease.

Trimmer

Cricut 12" Portable Trimmer with 15" swing-out arm helps you to precisely cut or score straight lines. Replacement blade storage compartments on the underside make fresh blades readily accessible on the go. this trimmer is a game changer. When you're working with materials, you'll always have to cut pieces away, right? Might as well make some straight lines! Seriously though, I love using this because it allows me to cut exactly what I need and cut it in straight lines. And you can easily measure what you need to cut on the trimmer, so you can make exact cuts! There is a swing-out arm that allows you to line your materials up straight, measure, and then cut exactly what you need. I think it saves a lot of material because you're precisely cutting what you need.

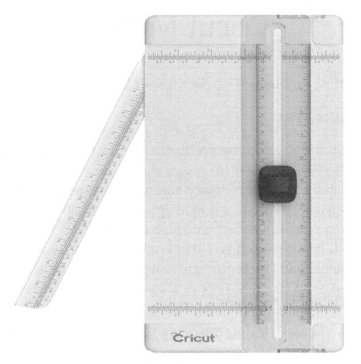

Chapter 5: How to Clean a Cricut Maker

Cricut Cutting Problems: Tips For Cleaner Cuts

1. Use A Sticky Mat

Your Cricut mat needs to be pretty sticky to get clean cuts. So if your cuts aren't clean, the first thing you should do is change your mat. I usually switch to a new or newer mat and it solves my problem right away. If you can't afford a new mat, you can try washing your mat with dishwashing soap and allowing it to air dry to get it stickier, but I'll be honest — it might still not be sticky enough. A sticky mat can make all the difference. And I prefer the green mats over the blue mats.

2. Use A Clean, Sharp Blade

You need to make sure your Cricut blade is clean and sharp. I do this by taking a sheet of aluminum foil and balling it up like this. Then I remove the blade from its housing, depress the plunger, and stick it in and out of the aluminum ball CAREFULLY over and over maybe 50 times. This cleans any debris from the blade, like bits of paper or vinyl that might be stuck to the blade, and also seems to sharpen it. (It may not be sharpening it, but it works!) This technique works for the Fine-Point and Deep-Point Blades. This technique works GREAT for me and I haven't had to buy a new blade in over a year. I always do this to my blades when I'm about to cut something with really intricate cuts.

3. Use Quality Materials

Your material can make a big difference in how it cuts, too. For example, not all paper is created equal. If the fibers are weaker or shorter in the paper, which you usually find in lower quality paper, you'll get more tearing. So if your paper doesn't seem to be cutting well even after using a sticky mat and a clean blade, the paper itself could be the culprit. There have been many times when I've had an issue and then changed to a new paper only to have everything work perfectly. Cricut paper is high quality, so is Recollections.

4. Check Your Settings

You must have got the right settings for your material. I find it works best to indicate the material settings in Cricut Design Space rather than on your Cricut dial. To do this on a Cricut Explore, just rotate the dial to Custom and you'll be prompted to choose your material before you cut it. (Note that the Maker has no dial you are on "customer settings" by default.) And if that still doesn't seem to help, try increasing the pressure of your cut. This is why I almost always have "More" pressure on my cuts, it seems to always help me get those clean cuts.

Tip: Sometimes when everything else seems right it can help to turn your custom settings to "Washi Tape" this seems to work best on intricate cuts on vinyl

5. Check Your Pattern

Not all patterns are going to cut cleanly. The smaller and more detailed and intricate they are, the harder it's going to be to cut them. Sometimes, they are just too small. So you can try making them larger if that is an option. If that doesn't work or is not an option, you can try setting your material to Intricate Cuts if you're cutting cardstock. Or try the washi tape set if you're cutting vinyl. Neither of these is guaranteed to work, but it's worth a try. In the end, some patterns may just be too tiny or detailed to be cut without issues. This doesn't mean all is lost, however you may still be able to cut it and just clean it up with scissors or a knife later.

These are all the tips I use each time I go to cut something, and I nearly always have clean cuts on all three of my Cricuts because of it. It does require a certain mindset you have to go into a project knowing you might need to tinker with it a bit to get it to cut properly. Testing can help a LOT. The key is not to give up. Be persistent and try new things. It always works for me!

Cleaning The Cricut Machines

- ❖ Gently wipe exterior panels with a damp cloth.
- ❖ Immediately dry any excess moisture with a chamois or other soft cloth.
- ❖ Do not use chemicals or alcohol-based cleaners (including, but not limited to, acetone, benzene, and carbon tetrachloride) on the machine. Scratchy cleansers and cleaning tools should also be avoided. Do not dip the machine or any component of it in water.
- ❖ Keep away from food and liquids, try not to eat and drink while using the machine.
- ❖ Keep in a dry, dust-free location.
- ❖ Avoid excessive heat or cold, do not leave the machine in the car, where excessive heat may melt or damage plastic components.
- ❖ Do not expose to direct sunlight for an extended period

Do's And Don'ts For Cleaning Your Cricut Explore

But now it is time to make sure you are taking good care of your investment right? With all the cardstock cutting, glitter paper cutting, vinyl cutting, and other materials that we all use, our Cricut Explore machines do tend to get a little dirty. I have a few tips I use to keep my Cricut Explore clean and beautiful as the day I received it and thought I would share with you.

Do's :

- ❖ Turn your machine off while cleaning
- ❖ Use a soft cloth to wipe down your machine...I use a non-alcohol baby wipe
- ❖ Clean off the rollers to remove residue...watch my video to see how I do this easily
- ❖ Clean out the blade housing to remove residue...important to keep this area clean at all times

- ❖ It's ok to gently move the housing unit to one side to clean the case

Don" Ts:

- ❖ Don't ever spray cleaner directly on your machine
- ❖ Don't ever wipe off the bar holding the housing...that grease is supposed to be on there
- ❖ Don't ever touch the gear chain at the back of the unit
- ❖ Don't clean while your machine is turned on

How To Clean Your Cricut Cutting Mat (And Restick It After)

This article will cover how to clean and maintain your cutting mats whether you're using a Cricut mat or a Silhouette. We all know how frustrating it can be when you start a project, and your material won't stick to the surface of your cutting mat. The questions I get the most are about cleaning and resticking cutting mats, especially after they've been used to cut felt. I'll explain how you can get rid of all the built-up gunk. We'll go over resticking your cutting mat when it's no longer working and end with some tips and answers to your frequently asked questions.

How To Clean Your Mat (Method 1: Gentle Cycle)

When you find that your Cricut mat is no longer sticky enough to properly hold your materials, try these methods to clean your mat and breathe some life back into it. As your mat accumulates grime and debris with your loving use, move down the list to more potent cleaning methods. Be gentle with your mats, and they may even last you through multiple rounds of holiday parties.

❖ **Sticky Lint Roller**

Run a sticky lint roller (or loop of masking tape) across your Cricut mat to remove dust, fibers, bits of paper, and hairs. This can be done every day, between projects, when you forget to cover your Cricut mats overnight, or simply whenever you notice bits and fibers accumulating on your mat. It's a great way to remove any remaining slivers or bits of paper, instead of trying to go after them all with tweezers. When the lint roller or masking tape is stickier than the mat, it pulls all the offending hairs and bits of paper right off the mat! It works especially well on the less-tacky cutting mats.

❖ **Baby Wipes**

Gently wipe down with unscented, alcohol-free, bleach-free baby wipes. Lotion-free, cornstarch-free. You want the absolute plainest wipes you can find, so you aren't coating your cutting mats with additional lotions, oils, or solvents that could interfere with the stickiness or break down the adhesive.

- ❖ Let dry before using.
- ❖ Soap and warm water
- ❖ Wash with soap and warm water.
- ❖ Dish soap is the best to use, and again you want to use soap that is free of lotions that could gunk up your mat.
- ❖ Gently scrub with a cloth, soft brush, soft sponge, or magic eraser, and rinse well.
- ❖ Let dry completely before using.

Warning: Do not use very hot water, as heat has been known to warp Cricut mats, making it so they won't fit well in your machine.

The Results

Often enough, simply washing your mat will be enough to rejuvenate its original sticky glory! After your cutting mat has completely dried, test out its stickiness with a scrap of the material you'll be using for your next project or a clean finger. If your mat has weathered enough seasons of projects, or been washed and scrubbed one too many times, you'll need to turn to something a bit stronger.

How To Clean Your Mat (Method 2: Heavy Duty)

If those gentle cleaning methods don't restore your cutting mat's functionality, you can try breaking out the big guns and use an adhesive remover to thoroughly clean your mat. The cleaning methods found on this page are not for the pink Cricut Fabric Grip mat. They are for blue, green, and purple Cricut mats. Don't put anything wet (including water) on your pink fabric mats.

What Is Adhesive Remover?

Adhesive removers are strong solvents that will dissolve some of the adhesive (the sticky glue) on your mat, helping you remove all the gunk that is stuck to it.

Warning: This process will strip your cutting mat of adhesive, so you may have to reapply adhesive to restick your mat. Don't worry, I'll walk you through it.

Which Adhesive Remover Should You Use?

I recommend using Goo Gone as it has been repeatedly and reliably used by the Cricut and crafting community. But you don't need to buy a whole new product for this! If you have any sort of adhesive remover lying around that you're comfortable with, it will likely work just fine. Other options are:

❖ 70% Isopropyl (rubbing) alcohol
❖ De-Solv-it Universal Stain Remover & Pre-Wash
❖ LA's Awesome All Purpose Concentrated Cleaner
❖ How to use an adhesive remover to clean your Cricut mat

- ❖ Read the directions of your adhesive remover, and adapt as necessary.
- ❖ Pour or spray a small amount onto your mat.
- ❖ Spread it around with a scraper, or any stiff piece of plastic like an old credit card.
- ❖ Let the solvent sit and work its magic. The longer you let the adhesive remover sit, the more stuff it will remove. The exact duration will depend on which solvent you use, so read the directions on your bottle. If this is your first time, I recommend just it sits for a few minutes to remove the dirty surface layer of adhesive. (If you have already restuck you mat a bunch of times and are ready for a fresh start, you can let it sit for up to 20-30 minutes.)
- ❖ Use your scraper to scrape the dirty adhesive off your mat. You can also wipe it off with a cloth or paper towels.
- ❖ Wash with soap and warm water to remove any leftover residue
- ❖ Let the mat dry completely.

How Do I Clean My Explore Machine?

Over time, and with use, your machine may collect dust or paper particles, or you may see some of the greases from the machine begin to build upon the carriage track. Cleaning it is easy! Consider the following tips when cleaning your Explore machine:

- ❖ Always disconnect the machine from power before cleaning it.
- ❖ The machine itself can be cleaned using glass cleaner sprayed on a soft clean cloth.
- ❖ If you observe static electricity build-up causing dust or paper particles to accumulate, you can simply wipe that away with a clean soft cloth.
- ❖ If you see a buildup of grease on the bar across which the carriage travels, you can use a cotton swab, tissue, or a soft cloth and gently remove it.

Important: Never use any kind of acetone, such as nail polish remover, as that will permanently damage the plastic surfaces of the machine.

Grease Application Instructions

- ❖ Turn off the Cricut Explore machine.
- ❖ Move the Cut Smart carriage by pushing it slowly to the left.
- ❖ Clean the Cut Smart carriage bar with a tissue, wiping around the entire bar (the carriage bar is the one the Cut Smart carriage slides on, just in front of the belt).
- ❖ Move the Cut Smart carriage by pushing it slowly to the right.
- ❖ Repeat the process of cleaning the Cut Smart carriage bar with a tissue, wiping around the entire bar.
- ❖ Slowly move the Cut Smart carriage to the center of the machine.
- ❖ Open the lubrication packet and squeeze a small amount of grease onto the end of the cotton swab.
- ❖ On both sides of the Cut Smart carriage, apply a light coating of grease around the bar to form a ¼" ring on each side of the carriage.
- ❖ Slowly move the Cut Smart carriage to the left and then to the right to distribute the grease evenly along the entire bar.
- ❖ Wipe off any grease buildup at the ends of the bar.
- ❖ Note: If your Explore machine is making a grinding noise, you can request a Grease Packet to be sent (US/Canada only) by contacting our Member Care team.

Important: Keep out of the reach of children. This product may irritate the skin or eyes. In the event of contact with skin or eyes, immediately rinse thoroughly with water and seek medical care if necessary. Wash hands thoroughly after handling.

Chapter 6 : How to Use Design Space

Are You Trying To Learn Everything About Cricut Design Space And You Don't Even Know Where To Start?

Learning a new hobby or skill can be intimidating at first. I get it; sometimes we don't even know where to start because there's so much information out there and it's just overwhelming. For me, the best way to learn and master Cricut Design Space is from the beginning. You see, when you have a clear concept of what every icon and panel is for, then you can truly dig in and start exploring further and further. Sometimes we are quick to jump from project to project – Hey That's ok too! BTDT – But I think that knowing your work area will help you to take your creativity to a whole new level. The purpose of this article is to teach you and show you an overview of every Icon, and Panel of the Cricut Design Space Canvas Area.

Cricut Design Space is an excellent tool for beginners, and if you have no experience with any other Design programs like Photoshop or Illustrator, you will find that although it looks overwhelming, it's quite easy. On the other hand, if you have preview experience with any of the Adobe Creative Cloud apps or Inkscape. You will see that this program is just a breeze. Design Space, it's mainly to touch up your projects and create minimal designs with Shapes and Fonts. If you want something more sophisticated, you are going to need your designs or Cricut Access. That's a membership where you get access to their supergiant library.

When you log into your Cricut Design Space account and want to start or edit a new project, you will do everything from a window called CANVAS. The Canvas Area in Cricut Design Space is where you do all of your editings before you cut your projects. There are so many buttons, options, and things to do that you might feel lost. Don't worry, I am here along the way, cheering you up and encouraging you to keep going. In this article, you are about to learn what EVERY SINGLE ICON on the Canvas area is for. To keep everything in order and easy to understand, we are going to divide the canvas into four areas and four colors:

- ❖ Top Panel Yellow – Editing Area
- ❖ Left Panel Blue – Insert Area
- ❖ Right Panel Purple – Layers Panel
- ❖ Canvas Area Green

Top Panel Cricut Design Space

The top panel in the Design Space Canvas area is for editing and arranging elements on the canvas area. From this panel, you can choose what type of font you'd like to use; you can change sizes, align designs, and more! This panel is divided into two sub-panels. The first one allows you to save, name, and finally cut your projects. And the second one will enable you to control and edit things on the canvas area.

Sub-Panel 1 Name Your Project And Cut It

This sub-panel allows you to navigate from the Canvas to your profile, projects, and it also sends your completed projects to cut.

- ❖ **Toggle Menu**

When you click on this button, another whole menu will slide open. This menu is a handy one. But it's not part of the Canvas, and that's why I won't be going into a lot of detail. Basically, from here you can go to your profile and change your photo. There are other useful and technical things you can do from this Menu like calibrating your machine, blades; also updating the Firmware Software of your device.

Note: On the settings option, you can change the visibility and measurements of the Canvas; this is explained better at the end of this post when I explain all about the canvas area.

❖ Project Name

All projects start with an *Untitled "title," you can only name a project from the canvas area after you've placed at least one element (Image, shape, etc.).

❖ My Projects

When you click on my projects, you will be redirected to your library of things you have already created; this is great because sometimes you might want to re-cut a previously created project. So, there's no need for you to recreate the same project over and over.

❖ Save

This option will activate after you've placed one element on your canvas area. I recommend you save your project as you go. Although the software is on the cloud, if your browser crashes, there goes your hard work with it!

❖ Maker – Explorer (Machine)

Depending on the type of machine you have you will need to select either the Cricut Joy, Maker, or the Cricut Explore Machine; this is very important because on the Cricut Maker you will find options that are only available to that particular machine. So, if you have a Maker and you are designing with the Explore option ON you won't be able to activate the tools that are for the maker.

❖ Make It

When you are done uploading your files, and ready to cut click on Make it!, Down below there's a screenshot of what you would see. Your projects are divided by mats according to the colors of your project.

From this window, you can also increase the number of projects to cut; this is great if you are planning on creating more than one cut.

Subpanel 2 – Editing Menu

It's extremely useful, and it will help you to edit, arrange, and organize fonts and images on the Canvas Area

Top Panel – Editing Menu

❖ **Undo & Redo**

Sometimes while we work, we make mistakes. These little buttons are a great way to correct them. Click Undo when you create something you don't like, or make a mistake. Click Redo when you accidentally delete something you didn't want to delete or modify.

❖ **Linetype And Fill**

line type and fill Cricut design space. This option will tell your machine what tools and blades you are going to use. Keep in mind that depending on the Machine you have selected on the top of the window (Maker, Explore, or Joy), you will have different options.

❖ **Linetype**

This option will tell your machine when you are cutting your project, what tool you will be using. Right now, there are eight options (Cut, Draw, Score, Engrave, Deboss, Wave, Perf, and Foil).

❖ **Line Type And Fill Per Machine In Cricut Design Space**

If you have a Cricut Maker, all options will be available; if you have an Explore, you will be able to Cut, Draw, Score, and foil; last, if you have a Cricut Joy, only Cut and Draw will be available.

Here Is A More In-Depth Explanation Of Each Tool.

❖ **Cut**

Unless you uploaded a JPEG or PNG image to the Canvas; "Cut" is the default line type that all of your elements on your canvas will have; this means that when you press MAKE IT, your machine will cut those designs. With the Cut option selected, you can change the fill of your elements, at the end of the day, this translates into the different colors of materials you will use when you cut your projects. If you need help with learning about the Cricut Blades and the differences, I recommend you this ultimate guide and tutorial I put together.

❖ **Draw**

If you want to write on your designs, you can do it with your Cricut!

When you assign this line type, you will be prompted to choose any of the Cricut Pens you have (You need specific pens, unless you have a 3rd party adapter). When you select a particular design, the layers on your canvas area will be outlined with the color of the pen you picked. With this tool, when you click Make it, instead of cutting, your Cricut will write or draw. Note: This option DOESN'T color your designs.

❖ **Score**

The score is a more potent version of the Scoring line located on the left panel. When you assign this attribute to a layer, all of the designs will appear scored or dashed. This time, when you click on Make it. Your Cricut won't cut, but it will score your materials. For these types of projects, you will need the scoring stylus or the scoring wheel. However, keep in mind The wheel only works with the Cricut Maker. If you have doubts about what materials you need, I suggest you read this article. It's the ultimate guide for you to learn, what accessories and materials you genuinely need.

❖ **Engrave**

Allows you to engrave different types of materials. For instance, you can create monograms on aluminum sheets or anodized aluminum to reveal the silver beneath.

❖ Deboss

This tip will push the material in, and it will create beautiful and detailed designs. The debossing tip will allow you to customize your designs to a whole new level. Just imagine debossing a beautiful gift box with flowers, hearts, stars, etc.!

❖ Wave

Instead of cutting on straight lines like the rotary or fine point blade, this tool will create wavy effects on your final cuts. Getting curved lines in Design Space is quite complicated, so this tool will come in handy if you like these sorts of effects.

❖ Perf

The Perforation Blade is a tool that allows you to cut your materials in small and uniform lines to create perfect and crisp tear effects like the ones you see in raffle tickets, coupons, tear-out cards, etc.

❖ Foil (New)

Foil is the newest Cricut tool and it allows you to make beautiful foil finishes on your projects with the Cricut foil transfer kit. When using this line type you have the option to choose between fine, medium, and bold finishes.

❖ Fill

The fill option is mainly to be used for printing and patterns. It will only be activated when you have Cut as a "line type." No Fill means that you won't be printing anything. The print is by far, one of the best features Cricut has because it allows you to print your designs and then cut them; this is fabulous, and honestly, it's what motivated me to get a Cricut in the first place.

Anyway, we are getting back to the Printing option. When this Fill option is active, after you click Make it; first, you'll send your files to your home printer and then have your Cricut do all the heavy lifting.

(Cutting) Another excellent option for the Print Type is Patterns!!! You guys, this is so cool. Use Cricut's choices, or upload your own; you can add a pattern to pretty much any kind of layer.

❖ **Select All**

When you need to move all of your elements inside the canvas area, you may struggle to select them one by one. Click Select all to select all of the elements from the canvas.

❖ **Edit**

This icon will allow you to cut (remove from the canvas), copy (copy the same item, leave original intact), and paste (insert copied or cut elements on the canvas area) items from the canvas.

The Edit Icon has a drop-down menu. The cut and copy option will be activated when you use have a selection of one or more elements from the canvas area. The Paste option will be enabled once you copy or cut something.

❖ **Align**

If you have previews experience with other graphic design programs, most likely you'll know how to use this menu. If you aren't familiar with the Align Tools, let me tell you something; the Align Menu is something that you want to master to perfection. I will be creating a full tutorial for this, but while it comes out; here's what every align function means:

- ❖ **Align:** This function allows you to align all of your designs, and it's activated when selecting two or more elements.
- ❖ **Align Left:** When using this setting, all of the elements will be aligned to the left. The furthest element to the left will dictate where all of the other elements will move towards.
- ❖ **Center Horizontal:** This option will align your elements horizontally; this will entirely center text and images.

- ❖ **Align Right:** When using this setting, all of your elements will be aligned to the right. The furthest element to the right will dictate where all of the other elements will move.
- ❖ **Align Top:** This option will align all of your selected designs to the top. The furthest element to the top will dictate where all of the other elements will move.
- ❖ **Center Vertically:** This option will align your elements vertically. It's handy when you are working with columns, and you want them organized and aligned.
- ❖ **Align Bottom:** This option will align all of your selected designs to the bottom. The furthest element to the bottom will dictate where all of the other elements will move.
- ❖ **Center:** This option is a very cool one. When you click on "center," you are centering, both vertically and horizontally, one design against another one; this is particularly useful when you want to center text with a shape like a square or a star.
- ❖ **Distribute:** If you want the same spacing between elements, it's very time consuming to do it all on your own, and it's not 100% right. The distribute button will help you out with that. For it to be activated, you must have at least three elements selected.
- ❖ **Distribute Horizontally:** This button will distribute the elements horizontally. The furthest left and right designs will determine the length of the distribution; this means that the items that are in the center will be distributed between the most distant left and right designs.
- ❖ **Distribute Vertically:** This button will distribute the elements vertically. The furthest top and bottom designs will determine the length of the distribution; this means that the items that are in the center will be distributed between the most distant top and bottom designs.

Align In Cricut Design Space

How To Align In Cricut Design Space

- ❖ **Arrange**

When you work with multiple images, text, and designs, the new creations you add to the canvas will always be in front of everything. However, some of the elements of your design need to be in the back or front. With the arrange option, you can organize the elements very easily. Something great about this function is that the program will know what item is on the front or back and, and when you select it, the Design space will activate the available options for that particular element. Cool right?

These are the options you get:

❖ **Send To Back:** This will move the selected element to the back.
❖ **Move Backward:** This option will move selected the item just one step back. So if you have a three-element design. It will be like the cheese in a cheese sandwich.
❖ **Move Forward:** This option will move the element just one step forward. Typically, you would use this option when you have four or more items you need to organize.
❖ **Sent To Front:** This option will move the selected element to the front.
❖ **Flip**

If you need to reflect any of your designs in Cricut Design Space, this is a great way to do it. There are 2 options:

❖ **Flip Horizontal:** This will reflect your image or design horizontally. Sort of like a mirror; It's handy when you are trying to create left and right designs. Example: You are building some wings, and already have the left side; with Flip, you can copy and paste the left-wing, and voila! Now you have both (left and right) wings!
❖ **Flip Vertical:** This will flip your designs vertically. Kind of like you would see your reflection on the water. If you want to create a shadow effect, this option would be great for you.
❖ **Size**

Everything you create or type in Cricut Design Space has a size. You can modify the size from the element in self (when you click on it). However, if you need an item to have an exact measurement, this option will allow you to do so. Something essential is the little lock. When you increase or reduce the size of an image, the proportions are always locked. By clicking on the small lock, you are telling the program that you don't want to keep the same dimensions.

❖ **Rotate**

Just like size, rotating an element is something you can do very quickly from the canvas area. However, some designs need to be turned on at a specific angle. If that's the case for you, I recommend you to use this function. Otherwise, you will spend so much time fighting to get an element angled the way you want it to be.

❖ **Position**

This box shows you where your items are on the canvas area when you click on a specific design. You can move your elements around by specifying where you want that element to be located on the canvas areas. It's handy, but it's a more advanced tool. I don't use it that much because I can get around better with the alignment tools I mentioned above.

❖ **Font**

When you click on this panel, you can select any font you want to use for your projects. You can filter them and search for them on the top of the window.

If you have Cricut Access, you can use any of all the fonts that have a little green A at the beginning of the font title. However, if you don't have Cricut access, Make sure you use your system's fonts; otherwise you will be charged when you send your project to cut.

❖ **Style**

Once you pick your font, you have the option to change its form. Some of the options you have:

- ❖ **Regular:** this is the default setting, and it won't change the appearance of your font.
- ❖ **Bold:** it will make the font thicker.
- ❖ **Italic:** it will tilt the font to the right.
- ❖ **Bold Italic:** it will make the font thicker and tilt to the right.
- ❖ **Font Size, Letter & Line Space**

Top Panel Font Spacing and size Cricut Design Space. I can't express enough how AMAZING these options are. Especially the letter spacing.

- ❖ **Font Size:** You can change it manually from here. I usually just adjust the size of my fonts from the canvas area.
- ❖ **Letter Space:** Some fonts have a considerable gap between each letter. This option will allow you to reduce the space between letters very quickly. It's seriously a game-changer.
- ❖ Line Space: this option will tackle the space between lines in a paragraph; this is very useful because sometimes I am forced to create a single line of text because I am not happy with the spacing between lines.
- ❖ **Alignment**

This Alignment differs from the other "alignment" I explained above. This option is for paragraphs. These are the options you have:

- ❖ **Left:** Align a paragraph to the left
- ❖ **Center:** Align a paragraph to the center
- ❖ **Right:** Align a paragraph to the right.
- ❖ **Curve**

This option will allow you to get extra creative with your text. With this function, you can curve your text the best way to learn it's by playing with the little slider. When you move the slider to the left, it will curve the text upwards; and when you move it to the right, it will bend the text inwards. Note: if you move the slider entirely to the left, or right; you will form a circle with your fonts.

❖ **Advance**

Advance is the last option on the editing panel. Don't be intimidated by the name of this drop-down menu. Once you learn what all of the options are for, you will see they are not that hard to use.

- ❖ **Ungroup To Letters:** This option will allow you to separate each letter, into a single layer (I will explain more about Layers down below); use this, if you have plans to modify every single character.
- ❖ **Ungroup To Lines:** This option is exceptional, and it will allow you to separate a paragraph on individual lines. Type your paragraph, then click on ungroup to lines, and there you have it; a separate line that you can now modify.
- ❖ **Ungroup To Layers:** This one is the trickiest of all of these options. This option is only available for Multi-Layer fonts; these kinds of fonts are only available for individual purchases and, or Cricut Access.

A multi-layer font is a type of font that has more than one layer; these fonts are great if you want to have some shadow or color around it. What if you like a font that is multi-layer and you don't want the added layer? Just select your text and then click on ungroup to layers to separate every single layer.

❖ **Left Panel – Insert Shapes, Images & More**

Left Panel

With the top panel (that I just explained in detail) you are going to edit all of your designs. But where do they all come from? They all come from the Cricut Design Space Left Panel. This panel is all about inserting shapes, images, ready to cut projects, and more. From here you are going to add all of the things you are going to cut. This panel has seven options:

- ❖ **New:** To create and replace a new project in the canvas area.

- ❖ **Templates:** this allows you to have a guide on the types of things you are going to cut. Let's say you want to iron on vinyl on an onesie. When you select the template, you can design and see how the design would look like.
- ❖ **Projects:** Add ready to cut projects from Cricut Access.
- ❖ **Images:** Pick single images from Cricut Access, and cartridges to create a project.
- ❖ **Text:** Click here to add text on your canvas area.
- ❖ **Shapes:** Insert all kinds of shapes on the canvas.
- ❖ **Uploads:** Upload your images and cut files to the program.

There's something fundamental that you need to consider on this panel; unless you have Cricut Access, Cricut Images, ready to cut projects, and Cricut fonts cost money. If you use them, you will have to pay before you cut your project. Now, that we saw a little preview of what everything was for on this panel. Let's see what happens when you click on each of those buttons.

❖ New

When you click on NEW, and if you are already working on a project, you will receive a warning on top of the window asking you whether you want to replace your project or not. If you want to replace your project, make sure to save all the changes from the current project; otherwise, you will lose all that hard work. After you save, a fresh new and empty canvas will open up for you to get started.

❖ Templates

Templates help you to visualize and see how your project will fit on a particular surface. I think this feature is just out of this world. If you want to personalize fashion items, this tool is marvelous because you can select sizes and different types of clothing. Plus they also have a lot of various categories that you can choose from.

Note: templates are just for you to visualize. Nothing will be cut when you finish designing and send your project to be cut.

❖ **Projects**

If you wish to cut right away, then Projects is where you want to go! Once you select your project, you can customize it; or click on make it, and follow the cutting instructions.

Tip: Most of the projects are available for Cricut Access members, or you can purchase them as you go. However, there are a handful of projects FREE for you to cut, depending on the machine you have. Just scroll to the bottom of the categories drop-down menu and select the device you own.

❖ **Images**

Images are perfect when you are putting together your projects; with them, you can add an extra touch and personality to your crafts. You can search by keyword, highlighted categories, themes, people, places, occasions. Cartridges are a set of images that you need to purchase separately; some of them come with Cricut Access, and some not.

Under "Highlighted Categories" Cricut has FREE images to cut every week. Anytime you click under any category a more powerful filter will appear. With this filter, you can narrow your search even further. I suggest you play with these filters so you find images more efficiently.

❖ **Text**

Anytime you want to type on the Canvas Area, you will need to click on Text; then, a little window that says "Add text here" will open on the canvas.

❖ **Shapes**

Being able to use shapes, it's essential! With them, you can create simple and less complicated, and (also) beautiful projects. There're nine shapes you can choose from:

❖ Square
❖ Triangle

- ❖ Pentagon
- ❖ Hexagon
- ❖ Star
- ❖ Octagon
- ❖ Heart

The last option is not a shape, but an amazing and powerful tool called Score Line. With this option, you can create folds and score your materials.

❖ Upload

With this option, you can upload your files and images. The internet is filled with them; there are tons of bloggers that create projects for free. I would love for you to be able to get access to all of them. It's 100% Free for my daydreamers (aka subscribers) check out a live preview here, or get access here.

Note: The uploads you see on the image right down below are inside my fantastic library!

Right Panel – Learn All About Layers

To set you up for success and before I explain to you what every icon is all about on the Layers Panel, let me give you a little introduction of what a layer is. Layers represent every single element or design that is on the canvas area.

Think of it like clothing; when you get dressed, you have multiple layers that make up your outfit; and depending on the day, or time of year, your outfit can be simple or complex. So, for a freezing day, your layers would be underwear, pants, shirt, jacket, sock, boots, gloves, etc.; and for a day at the pool, you would only have one layer, a Swim Suit!, The same happens with a design; depending on the complexity of the project you are working on, you'll have different types of layers that'll make up your entire project.

❖ **Group, Ungroup, Duplicate And Delete**

These settings will make your life easy when moving things around the canvas area, so make sure to play around with them.

Group: Click here to group layers. This setting is handy when you have different layers that make up a complex design.

Let's say you are working on an elephant. Most likely (and if this is an SVG or cut file) the elephant will be composed of different layers (the body, eyes, legs, trunk, etc.); If you want to incorporate, extra shapes, and text; most likely is that you will be moving your elephant across the canvas area a lot. Therefore, by grouping all of the elephant layers, you can make sure that everything will stay organize and nothing will get out of place when you move them around the canvas.

Ungroup: This option will ungroup any grouped layers you select on the canvas area or layers panel. Use this option if you need to edit (size, type of font, etc.) a particular element or layer from the group.

Duplicate: This option will duplicate any layers or designs you have selected on the layers panel or canvas.

Delete: This option will delete any elements you have selected on the canvas or layers panel.

❖ **Linetype/Fill**

Every item on the Layers Panel will show what Linetype or Fill you are using (Cut, Write, Score, Perf, Wavy, Print, etc.).

❖ **Layer Visibility**

The little eye that appears on every layer on the layers panel represents the visibility of a design. When you are not sure whether an element looks good, instead of deleting it, click on the little eye to hide that design. Note: When you hide an item, the eye will have a cross mark.

Tip: By clicking on a layer and dragging it, you can move a particular design on top or under; you could say that this works like the Arrange option (sent to the front, back, etc.).

❖ Blank Canvas

This "layer" allows you to change the color of your canvas; if you are trying to see how a particular design looks with a different color. The power of this setting is unleashed when you use it along with the Templates tool because you can modify the color and the options of the template itself.

❖ Slice, Weld, Attach, Flatten And Contour

These tools you see here are incredibly important! So make sure you master them to perfection. I won't go into a lot of detail on them because they deserve tutorials on their own. However, I will give you a brief explanation of what they are all about by using the graphic down below.

❖ Slice, Weld, Attach, Flatten, And Contour Info-Graphic

As you can see in the graphic, the original design is a pink circle and a teal square. Now let's see what happens when I use all of these options.

❖ Slice

The slice tool is perfect for cutting out shapes, text, and other elements, from different designs. When I selected both shapes and clicked on slice, you can see that the original file got all cut up; to show you what the outcome was, I copied and pasted the "slice result" and then separated all of the pieces that resulted from slicing.

❖ Weld

The welding tool allows you to combine two or more shapes in one. When I selected both shapes and clicked on Weld, you can see that I created a whole new shape. The color is determined by the layer that is on the back, that's why the new shape is pink in color.

❖ Attach

Attach works like grouping layers, but it's more powerful. When I selected both shapes and clicked on attach, you can see that the layers just changed color (determined by the layer that is on the back). However, the shapes are connected, and this attachment will remain in place, even after I send my project to be cut.

❖ Flatten

This tool is extra support for the Print then Cut Fill setting; when you change the fill from no fill to print, that applies to just one layer. But what if you wish to do it to multiple shapes at the time?

When you are done with your design, select the layers you want to print together as a whole, and then click on flatten. When you are done with your design (you can't reverse this after exiting your project), select the layers you want to print together as a whole, and then click on flatten.

❖ Contour

The Contour tool allows you to hide unwanted pieces of a design, and it will only be activated when a shape or design has elements that can be left out. For this example, I combined the original design in one shape with the weld tool; then I typed in the word contour and sliced it against the new shape, and used the Contour tool to hide the inner circles of the two letters O and the inner part of the letter R.

❖ Color Sync

Color Sync is the last option of the layers panel. Every color on your canvas area represents a different material color. If your design has multiple shades of yellows or blues; are you sure you need them? If you only need one shade of yellow, like this example. Just click and drag the tone you want to get rid of and drop it on the one you want to keep.

❖ Canvas Area

The canvas area is where you see all of your designs and elements. It's very intuitive and effortless to use!

❖ Canvas Grid And Measurements

The canvas area is divided by a grid; this is great because every little square you see on the Grid helps you to visualize the cutting mat. In the end, this will help you to maximize your space. You can change the measurements from inches to cm and turn the grid on and off when you click on the top panel toggle and then select Settings. Turn the Grid off and on

❖ Selection

Anytime you select one or more layers, the selection is blue, and you can modify it from all of the four corners. The "red x" is for deleting the layers. The right upper corner will allow you to rotate the image (although if you need a specific angle, I recommend you to use the rotate tool on the editing menu). The lower right button of the selection, "the small lock," keeps the size proportional when you increase or decrease the size of your layer.

❖ Zoom In And Out

Last but not least. If you want to see on a bigger or smaller scale (without modifying the real size of your designs), you can do it by pressing the "+ and -" signs on the lower-left corner of the canvas.

Chapter 7 : Design Space Troubleshooting

Cricut Design Space Not Working? Common Issues & Fixes

If you have a Cricut Maker, a Cricut Easy Press, or a Cricut Explore, then you'll be familiar with Cricut Design Space. This is the software that lets you design and cut your images. If you're new to creating and cutting your designs, then it has lots of good features to help you get started.

- ❖ It works with most recognised image types: .jpg, .gif, .pgn, .svg and .dxf
- ❖ It has more than 60,000 images for you to start with

And it includes some pre-prepared projects so that you can get used to creating and designing. One potential drawback is that you need to keep connected to the internet and this can sometimes cause problems, so what can you do if your Cricut Design Space isn't working?. There is no simple answer and some things are tried and tested ways of fixing other problems too, but here are some ways to fix some of the most common errors.

Program Lagging Or Freezing

One thing you may experience is the program freezing or taking a long time to do anything. If you do, then first check your internet speed as a slow speed can cause this. You may be paying for a high speed, but in reality, you may not be getting this.

1. Run A Speed Test

There are many sites where you can run a free speed test. To run Cricut Design space you will need both good upload and download speeds.

- ❖ Recommended minimum download speed: 5 Mbps
- ❖ Recommended minimum upload speed: 1.0 Mbps

If either your upload or download speeds are not enough, the best thing to do is get in touch with your internet service provider. They can often tell you the best way to increase these or upgrade your contract so you can get the desired speed. It's possible you may need a new modem or router and they will be able to tell you.

2. Check What Else Is Connected

Most households these days have several people sharing one internet connection. This can put a strain on it and even slow it down. Streaming movies and TV programs can affect the speed of everyone else in the house. If you find your Cricut Design space is lagging or freezing, check to see what else is being used, and if necessary turn it off. This could give you the extra speed you need. You also need to look at your computer to see what's running in the background. It's sometimes easy to forget that you have other programs open and these can be slowing your system down. If you can hear the processor working hard, then something is using it. Some of the things to look out for are:

- ❖ If you are using a Windows machine, Windows may be updated in the background.
- ❖ Anti-virus programs run scans and updates, and you may find this is running and causing problems. If it is, then you can stop the scan until you have finished working.
- ❖ If you are streaming while working, that might prevent your Cricut Design Space from running smoothly.
- ❖ Similarly having too many pages open such as Facebook, Skype, Twitter, Newsfeeds, and sites like Ebay, can all slow things down.
- ❖ If you cannot see anything running in the background, try restarting your computer. This often works to speed things up, particularly if it's not been turned off for several days.

3. Restart The Router

Now and then it can help to turn off your router and restart it. Many people don't like to do this, but it can help to keep your connection running smoothly.

4. Check Your Computer

If your computer doesn't meet the required specifications for using Cricut Design space, then you may experience freezing. The recommendations for a Windows machine are:

- ❖ Windows 8 or later
- ❖ Intel Core series or AMD processor
- ❖ 4GB of Ram but 8GB will help
- ❖ At least 50MB of free disk space
- ❖ A spare USB port or Bluetooth connection

If you use Windows, then always use the most up to date version of your chosen browser. Cricut Design space will work in Chrome, Firefox, and Edge, but if you notice lag, check to see if there's an update to your browser. The recommendations for Apple machines are:

- ❖ Mac OS X 10.12 or later
- ❖ CPU of 1.83 GHz
- ❖ Minimum 4GB Ram
- ❖ 50MB free disk space
- ❖ A spare USB port or Bluetooth connection

If you do not have the required specification, you may need to look at upgrading your computer.

5. Clear Your Cache

Over time your cache can get very cluttered, and if you don't turn your PC off every night, you might find things slowing down. Clearing your cache can improve your speed.

6. Shockwave Issues

Like a lot of software, Cricut Design Space uses Flash. This can cause problems of its own. If you start working on a project and leave it open while you have a break, then you may come back to a message telling you that Flash is not working. This is because it has an automatic time limit and if you do not complete what you are doing within that time, it closes down. There is no easy way around this one but make sure you save your work regularly so you still have it if you encounter a Shockwave error.

7. Reinstall

Sometimes when you encounter problems, all you have to do is close the program and re-open it. If all else fails, then you may need to uninstall the software and reinstall it. This can be done using the same method that you use for uninstalling other programs, but you may need to restart your pc before you reinstall it.

Design Space Problems

When you're working with images and design software there are many problems you can encounter. Some may require technical help but the three most common are these:

1. The Program Won't Open

As Cricut Design Space uses Flash you will need to install Adobe Flash before you use it. This is free software which you can download from the Adobe website. Some browsers such as Chrome will ask you every time you open Design Space if you want to allow Flash to run. You must click to allow this or you won't be able to use the software.

2. Cannot Locate The Image Files

The preloaded files are in a ZIP folder so you will need to unzip them before you can use them. There are free unzip programs available or you may already have one installed. When you import your files, you should get an editing window to appear. If it does not, find the files in

Design Space and click on the button which says 'insert images'. If you're not sure which ones they are, they should have a green tick next to them.

3. Imported Images Do Not Look Right

If you find that your image has gaps or is all one color after you've uploaded it then this is most likely to be a problem with the layers. Click 'Ctrl+A' to select all of the elements of your design, and then change the fill color so that it is transparent. You may find that you have a hidden layer that was causing the problems. Now that you can see it, you can continue your editing. As with all programs, you may experience a problem when you first start to use Design Space. As you get more experienced and try more features you will soon be able to troubleshoot when you have any problems.

Chapter 8: Best Software to Use With Cricuit Machine

What Is The Best Software To Use With Cricut?

1. Adobe Illustrator

No type of graphics design can be discussed without mentioning one of the best tools in the trade. Adobe Illustrator is a vector-based image editor that allows you to create pretty much anything that has shape or color. In the case of Cricut designs, this means being able to create complex and beautiful patterns, and that is something that Adobe Illustrator can do without much effort.

The expanded toolset allows you to create models that are both precise and intricate, and the file formats are perfectly compatible with Cricut hardware. More so, once you are done designing your Cricut patterns, you should know that the software tool can be used for pretty much anything else, as it is not a program with a singular purpose. Let's quickly look at its key features:

- ❖ Great for creating intricate and precise patterns
- ❖ File formats supported by a wide range of hardware and software
- ❖ Its popularity makes it so that tutorials and guides are not hard to find
- ❖ The toolset can be further expanded using plug-ins
- ❖ Can be tested for free

2. Adobe Photoshop

The world's best imaging and graphic design software need little or no introduction at all, so we're going to jump straight to it. Just like Illustrator, this amazing tool can be paired with your Cricut machine to achieve sophisticated patterns executed with supreme precision. And just like its vector-based sibling, Photoshop is a hugely versatile software that can be used to create pretty much anything your imagination can conceive.

Needless to say that such powerful features cannot be confined to a singular platform or workspace and that is precisely why you can use Photoshop whenever your Cricut inspiration strikes. From PC to mobile workstations, your progress will be instantly updated across all platforms. Since so many artists all around the globe are already used to working in Photoshop, creating Cricut files is rather straightforward and comfortable, we may add.

Just open Adobe Photoshop, then click on Place Embed to add all the PNGs (or other file formats) you want. Then start making use of the powerful editing toolset to resize, rearrange, adjust, add layers, group images, and much more until you are perfectly satisfied with the result. Eliminate the white background (more tools are available for this task – don't be afraid to explore them at your own pace). Once you're satisfied with the outcome, go to the File menu, name your project and choose to save it as PNG. Finally, upload your design in the Cricut tool and you're all set. Let's quickly look at its key features:

- ❖ Robust editing toolkit (crop, combine, retouch, resize images to perfection)
- ❖ Cross-platform integration (from desktop to mobile station)
- ❖ Fully compatible with touch and pen technology
- ❖ Unlimited layers, masks, filters, and brushes
- ❖ your work is automatically saved to the cloud
- ❖ Adobe Fonts integration to automatically detect all missing fonts
- ❖ Object Selection tool to create fast and precise selections

3. Cricut Design Space

Design Space is cloud-based design software that is both easy to learn and lightweight. Use it whenever inspiration strikes and take advantage of its cross-platform compatibility that stretches from laptop to Mac, iOs, and Android devices. You can even use it offline! So what's there not to like?

Let's quickly look at its key features:

- ❖ Extensive assets library (images, fonts, pre-made templates, and more)
- ❖ Advanced editing toolkit to personalize your project
- ❖ Create complex details with unmatched precision
- ❖ Step-by-step tutorials and instructional videos
- ❖ Extended chat and phone support

4. CorelDRAW

CorelDRAW Graphics Suite is one amazing all-in-one graphic design software to meet every single one of your needs. From apparel and textiles to blueprints and maps and all way to sophisticated illustrations, this feature-rich design suite delivers all the tools you need to conceptualize your ideas and take them one step closer to materialization.

If you've simply outgrown your cartridge collection, it's time to take your Cricut skills up a notch and invest in performant design software that is perfectly adapted for Cricut Machines such as CorelDRAW. This vector-based tool is preferred by many professional cutters who enjoy its complex functionalities, but home cutter crafters will enjoy it just the same. With beautiful typography, support for TTF files, and seamless integration with popular plugins for cutting, CorelDRAW is a great solution to use with your Cricut.

5. Silhouette Software

The final product on our list is not a standalone software, but an already built-in solution meant to facilitate the design process for you. Indeed, some cutters come with full-featured design software and

Silhouette Studio is such a tool that allows you to create designs and send them to a Silhouette machine.

As far as we are concerned, the tool does a pretty good job at meeting your basic needs by allowing you to import, customize, and create cutting files. However, if you want to export your work in formats that can be used with other cutters, you will need to adhere to a subscription plan. The premium versions of this software are Designer Edition, Designer Edition +, and Business Edition. To make the most out of your Cricut die-cutting unit, we strongly recommend that you consider these fantastic design software apps that are compatible with Windows systems.

Pair them up with some amazing photo editors or with some 2D digital pixel art tools for the best experience possible. No matter which one you decide to use, you will be able to take control of your creativity, and you'll finally manage to use the Cricut die-cutting system the way that you always wanted to.

Pros

- ❖ Works well with a wide array of file formats
- ❖ Delivers potent and uniquely helpful editing tools
- ❖ Highly compatible with Cricut and other die-cutting machines
- ❖ Merges well with other crafting & editing applications

Cons

- ❖ Some functions are paid only
- ❖ Installing & activating can be tricky

6. Sure Cuts A Lot

This is the most popular option behind Cricut Design Space. And it happens because it works well with a wide array of Cricut machines, going from the Cricut standard to the Silhouette, the Craft ROBO, and even the Wishblade – among many others. You will have the chance to draw, design, color, and edit all kinds of stuff so you can create the most interesting drawings. At the same time, it offers the chance to transform random images into die-cut designs, for even better results no matter what you're looking for. Sure enough, Sure Cuts a Lot is also a piece of cake to use and delivers excellent features that you won't find in other programs. Here's a better idea of the different functions and benefits that Sure Cuts a Lot offers:

- ❖ Easy Operation
- ❖ High Compatibility
- ❖ Extra Plugins & Functions

Pros

- ❖ Offers total control of the designs & interface
- ❖ Works well with most die-cutting machines & computers
- ❖ Updates automatically with complete support
- ❖ Offers tons of plugins and extra features

Cons

- ❖ Some features may not be compatible with Mac computers
- ❖ Only allows one project at a time

7. Make The Cut

Another third-party software system you can use to edit die-cutting designs is Make the Cut or MTC. It offers precisely what Cricut Design Space offers, going from maximum design features to excellent compatibility with most machines. From editing shapes and coming up with unique designs to adding exciting effects and even marking the Cricut pattern – Make the Cut offers it all. But the real advantage comes from its capacity to work with a wide array of files. So it does not only offer the chance to enjoy excellent editing but also unbeatable compatibility. Another advantage is how long it's been in the market – making it a hugely prestigious and reliable option to have. Want to have a more in-depth idea of what it offers? Here are some of its features:

- ❖ Convenient Editing
- ❖ Next-Level Compatibility
- ❖ Fast and Well-Made

Pros

- ❖ Fully-equipped editing with tons of features
- ❖ Compatible with most die-cutting machines
- ❖ Superb file format compatibility
- ❖ Reliable and fast system

Cons

- ❖ Not compatible with Cricut machines
- ❖ Faulty compatibility with Mac computers

8. Inkscape

In contrast with the two previous apps, Inkscape is an open-source program. That means you can get it for free, and it will deliver all the best features at no cost. That means you get everything from object creation and manipulation like drawing, cloning, layering, and transforming, to rendering, importing, and exporting files with maximum support. There's a unique vector path system as well, the capacity to create logos, charts, lines, text designs, and even import the most elaborate pieces of art to edit them. And being an open-source program, you can expect it to have excellent support in every way, as well as tons of tutorials and guides to follow when necessary. There's a lot you get with Inkscape, so we decided to summarize it for you:

- ❖ Powerful Editing
- ❖ Outstanding Import & Export
- ❖ Best Compatibility

Pros

- ❖ Works with almost all design file formats
- ❖ Compatible with Linux, Windows, and macOS
- ❖ Won't cost you a single dime to use

334

Cons

- ❖ Editor tends to lag in large projects
- ❖ Slightly complex interface.

Chapter 9 : Quick Tips to Keep Cricuit Maker Efficient

Tips For Getting The Most Out Of Your Cricut Cutter

Whether you've just bought a Cricut machine, or you're wondering if it's worth the investment, there are a lot of things to learn before you can operate them effectively. Different Cricut cutters have unique features and abilities, so you should do your research before choosing a Cricut machine that's right for your intended projects. You can use this guide to learn some Cricut tips for beginners and about the best Cricut accessories.

What Is A Cricut Cutter?

A Cricut is a machine that writes, scores, and cuts to help you design DIY projects. In this guide, we will answer the following questions:

- ❖ Which Cricut cutter should you buy?
- ❖ How do you know which one is right for your projects?
- ❖ What type of mats should you use?
- ❖ What materials can you use with a Cricut?
- ❖ What can you make with a Cricut machine?
- ❖ How do you get the most out of your Cricut cutter?

With a Cricut cutter, the possibilities are endless. You can create a vast array of projects with over 100 materials that can be designed from your computer and add creative flair to your home decor with your Cricut machine.

Which Cricut Cutter Should You Buy?

The Cricut cutter is currently available in four different models — the Maker, the Explore One, the Explore Air, and the Explore Air 2. As you consider which Cricut cutter you should buy, think about how you want to use it and how much you're willing to spend.

❖ Cricut Maker

Out of all four models, the Cricut Maker has the most features and is available in six colors: champagne, lilac, mint, blue, raspberry, and rose. Its rotary blade can cut unbonded fabric, and its knife blade can cut thick materials, such as balsa wood and leather. The Cricut Maker also uses a rotary cutter for fabric and crepe paper.

The Maker's Scoring Wheel can score practically any material for any project. This machine features an adaptive system that allows it to use a wide array of tools. Plus, since it's Bluetooth enabled, the Cricut Maker can easily connect to your electronic device.

❖ Cricut Explore One

The most basic model is the Cricut Explore One in standard white. You can cut almost 100 materials with this basic machine without compromising on the writing, scoring, and cutting features of the Cricut Explore Air. This machine doesn't offer Bluetooth, so you will have to connect a wire from your computer or electronic device to your Cricut Explore One. This model also doesn't have a double cartridge feature, so you cannot write and cut at the same time.

❖ Cricut Explore Air

The Cricut Explore Air model contains all the same features as the Explore One, but it can also connect to Bluetooth and has the double cartridge feature. Since it's comparable to the Cricut Explore Air 2 with only a small price bump, you may want to invest in the newer model because of the Explore Air 2's speed and efficiency.

❖ Cricut Explore Air 2

The Cricut Explore Air 2 can cut twice as fast as its predecessor. The Explore Air 2 also comes in different colors, including rose, lilac, mint, raspberry, black, blue, Fuschia, sky, and peach kiss. A rotary blade is also compatible with this machine to cut thicker materials.

How To Know Which Cricut Cutter Is Right For Your Project

If you're a beginner, you'll most likely want a cheaper machine so you can grow your Cricut skills before splurging on an expensive, more versatile model. As you advance in your Cricut skills, you can buy a model that specializes in the projects you enjoy. Use this guide to help you decide which Cricut machine matches your skill level and needs:

1. When To Buy The Cricut Explore One: Since the Cricut Explore One is the most basic model, it may be best for you if you're a beginner. You'll need to use a wire to connect your Cricut machine to your computer. To add Bluetooth to your Cricut machine, you can spend a few extra dollars and upgrade to the Cricut Explore Air. You can also buy a Bluetooth adapter that is compatible with your Mac, PC, iPhone, or iPad.

2. When To Buy The Cricut Explore Air: With the double cartridge feature, you can cut and write at the same time, easing the process of making cards and other projects. The design software and cutting process are slower, so if you want a more efficient product, you can upgrade to the Cricut Explore Air 2.

3. When To Buy The Cricut Explore Air 2: If you have your own business and need to have a quick turnaround for your products, the Cricut Explore Air 2 can efficiently produce your projects. Plus, since it comes in more colors, you have more versatility in the appearance of your machine. You can design projects with almost any material with the Cricut Explore Air 2.

4. When To Buy The Cricut Maker: Since the Cricut Maker does it all, this model would be ideal for you if you need it for your business operations or if you want to design projects with wood, fabric, and crepe paper. If you enjoy crafting and you'll use your Cricut cutting machine often, consider investing in the Cricut Maker.

338

❖ Cricut Cutter Mats

Cricut cutter mats contain grid lines that will help you measure and precisely place each material on your mat. Cricut cutter mats have different levels of adhesiveness, depending on the grip strength required for each material. You will need the following types of Cricut cutter mats for each of your projects:

- ❖ **Blue Mat:** Light grip ideal for office paper, vellum, and light cardstock.
- ❖ **Green Mat:** Standard grip ideal for vinyl, iron-on, patterned paper, and cardstock.
- ❖ **Purple Mat:** Strong grip ideal for thick cardstock, poster board, chipboard, glitter cardstock, and other thick materials.
- ❖ **Pink Mat:** Fabric grip ideal for machines that use Rotary Blades or Bonded-Fabric Blades to cut through fabrics.

All cutting mats also come in two different sizes: 12 by 12 inches and 24 by 24 inches. To use the Cricut cutter mat, stick the material you want to cut on the mat and load both the mat and the material into your Cricut cutting machine. After you press the load button, your Cricut cutting machine will cut your design for you.

Tips For Caring For Your Cricut Cutter Mats

To prolong the life of your Cricut cutter mats, follow these tips:

1. Using Your Mat: Only cut the recommended materials when using each mat. For example, if you use a purple mat for office paper, it may get stuck on the mat, adding wear and tear to your mat over time. As you transfer your project, keep your fingers off the grip.

2. Cleaning Your Mat: For blue, green, and purple grip mats, you can use a scraper to remove excess pieces and use a spatula to remove your finished cut projects. You can also use non-alcoholic baby wipes, a lint roller, or soapy water to clean your mat. Alternatively, for a pink mat, you should only use a lint roller or transfer tape to clean stray pieces off your mat. A scraper might pull off the grip adhesive of your fabric mat.

3. Safely Storing Your Mat: Your Cricut cutter mats come with clear film covers. Cover your mat with a clear film cover to protect it from debris and dust.

Transfer Tips For Your Cricut Projects

Transfer tape is an efficient way to transfer your vinyl projects from the adhesive mat cover to your wall or other surfaces. With a removable adhesive on the side of your transfer tape, you can use vinyl to stick decals on water bottles, journals, windows, cell phone covers, and more. You should also use transfer tape for easy project handling on your Cricut cutter mats.

To use transfer tape for your vinyl projects:

- ❖ Cut your design with a kiss cut a shallow cut that doesn't break through the paper backing and weed out the excess vinyl.
- ❖ Cut out a piece of transfer tape that will fit over your vinyl project and completely smooth it over the vinyl.
- ❖ As you peel the adhesive side off of the vinyl backing, the decal should come with the adhesive.

If any pieces continue to stick to the backing, smooth the tape over the vinyl in those spots until it completely comes off the backing. When choosing what type of transfer tape is right for your project, you should consider the tape's tack level, transparency, and width:

Paper Transfer Tape For Crafters: This premium, multi-use transfer tape provides medium and high tack levels for vinyl projects. It is perfect for crafters and includes a blue alignment grid suitable for the precise application of vinyl stickers, graphics, and letters. It also has an easy-release liner to make the vinyl application quick, simple, and hassle-free.

Clear Transfer Tape: This type of transfer tape is more versatile than paper transfer tape in terms of tack levels and width. It is available in medium-high and low tack levels and is available in widths between 6 inches and 48 inches. Since clear transfer tape is transparent, you can use this tape for projects where the vinyl design needs to be visible.

What Type Of Material Should You Use For Your Project?

Your Cricut machine can write, cut, and score more than 100 different materials. You can also use your Cricut machine's custom setting to cut and style a different material. Besides bonded fabric and poster board, most materials can be cut with a fine blade included with your Cricut machine. The most common materials for your Cricut project ideas are:

- ❖ Paper

In addition to office paper, you can also use a Cricut for wrapping paper, tissue paper, crepe paper, and more.

You can use paper to make:

- ❖ Invitations
- ❖ Wall decorations
- ❖ Paper flowers
- ❖ Cards
- ❖ Decorative bags

You can also use your Cricut machine to write on envelopes to send with your invitations and cards.

- ❖ Vinyl

You can use vinyl to make decals for:

- ❖ Mugs
- ❖ Walls
- ❖ Car windows
- ❖ Candleholders
- ❖ Journals

You can use different colors of vinyl, including holographic and glitter vinyl, to take any ordinary object and add a design to it.

❖ Iron-On Vinyl

Instead of stick-on vinyl, you can use iron-on vinyl to iron a pattern onto fabric, wood, paper, or metal. You can use iron-on vinyl to decorate:

❖ Baby onesies
❖ T-shirts
❖ Sweaters
❖ Dresses
❖ Towels
❖ Light Cardstock

With paper slightly thicker than office paper, you can use light cardstock for:

❖ Posters
❖ Cake and cupcake toppers
❖ Party decorations
❖ Gift tags
❖ Goodie bag tags
❖ Cardstock

You can use thicker cardstock for office supplies and decorations like:

❖ Bookmarks
❖ Cards
❖ Place cards
❖ Invitations
❖ Posters
❖ Bonded Fabric

If you have a Cricut Maker, you can use it for fabric projects, like:

❖ Quilts
❖ Dolls and stuffed animals

- ❖ Baby and kids clothes
- ❖ Christmas stockings
- ❖ Pillows and cushions
- ❖ Poster Board

You can use poster board to make:

- ❖ Gift boxes
- ❖ School projects
- ❖ Bulletin board lettering

Tips And Tricks For Using Your Cricut Cutter

Now that you know the types of Cricut cutters, the mats you should buy, and the materials you can use for your projects, you can begin using your Cricut cutter machine. Here are some tips and tricks to keep in mind:

Other Helpful Tools And Accessories To Consider Purchasing

Cricut Design Space is a free software included with your Cricut machine that allows you to do everything from uploading images to editing designs to scoring and finalizing your project. You should make yourself familiar with Design Space and all it has to offer before you start using your Cricut machine. Design Space features project ideas, SVG files you can print on your products, and other helpful tips for your DIY Cricut projects.

In addition to your Cricut cutter and all that is included with it, you can also buy a Cricut Machine Beginner Set, which includes the following Cricut tools:

1. Weeders: These tools pull stray pieces out from adhesive vinyl or heat transfer vinyl patterns. You should weed your project while it's still on the mat.

2. Scraper: These scrape stray pieces off of your Cricut cutter mats. You can also use your scraper to smooth your adhesive vinyl project onto the transfer paper.

343

3. Tweezers: With their reverse grip design, tweezers can help you lift and secure small pieces with ease.

4. Spatula: The spatula allows you to remove projects from your Cricut cutter mat.

5. Scissors: The stainless steel blades of these scissors precisely cut through materials such as paper, cardstock, fabric, and vinyl.

6. Trimmer: With a trimmer, you can accurately cut and score straight lines.

7. Scoring Stylus: Use this tool to score fold lines for cards and other projects. For the Cricut Maker, you would use a Scoring Wheel.

Cricut pens are included in your Cricut Machine Beginner Set, but you can also use other thick pens if you have some available. Always keep your vinyl scraps and weeded pieces for future projects. Design Space can also help you minimize waste by moving all the shapes closer together. You'll eventually need to replace the blade included with your Cricut machine. You know you'll need a new blade for your Cricut machine when the blade isn't cutting all the way through or tearing the material from your mat.

Creative Ways To Use The Cutter

Before you start crafting your DIY Cricut creations, you can find inspiration online through Design Space and free blogs. Bloggers are eager to share their creative ideas with you, and you can find both beginner and advanced projects online. Your Cricut machine has the following features:

1. Print And Cut: Use an inkjet printer and print out your design with registration marks around it. Your Cricut machine will recognize the design and use the print and cut feature to create your design.

2. Write: Your Cricut machine comes with special Cricut pens, but you can use other types of pens to write your design. You can also find free font designs online.

3. Score: Scoring makes folding easier. You can put your Scoring Stylus in your Cricut's pen holder.

4. Emboss: Program your Cricut to cut, but if you put your accessory adapter in place of the blade and your Scoring Stylus in place of your pen, your Cricut will emboss the material instead.

Your Cricut machine software helps you create the best projects from choosing the right materials for your project to loading the machine properly. Follow the prompts that arise as you complete your projects on your computer. As you create your first project, start small, and use test cuts to get a feel for the machine. In older models, Cricut machines used cartridges to remember what designs you've saved. You can now save your projects online with newer models, but if you replace your Cricut machine, use any old cartridges to link to your account and retrieve old projects.

Tips For Using The Machine

Before you use your Cricut cutting machine, you'll need to prepare properly, by:

1. Reading The Instructions Before Use: The box will have information regarding what's included with your Cricut and how to take care of it. Read the manual and the instructions on the box before you use your product.

2. Watching Tutorial Videos: You can find videos online for safety tips and creative ideas. Design Space has videos that are related to each type of Cricut machine.

3. Setting Up Your Workspace: Clear the clutter from your office table and place your Cricut on a flat surface before use. You should also organize your Cricut supplies and materials so you can begin your projects without getting overwhelmed.

Finally, Here Are Some Troubleshooting Tips For Using Your Cricut Machine:

1. Mirror Image Iron-On Vinyl: Put the iron-on paper upside-down to print your design on iron-on vinyl. Cricut machines have a mirror-image setting. For HTV Heat Transfer Vinyl put the vinyl right side up.

2. Load Mat Correctly: Your mat should slip below the rollers. Your machine may not run if you load the mat incorrectly.

3. Use The Right Material Setting: With each new project you do, make sure you use the right setting for the material you use. Check the material setting dial each time you're about to start a new project.

4. Replace Your Pen Caps After Use: After you're finished with your project, you should replace the pen caps, so you don't dry out your Cricut markers.

15 Cricut Hacks You Probably Didn't Know About

- ❖ Use Glad Press 'n Seal instead of transfer paper as a very cheap substitute!
- ❖ Remove tiny pieces from Cricut cutouts with a sticky lint roller.
- ❖ Use Dollar Store pencil grips to get Sharpies to fit in the Cricut Explore pen holder
- ❖ Cheap Way to Clean Your Cricut Mat
- ❖ How to "Resticky" Your Cutting Mat
- ❖ Use a tennis ball to get the vinyl to stick to textured walls.
- ❖ If you lose your burnishing tool, use a credit card or old gift card to rub the design well for an easy transfer after weeding.
- ❖ Cut freezer paper using your Cricut to create a practically free stencil.
- ❖ Keep the plastic sheet that comes with your mats and put it back on after use to prevent pet hair or dust from sticking to them.
- ❖ Store your vinyl rolls in an Ikea holder on a lazy susan.
- ❖ Wrap masking or painter's tape around your hand to easily remove scraps when weeding.
- ❖ Mark the top side of your cutting mat to make sure you load it correctly.

❖ To sharpen your Cricut blade, poke it in and out of a ball of aluminum foil.
❖ Spice up your designs with new fonts! Find a TON of free ones at dafont.com.
❖ Download Inkscape to create your SVGs for free

Conclusion

Learning a new hobby or skill can be intimidating at first. I get it; sometimes we don't even know where to start because there's so much information out there and it's just overwhelming. For me, the best way to learn and master Cricut Design Space is from the beginning!, You see, when you have a clear concept of what every icon and panel is for, then you can truly dig in and start exploring further and further. Sometimes we are quick to jump from project to project but I think that knowing your work area will help you to take your creativity to a whole new level.

So which one is better? If you're looking for versatility and features, the Cricut Maker has the upper hand here. It cuts through so many different materials. Plus, it uses Adaptive Technology so that the blades' pressure changes depending on the material. If you're looking for an affordable cutting machine, then the Explore Air 2 is the more ideal model. It's not as powerful as the Cricut Maker, but it's versatile and advanced for its price. Cleaning your Cricut mat is important so you can use precision techniques without worrying about dirt, dust, or lint getting in the way. We'd recommend taking care of your mat's surface and regularly cleaning it with the methods mentioned above.

Also, resticking your Cricut mat allows the material to slide evenly into the cutting machine and kept intact throughout the process. Why spend hard-earned money on buying a new mat when the old one is perfectly serviceable? Rejuvenating and making it sticky again only takes a few minutes and it's not that expensive. That's it – You are not a beginner anymore! , I hope this tutorial was useful for you! If you read it and studied it consciously, let me tell you something that you are not a beginner. Cricut machines are great pieces of hardware that allow you to cut magnificent patterns into pretty much any material.

As you can see, finding a Cricut Design Space alternative is not hard. There are many options you can go for, and they all offer amazing features to consider. So, it's all up to you. Find the best model according to our small reviews and make sure it matches your standards. Then, you'll have the chance to enjoy excellent Cricut designs without having to waste any time or effort looking for the ideal tool out there. Hope you find an alternative to the Cricut design space.

As you can see, you can do a wide array of projects when using Cricut machines. These tools are proven effective in cutting both thin and thick materials. Also, they can print images on the printer through the help of Cricut design software included in the machine. Hence, you can use a Cricut machine in cutting out clip art, printed photos, and other images.

Cricut machines might be useful for various tasks. Their versatility and effectiveness are making them popular options when it comes to die-cutting. That is why you need a Cricut machine, particularly when you're a skilled crafter. If you're a newbie, the best cutting machine for you will be the multi-featured one and is easy to use.

CRICUT ACCESSORIES

A Practical Guide to Mastering Your Cricut Machine. A step-by-Step Manual with Illustations and Examples to Improve your Ability with Accessories and Materials

Kimberly Johnson

Introduction

Cricut is a brand of cutting plotters, or computer-controlled cutting machines, designed for home crafters. Consumers often use the machines for cutting paper, felt, vinyl, fabric, and other materials such as leather, matboard, and even wood. A Cricut is a cutting machine and is a dream come true for many crafters out there. You can use it for several different things like card making, home decor, etc.

Do you craft or find yourself in a position where you need to cut a lot? If the answer to that is yes. Then you will benefit from having a Cricut. However, if you are not into crafty things. Let's face it! a Cricut is not something you will benefit from. The original Cricut machine had cutting mats of 6 × 12 inches, the larger Cricut Explore allows mats of 12 × 12 and 12 × 24. The largest machine will produce letters from a half-inch to 231/2 inches high. Both the Cricut and Cricut Explore Air 2 require mats and blades which can be adjusted to cut through various types of paper, vinyl, and other sheet products. The Cricut personal paper cutter operates as a paper cutter based upon cutting parameters programmed into the machine and resembles a desktop printer. Cricut

Cake produces stylized edible fondants cut into various shapes from fondant sheets, and is used by chefs in the preparation and ornamentation of cakes.

What Is A Cricut?

A Cricut machine is a cutting machine. It cuts shapes, text, and photos. While many people think of a Cricut as something that cuts card stock or vinyl only, it can cut faux leather, adhesive foil, balsa wood, and more. With the Cricut Explore One, Cricut Explore Air, and Cricut Explore Air 2 (the current models sold by Cricut), the machine has a writing and scoring adapter in addition to cutting. A Cricut is popular with crafters, party planners, DIY enthusiasts, and more!

The Cricut Explore Air is a die-cutting machine (aka craft plotter or cutting machine). You can think of it like a printer; you create an image or design on your computer and then send it to the machine. Except that instead of printing your design, the Cricut machine cuts it out of whatever material you want!

What Can I Do With A Cricut?

Wow! Listing everything would be a long list! But, here's a shortlist of Cricut project ideas.

1. School Projects: My elementary-aged daughter can use my Cricut machine. She has used it on several projects this year already!

2. Card Stock Projects: Crafters and party planners can make greeting cards, party invitations, party decorations, costume pieces, Bible journaling embellishments, and more!

3. Vinyl Projects: Use permanent vinyl for outdoor projects (update a mailbox maybe) and kitchen items (like mugs) that can be hand washed. Use removable vinyl for wall projects.

4. Iron-On Projects: One of the most popular uses for the Cricut, iron-on vinyl (also known as heat transfer vinyl) is used to make custom shirts, bags, hats, and more!

5. Craft Foam Projects: Craft foam projects are fun for kid crafts, wreaths, and more.

6. Window Cling Projects: Imagine making your window clings for holidays! With the Cricut, easily cut window cling material into different shapes and decor, like these Preschool Shape ideas.

7. Print And Cut Projects: Working in conjunction with your home printer, the Cricut allows crafters to print photos or images out on their computer and then cut them with the Cricut. From printable magnets to sticker paper, there are so many options for customized gifts or favors for weddings, etc.

8. Faux Leather Projects: One of my favorite mediums, create lovely jewelry items or fashion accessories with faux leather or add a leather look to cards, pillows, and more.

9. Adhesive Foil And Washi Sheet Projects: Would you like to add a custom look to a photo frame or your phone case? Adhesive foil and washi sheets are excellent for these projects! The adhesive foil adds a shiny, metallic look to any project, like these pretty Family Ornaments that I made last year.

10. Stenciled Wood Projects: I discovered stencil vinyl this year, and I love it! Create your adhesive stencil with stencil vinyl, adhere it to wood, and then paint. Remove the stencil vinyl after the paint has dried, and, there you go! Create custom wood signs and more with stencil vinyl.

How Cricut Machines Work

You can connect a Cricut to your computer wirelessly, create or download designs onto your computer, and then send them to your Cricut for cutting. Cricut has software called Design Space (available for Windows, MAC & smartphone) that allows you to create and import designs to cut with your machine. The Cricut houses a tiny blade (or rotary cutter, or pen, or scoring tool) inside. Once you have a design ready to cut in Design Space, you can fasten your desired material onto a 12 inch wide cutting mat, send your design from your computer to your Cricut wirelessly, and then load your material into your machine.

Are Cricut Machines Hard To Use?

Cricut machines come with a thorough online manual and there are a lot of other Cricut resources online, so they are fairly easy to learn how to use. Design Space and the Cricut machine itself are both designed to be very user-friendly, and you don't need lots of graphic design experience to use them (though it does help if you want to create your designs from scratch). There's a library of images and designs in Cricut's Design Space that are simple to import as a new project. Some are free, and some can be purchased at a low cost.

Are Cricut Machines Worth It?

If you love to craft especially with paper and vinyl a Cricut machine is a good investment. It will make your cut projects look crisp and professional, and once you are confident using it, your crafts will be much quicker to create. There are also many ways you can make money with your Cricut, like selling custom t-shirts, mugs, decals, etc. online or at craft fairs. I have used my Cricut machines a lot, and continue to get more and more ideas on things I could create with them!

Chapter 1 - Cricut Accessories and How to Use Them

What Cricut Accessories Do I Need?

What tools and gadgets you need will vary wildly depending on what you want to do with your Cricut. If you are cutting lots of vinyl then you need a wedding toolset and a scraper as well as a heat source. If you are cutting fabric then you'll want some pink mats and a brayer. No matter what you are cutting I have put together a huge list of useful and fun accessories.

Cricut Weeding Tool

This Cricut Weeding Tool which looks a bit like something you'd find in the dentist's office is ideal for poking out tiny pieces of cut-out paper (or other substances). It's also helpful for picking up items with adhesive on it (so they don't stick to your fingers). And take advantage of the curved section of the hook to hold down pieces when you're making complicated projects. You'll appreciate this tool when your nail or the pointy end of a scissor is too big for the task.

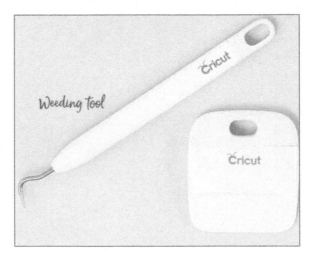

Cricut Infusible Ink Pens

Use these markers to create transfers that can then be used on Cricut blank products such as t-shirts, tote bags, coasters, and more. These heat-transfer inks adhere to the end product completely which means you'll never have a stiff line or fraying edge around a transfer, as you would with an iron-on transfer. The colors are rich and vibrant.

Cricut Standard Grip Cutting 12x12 3-Pack

Hear us out: Yes, your Cricut comes with a mat. But once you're cranking on a project, you'll appreciate the convenience of having several available. As one reviewer notes, it's not uncommon for projects to call for upwards of 15 mats. And while you can pull the paper off after it runs through the Cricut machine, then reuse the mat, that's a slow process having more mats available is a huge time-saver. These mats can be used with the Cricut Maker and Cricut Explore machines. Make sure to pick the mat that's right for your needs each three-pack is intended for different usages, such as with fabric or cardstock.

Cricut Tools Scoring Stylus

Use this stylus in your Cricut Explore machine to score lines it's perfect if you're making things that you want to fold up, like a greeting card or anything three-dimensional. If you're making many cards (hello, winter holidays or wedding invites!) you'll appreciate this time-saving device, and that it will prevent you from frustratingly uneven folds. Just note that some reviewers felt that the stylus did not score deeply enough.

Cricut Tools, XL Scraper

Make clean-up a breeze with help from this scraper, which scoops up tiny scraps of paper with ease. Plus, you can also use it to smooth out vinyl (bubble-free!). It's significantly larger than the scraper that comes in starter packs or that may have accompanied your machine. It especially comes in handy when it's time for bigger projects with lots of little pieces floating around.

Cricut Brayer

Before you get started on a project with a soft material, like vinyl or fabric, you want to make sure it is laying completely flat on the mat to avoid puckers and bubbles from ruining your designs. Press the Cricut Brayer along on top of the materials on your cutting mat to smooth lines and move air bubbles after you lay your material down. Reviewers note that it has a nice weight in the hand and is super simple to use.

Cricut Bright Pad

Do your eyes ache while weeding as you struggle to figure out what to remove? The Cricut Bright Pad is a major convenience. This illuminated pad has an adjustable LED light so that you can weed and trace with ease the backlight makes it easier to spot the scores in the paper, so you can easily take your weeding tool and get to work.

Cricut Ultimate Fine Point Pen Set

This set of 30 pens works in all Cricut Explore machines, including the Cricut Joy. (Note: With the Cricut Explore One machine, an adapter is required, per the manufacturer.) Use these pens to transfer drawn designs onto paper via your Cricut's design software or just use them to freestyle draw without the machine.

Reviewers appreciate the pens' vibrant colors other packs are available with different color palettes and finished. According to Cricut, these pens are nontoxic, and after drying, the ink will stay in place permanently.

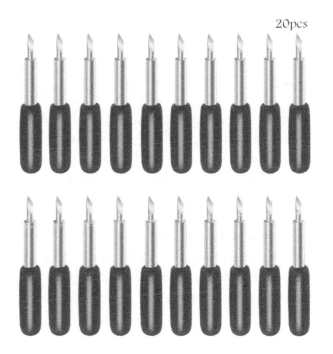

20pcs

All Purpose Mat Set

Cricut has 4 different colors of mats right now. The pink mat (not listed or pictured) is designed for cutting fabric. The blue mat is the light grip mat that you will use with paper and other lightweight materials like crepe paper. This mat has less adhesive and allows you to cut materials that previously would have stuck to a traditional mat. The trick for using the blue mat is to turn the mat over and peel the mat away from the paper rather than peeling the paper away from the mat. The green mat is your standard mat that works well with vinyl, iron-on, and I also use it for felt. The purple mat is the heavy-duty mat that you will use for thicker items like wood veneer and other heavy-duty materials. The extra ling mats are great for making multiples or larger designs. This bundle is a great deal and a great way to stock up on mats.

- ❖ LightGrip Mat – Blue: Thin materials like paper
- ❖ Standard Mat – Green: Medium Weight Materials like cardstock
- ❖ StrongGrip Mat – Purple: Thick materials like poster board and wood
- ❖ FabricGrip Mat – Pink: Designed for fabric only.

Rolling Craft Tote

If you don't have a table or counter space for your machine then you must have a great place to store it. Grab this tote to store all of your Cricut accessories. It rolls so you can roll it right into your storage closet or roll it out the door to a friend's house for a day of cutting and crafting. The fabric is beautiful and it just screams for some customization with iron-on! Right? Then pair it with this machine tote. These used to come as a set, but now you can easily get them separately and set the machine tote right on top of the craft tote. Use a cute belt or a bungee cord to hold the machine tote on top when you are headed out for a day of crafting!

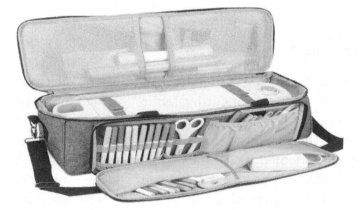

Wavy Blade

The wavy blade is amazing for use with fabric and felt. The wavy blade adds a curved edge to any project. It is also great for use with paper and would be an amazing addition to your tool kit if you are creating flowers with your machine. The wavy blade is one of the newest blades for the Cricut Maker and cannot be used with the Explore line of machines.

Blades

- ❖ Fine Point Blade: Medium Weight Materials
- ❖ Deep Point Blade: Thick Materials (2 mm)
- ❖ Bonded Fabric Blade: Only to use with fabric and backing material
- ❖ Rotary Blade (Cricut Maker only): Fabric, not backing needed
- ❖ Knife Blade (Cricut Maker only): Thick and dense materials like basswood

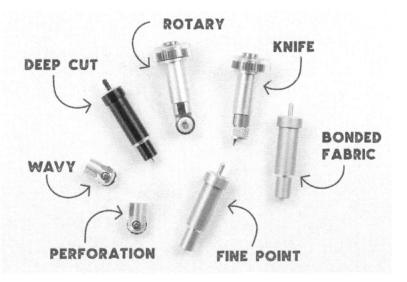

Chapter 2 - Cricuit Tools and How to Use Them

Once you get your Cricut, it can be easy to get overwhelmed with everything there is to learn. There are so many materials and tools out there to work with! How do you know what to buy? How do you know which tools are most helpful for you and your crafting? We've been there and we want to help you out! In this post today, we're going to show you ten Cricut tools that we faithfully use in our crafting. These essential tools are everything you need for a Cricut crafting session.

Scissors

Cricut Scissors have hardened stainless steel blades for durability and smooth, even cuts. The micro-tip blade gives you greater precision on all materials. A removable cover protects the blades.

Tweezers

Cricut Tweezers lift and secure in one step with their reverse grip design - squeeze the handle together to open, and release pressure to clamp together. Smooth interior points help prevent tearing or marring your materials.

Weeder

Cricut Weeder is for "weeding," or removing negative pieces around a cut image. When working with iron-on or vinyl images, it helps you precisely remove everything that isn't part of your design from the carrier sheet. It's also great for poking out tiny negative pieces from a cut cardstock image. This tool truly is a must-have when it comes to Cricut crafting! If you aren't familiar with weeding yet, you will be soon. When your Cricut cuts materials like vinyl or iron-on, you'll need to remove the excess material from around your design and also inside of the design. You're removing negative space so you can get to your design.

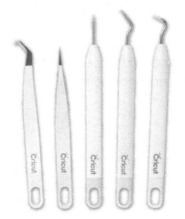

Scraper/XL Scraper

Cricut Scraper is custom designed to clean unwanted scraps from the Cricut cutting mats, contributing to a longer-lasting mat. It can also be used to smooth materials onto the mat or burnish materials such as vinyl to remove air bubbles or wrinkles. The scraper is another must-have tool because you will use this almost every time you use your Cricut! You can use your scraper in several different ways in your Cricut crafting. First, it will help to apply materials to the mat before you cut. Before you cut your material, you want to make sure that the material is completely flat on the mat the scraper will help to remove any debris you may have stuck on the mat and also any air bubbles. The scraper tool can also be used to help remove materials from the mat and apply vinyl/transfer tape onto surfaces.

Spatula

Cricut Spatula precisely lifts images from the Cricut cutting mat, preventing intricate images from tearing or curling. The angled head of the spatula allows it to slide underneath the material with ease.

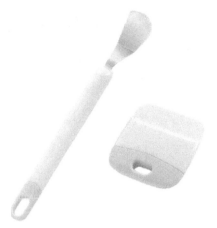

Trimmer

Cricut 12" Portable Trimmer with 15" swing-out arm helps you to precisely cut or score straight lines. Replacement blade storage compartments on the underside make fresh blades readily accessible on the go. this trimmer is a GAME CHANGER. When you're working with materials, you'll always have to cut pieces away, right? Might as well make some straight lines! Seriously though, I love using this because it allows me to cut exactly what I need and cut it in straight lines. And you can easily measure what you need to cut on the trimmer, so you can make exact cuts! There is a swing-out arm that allows you to line your materials up straight, measure, and then cut exactly what you need. I think it saves a lot of material because you're precisely cutting what you need.

Chapter 3 - Cricuit Materials

Which Materials Can I Cut With Cricut Joy?

Cricut Joy can cut a range of basic materials for all your DIY projects. Here's a list of the ones we've qualified with Cricut Joy. Cut settings for these materials are already in Design Space. We will continue to add to this list as more materials are tested.

Art Board

- ❖ Corrugated Cardboard
- ❖ Flat Cardboard
- ❖ Foil Poster Board

Cardstock

- ❖ Glitter Cardstock
- ❖ Insert Card - Cardstock
- ❖ Medium Cardstock - 80 lb (216 gsm)

Iron-On

- ❖ Everyday Iron-On Mesh
- ❖ Everyday Iron-On Mosaic
- ❖ Glitter Mesh Iron-On
- ❖ Holographic Iron-On
- ❖ Infusible Ink Transfer Sheet
- ❖ Smart Iron-On
- ❖ SportFlex Iron-On

Leather

❖ Faux Leather (Paper Thin)

Paper

❖ Deluxe Paper
❖ Deluxe Paper, Adhesive Backed
❖ Deluxe Paper Foil Embossed
❖ Foil Paper – 0.36mm
❖ Pearl Paper
❖ Shimmer Paper
❖ Smart Label Writable Paper
❖ Sparkle Paper
❖ True Brushed Paper

Plastic

- ❖ Foil Acetate

Vinyl

- ❖ Adhesive Foil
- ❖ Chalkboard Vinyl
- ❖ Dry Erase Vinyl
- ❖ Holographic Sparkle Vinyl

Premium Vinyl

- ❖ Premium Vinyl – Frosted Glitter
- ❖ Premium Vinyl – Frosted Gray
- ❖ Premium Vinyl – Frosted Opaque
- ❖ Premium Vinyl – Holographic
- ❖ Premium Vinyl – Textured Metallic
- ❖ Premium Vinyl – True Brushed

Stencil Vinyl

- ❖ Smart Label Writable Vinyl
- ❖ Smart Vinyl – Holographic Patterns
- ❖ Smart Vinyl – Matte Metallic
- ❖ Smart Vinyl – Permanent
- ❖ Smart Vinyl – Removable
- ❖ Smart Vinyl – Shimmer

1. Paper, Cardstock, Art Board, Insert Cards

I. Glitter Cardstock Instructions

Add instant sass, glam, or festive style to your cards, paper crafts, school projects, and decor with Cricut Glitter Cardstock.

What You Need

- ❖ Cricut smart cutting machine
- ❖ Cricut Design Space on computer or mobile device, or Cricut Joy app
- ❖ LightGrip machine mat
- ❖ Fine Point or Premium Fine Point blade
- ❖ Cricut Glitter Cardstock
- ❖ Glue/adhesive to assemble your project (optional)

Design And Cut

- ❖ Customize your design.
- ❖ Select Glitter Cardstock from the list of materials
- ❖ If using a Cricut Explore machine, turn Smart Set dial to Custom.
- ❖ Place Glitter Cardstock onto LightGrip cutting mat.
- ❖ Load mat into the machine.
- ❖ Press Go.
- ❖ Remove cut design from cutting mat and add to your project.

II. Paper Instructions

Cricut Deluxe Paper is perfect for elevated paper crafts, cards, décor, and more.

What You Need

- ❖ Cricut smart cutting machine
- ❖ Cricut Design Space on computer or mobile device, or Cricut Joy app

- ❖ LightGrip machine mat
- ❖ Fine Point or Premium Fine Point blade
- ❖ Cricut Deluxe Paper
- ❖ Glue/adhesive to assemble your project (optional)

Design And Cut

- ❖ Select and size your design in the software.
- ❖ Select Deluxe Paper from the list of materials.
- ❖ If using a Cricut Explore machine, turn Smart Set dial to Custom.

Place Deluxe Paper Onto Lightgrip Mat.

- ❖ Load mat into the machine.
- ❖ Press Go.
- ❖ Remove cut design from the mat and add it to your project.

III. Insert Cards And Card Mat

Cricut Joy Insert Cards are designed for use with ready-to-make projects and require Cricut Joy Card Mat (sold separately). Cricut Joy Card Mat Mat is uniquely designed with a divider to protect the back of the folded Cricut Insert Card while cutting a design on the front.

What You Need

- ❖ Cricut Joy smart cutting machine
- ❖ Design Space software on computer or mobile device
- ❖ Cricut Joy Blade and Housing
- ❖ Cricut Joy Insert Cards
- ❖ Cricut Joy Card Mat
- ❖ Cricut Joy Pens or Markers (optional)

Instructions

- ❖ Select Insert Card design you want, then Make It.
- ❖ Choose On Card Mat. Then select Continue.
- ❖ Select Browse All Materials and choose Insert Card - Cardstock.
- ❖ Remove protective cover from the mat.

- ❖ Open card. From the left, slide one side of the folded card under the plastic divider.
- ❖ Ensure the card is aligned to the top left corner of the mat. Push card up until it's flush with the top, then align the inside fold of the card against the plastic divider.
- ❖ Press the front of the card into the adhesive on the mat.
- ❖ Insert mat into machine, arrow end first.
- ❖ When the cut is complete, peel the mat away from the card.
- ❖ Tuck insert in to corner notches in the card.
- ❖ Enjoy!

Tips

- ❖ To write or draw on the inside of your card, fold the card inside out and repeat the steps above. Be sure that your Draw design is properly oriented and positioned on the project preview screen.
- ❖ The cuts will leave impressions on your mat. This is normal.
- ❖ If the material is not adhering well to the mat, use a brayer to create a firm bond. Cricut Joy Card Mat will lose stickiness with use and will eventually need to be replaced.
- ❖ Cricut Insert Cards are compatible with all Cricut Joy Pens and Markers.

2. Vinyl

I. Chalkboard Vinyl: Cutting And Application Instructions

- ❖ Cutting Chalkboard Vinyl with a Cricut Machine
- ❖ Place vinyl (liner side down) onto Cricut cutting mat.
- ❖ Select images and size and load the mat into the machine.
- ❖ Refer to the Vinyl Kiss Cut guide table below to adjust machine settings.
- ❖ Press CUT.

Preparation With Cricut Transfer Tape

- ❖ Remove the negative pieces from each of the images using the hook found in the Cricut Tool Kit, leaving the liner intact. This process is known as weeding.
- ❖ Remove the liner from the transfer tape liner. Take the transfer tape in each hand with the adhesive side facing down.

- ❖ Gently place the transfer tape over the images. To prevent bubbles, start in the center and move out toward the edges. Use a craft stick or Scraper found in the Cricut Tool Kit to burnish (rub or polish) the tape onto the vinyl.

- ❖ Peel the vinyl away from the vinyl liner at a 45-degree angle. If the vinyl does not separate from the liner, simply burnish the transfer tape onto the vinyl again and then continue to peel the vinyl away from the liner.

Application

- ❖ Make sure your project surface is clean and dry. Carefully place the transfer tape with vinyl images onto your surface, making sure the images are straight.

- ❖ Starting in the center and moving out toward the edges, burnish transfer tape onto the surface. Use a craft stick or Cricut Scraper.

- ❖ Peel the transfer tape away from the vinyl at a 45-degree angle. If the vinyl sticks to the transfer tape, simply burnish the vinyl onto the surface again. Then continue to peel the transfer tape away from the vinyl.

II. Glitter Vinyl: Cutting And Application Instructions

- ❖ Cutting Glitter Vinyl with a Cricut Machine
- ❖ Place vinyl liner side down onto LightGrip Mat.
- ❖ Select images and size and load the mat into your machine.

- ❖ Refer to Glitter Vinyl Kiss Cut Guide below to adjust machine settings (a kiss cut goes through the vinyl film and leaves the liner intact).
- ❖ Press the flashing Go button.

Preparation With Stronggrip Transfer Tape

- ❖ Remove the negative pieces from each of the images, leaving the liner intact. This process is called weeding. Using a weeding tool found in a Cricut Basic Tool Set or Weeding Tool Set can make this process faster and easier.

- ❖ Remove the Transfer Tape liner.

- ❖ Gently place the Transfer Tape (adhesive side down) over your images. To prevent bubbles, start in the center and move out toward the edges. Use a craft stick or the Scraper found in the Cricut Basic Tool Set to burnish (rub or polish) the tape onto the vinyl.

- ❖ Peel away the vinyl liner at a 45-degree angle. If the vinyl does not separate from the liner, simply burnish the Transfer Tape onto the vinyl and peel away again.

Application

- ❖ Make sure your project surface is clean and dry. Carefully place the Transfer Tape with vinyl designs onto your surface as you would like them to appear.
- ❖ Now burnish Transfer Tape onto the surface, starting in the center and moving out toward the edges. Use a craft stick or Cricut Scraper.

- ❖ Peel away the Transfer Tape from the vinyl at a 45-degree angle. If the vinyl sticks to the Transfer Tape, simply burnish the transfer tape onto the vinyl and peel away again.

III. Cricut Joy Smart Vinyl Instructions

Follow the instructions below to cut and apply Cricut Joy Smart Vinyl.

- ❖ What you need
- ❖ Design, cut, and weed
- ❖ Apply Transfer Tape
- ❖ Apply to project surface

What You Need

- ❖ Cricut Joy smart cutting machine
- ❖ Cricut Joy app, or Design Space software on computer or mobile device
- ❖ Cricut Joy Blade and Housing
- ❖ Cricut Joy Smart Vinyl
- ❖ Weeder
- ❖ Cricut Transfer Tape
- ❖ Burnishing tool, such as a Scraper

Design, Cut, And Weed

- ❖ Customize your design in the Cricut Joy app or Design Space, then select Make It.
- ❖ Select your material load style (Without Mat) and your specific material type.
- ❖ Using both hands, insert material under guides. Continue feeding into the machine until rollers grip material.
- ❖ For best results, make sure your material has a straight edge.
- ❖ Once the machine senses materials under the rollers, it measures your material to ensure there's enough for your project.
- ❖ Leave 10 inches of space behind your machine and guide vinyl into a roll as it feeds out the back of your machine.
- ❖ Smart Materials may bow in the middle when loading. If your material isn't lying flat by the end of the measuring process, select Unload in the software, then reload.
- ❖ Select Go and watch the magic happen!

- ❖ When the cut is complete, select Unload.
- ❖ Use a weeder to remove the excess vinyl from in and around your design, leaving the design on the liner.

Apply Transfer Tape

- ❖ Peel liner from Transfer Tape.
- ❖ To place Transfer Tape on your design carefully follow these steps:
- ❖ Attach a small area of Transfer Tape to your design. This can either be the center or one end of your design.
- ❖ Use a Scraper to burnish Transfer Tape onto your design, working outward from where you attached the small area.
- ❖ Flip design and burnish.

Apply To Project Surface

Important: Application of long designs requires care and planning. Take time to plan your approach.

1. Make sure the project surface is clean and dry.

2. Peel vinyl liner away from Transfer Tape and design.

- ❖ If the vinyl doesn't separate from the liner, simply burnish liner back onto the vinyl and peel away again.

3. To transfer the design to your project surface carefully follow these steps:

- ❖ Attach a small area of the design onto your surface. This can either be the center or one end of your design.
- ❖ Use a Scraper to burnish design onto your surface, working outward from where you attached the small area.

4. Peel Transfer Tape away from the design.

❖ Work carefully. If vinyl peels up with Transfer Tape, simply burnish Transfer Tape and vinyl back down to the project surface and peel away again.
❖ For best results, peel Transfer Tape at an acute angle.

3. Iron-On

I. Cricut Joy Smart Iron-On Instructions

Follow the instructions below to cut and apply Cricut Joy Smart Iron-On.

❖ What you need
❖ Preparation
❖ Design, cut, and weed
❖ Apply

What You Need

❖ Cricut Joy smart cutting machine
❖ Cricut Joy app, or Design Space software on computer or mobile device
❖ Cricut Heat Transfer Guide
❖ Cricut Joy Blade and Housing
❖ Cricut Joy Smart Iron-On
❖ Weeder
❖ Cricut EasyPress
❖ Cricut EasyPress Mat or towel
❖ Base material

Preparation

Prewash fabric base materials without fabric softener to pre-shrink and remove chemicals that may prohibit strong adhesion.

Recommended: Make a test cut using a small basic shape to verify the cut setting.

Recommended: Apply test cut in an inconspicuous area on the base material to verify application settings.

Design, Cut, And Weed

- ❖ Customize your design in the Cricut Joy app or Design Space.
- ❖ Select your load style (Without Mat) and your specific material type.
- ❖ When using Design Space, make sure to mirror your design before cutting. In the Cricut Joy app, Mirror is enabled automatically when you select a heat-transfer material.
- ❖ Using both hands, insert material (shiny liner side down) under guides until rollers grip material.
- ❖ For best results, make sure the material has a straight edge.
- ❖ Once the machine senses materials, it measures your material to ensure there's enough for your project.
- ❖ Leave 10 inches of space behind your machine and guide iron-on into a roll as it feeds out the back of your machine.
- ❖ Smart Materials may bow in the middle when loading. If your material isn't lying flat by the end of the measuring process, select Unload in the software, then reload.
- ❖ Select Go and watch the magic happen!
- ❖ When the cut is complete, select Unload.
- ❖ Use a weeder to remove excess iron-on from in and around your design, leaving the design on the liner.

Apply

- ❖ Place design on your base material, shiny liner side up. Press as instructed (see Heat Transfer Guide).
- ❖ Leaving the liner in place, flip the base material over and apply heat to the back of the design as instructed
- ❖ Peel the liner away from the design at the temperature instructed (see Heat Transfer Guide).
- ❖ Enjoy!

II. Everyday Iron-On Instructions

Cricut Everyday Iron-On works fabulously with the widest variety of base materials, including wood! Intricate designs are simple to cut with your Cricut machine, and you'll weed with ease to prep for flawless application. Find the cutting and application instructions and tips below.

- ❖ What you need
- ❖ Preparation
- ❖ Design, cut, and weed
- ❖ Apply
- ❖ Care

What You Need

- ❖ Cricut smart cutting machine
- ❖ Cricut Design Space on computer or mobile device, or Cricut Joy app
- ❖ Cricut Heat Transfer Guide
- ❖ StandardGrip machine mat
- ❖ Fine Point or Premium Fine Point blade
- ❖ Cricut Everyday Iron-On
- ❖ Weeder
- ❖ Cricut EasyPress, heat press, or household iron
- ❖ Iron-On Protective sheet (optional)
- ❖ Base material

Preparation

Pre-wash fabric base materials without fabric softener to pre-shrink and remove chemicals that may prohibit strong adhesion.

Recommended: To verify the cut setting, perform a test cut using a small basic shape.

Recommended: To verify application setting, apply test cut in an inconspicuous area on the base material.

Find your pressing surface. If it's firm, flat, and around waist-high, you're golden. Be sure to avoid flimsy ironing boards.

Design, Cut, And Weed

Select and size your design in the software. Be sure to Mirror your mats before cutting if using Design Space. In the Cricut Joy app, Mirror is enabled automatically when you select a heat-transfer material.

- ❖ Select Everyday Iron-On from the list of materials.
- ❖ If using a Cricut Explore machine, turn Smart Set Dial to Custom.
- ❖ Place Iron-on sheet, liner side down, onto Cricut standard grip cutting mat.
- ❖ If using Smart Iron-On with Cricut Joy, it may be loaded into the machine without a mat.
- ❖ Load it into the machine and cut your design.
- ❖ When the cut is complete, weed your image.

Apply

- ❖ Preheat base material as instructed
- ❖ Place the cut design on the base material with the shiny liner side up. Apply heat as instructed.
- ❖ Flip the base material over and apply heat to the back of the design as instructed.
- ❖ Use a cool peel to remove the liner.

Care

- ❖ Wait 24 hours before washing the embellished item.
- ❖ For the longest life, wash and dry the embellished item inside-out.
- ❖ If areas of Iron-On material lift after washing, simply follow the complete application instructions to reapply.

3. Glitter Iron-On Instructions

Cricut Glitter Iron-on lets you customize T-shirts, team or club wear, bags, home decor, and more! Cute shapes, letters, and designs are all a cinch with this easy heat-transfer material. Find the cutting and application instructions and tips below.

Cutting Glitter Iron-On With A Cricut Machine

- ❖ Place iron-on sheet, shiny liner side down, onto StandardGrip Mat.
- ❖ Adjust your machine settings according to the Iron-on Kiss Cut Guide below (a kiss cut goes through the iron-on film and leaves the liner intact).
- ❖ Select and size the image(s) you want to cut. Be sure to Mirror all images before cutting.
- ❖ Load the mat into the machine and press the flashing Go button.

Application Instructions

- ❖ Remove negative pieces from each of the images leaving the liner intact. This process is called weeding. Using the weeding tool found in a Cricut Basic Tool Set or Weeding Tool Set can make this process faster and easier.

- ❖ Set your iron to the Cotton/Linen setting (generally the highest temperature setting). Make sure the steam setting is OFF for steam irons.

- ❖ Use the iron to preheat your base material for 10-15 seconds.

- ❖ Place the weeded image, shiny liner side up, onto the preheated material. Apply medium pressure to each area of your design with the iron for 25-30 seconds.

- ❖ Flip the base material over and apply medium pressure with the iron to the back of the material for an additional 25-30 seconds.

- ❖ Use a cool peel to remove the liner.

385

Application Tips

- ❖ Find your surface. If it's firm, flat, and around waist-high, you're golden. Be sure to avoid flimsy ironing boards.

- ❖ Iron with a press cloth or piece of cotton fabric (such as a dish towel) over your material and design to protect it from the heat of the iron.

- ❖ Do not layer on top of Holographic, Holographic Sparkle, Foil, Glitter, Glitter Mesh, or flocked iron-on.

- ❖ If a portion of the image isn't sticking, replace the liner over the iron-on film and iron that section with the iron tip for an additional 10 seconds, moving it back and forth with firm pressure directly over loose edges.

- ❖ Using the Cotton/Linen setting of the iron provides the best results for most materials. Protect more delicate materials by using a press cloth or piece of cotton fabric (such as a dishtowel).

- ❖ For steam irons, turn the steam setting OFF when applying Cricut iron-on.

4. Felt, Foam, Foil & Metal

I. Craft Foam: Cutting Instructions

Give DIY projects and layered accents a new sense of depth with uniquely textured Craft Foam for Cricut Maker and Cricut Explore. Cut shapes to make one-of-a-kind 3D accents, stencils, embellishments, and kid's games. Read on for cutting instructions and tips.

- ❖ Cutting Cricut Craft Foam with Cricut Explore or Cricut Maker

- ❖ Place Craft Foam onto Cricut StrongGrip Machine Mat. Ensure grain runs vertically.
- ❖ Select images and size, then load the mat into your machine.
- ❖ On a Cricut Explore turn the Smart Set Dial to Custom. Then select Browse all materials and select Craft Foam. For Cricut Maker, select Browse all materials, then select Craft Foam from the list of materials.
- ❖ Press the flashing Go button.

Ii. Adhesive Foil, Matte: Cutting And Application Instructions

Cricut Adhesive Foil lets you customize without a commitment! Create easily removable decals, labels, home décor, media covers, and more. Use with all Cricut cutting machines. Find the cutting and application instructions below.

- ❖ Cutting Adhesive Foil with a Cricut Machine
- ❖ Place Adhesive Foil (liner side down) onto Cricut standard grip cutting mat.
- ❖ Select images and size, and load the mat into the machine.
- ❖ Refer to the Custom Cut Guide table below to adjust machine settings.
- ❖ Press CUT.

Preparation With Cricut Transfer Tape

- ❖ Remove the negative pieces from each of the images using the Weeder found in the Cricut Tool Kit, leaving the liner intact. This process is known as weeding.
- ❖ Remove the transfer tape liner.
- ❖ Gently place the transfer tape (adhesive side down) over the images. To prevent bubbles, start in the center and move out toward the edges. Use a craft stick or the Scraper found in the Cricut Tool Kit to burnish (rub or polish) the tape onto the Adhesive Foil.

❖ Peel away the Adhesive Foil liner at a 45-degree angle. If the Adhesive Foil does not separate from the liner, simply burnish the transfer tape onto the Adhesive Foil and peel away again.

Application

❖ Make sure your project surface is clean and dry. Carefully place the transfer tape with Adhesive Foil images onto your surface how you would like them to appear.

❖ Now burnish transfer tape onto the surface, starting in the center and moving out toward the edges. A craft stick or the Scraper found in the Cricut Tool Kit can be used.

❖ Peel away the transfer tape from the Adhesive Foil at a 45-degree angle. If the Adhesive Foil images stick to the transfer tape, simply burnish the transfer tape onto the foil and peel away again.

5. **Plastic, Leather, Wood**

I. Cricut Genuine Leather: Cutting Instructions

Cut custom designs for unique leather creations with Cricut Genuine Leather. Ideal for fashion, accessories, jewelry, home décor, embellishments, and more! Find the cutting instructions below. Cricut Genuine Leather can be cut with Cricut Maker and Cricut Explore machines. Select the tabs below to view information and recommendations for cutting with each machine.

❖ Place Cricut Genuine Leather face down onto clean Cricut StrongGrip (purple) cutting mat.
❖ Create a firm bond between the leather and the cutting mat by burnishing with a scraper or rolling a brayer over the leather.
❖ Move star wheels to the right.

- ❖ Select and size images in Cricut Design Space and load the mat into the machine.
- ❖ Select Browse All Materials and choose Genuine Leather.
- ❖ Follow prompts in Cricut Design Space to complete the cut.
- ❖ Before unloading the mat, check the material to ensure it is cut all the way through.

II. Cricut Natural Wood Veneers Instructions

Made from genuine wood, these versatile, ultra-slim, and spectacularly smooth veneers are ready for your making! Cut and craft each sheet into enviable, one-of-a-kind projects that showcase the wood's natural color and grain – from gorgeous gift boxes to mid-century lampshades, home decor, and more. For use with Cricut Maker or Cricut Explore family machines and Deep-Point Blade.

What Is A Wood Veneer?

A veneer is a very thin sheet of material that is applied to another surface for protection or decoration. Cricut Natural Wood Veneers are thin slices of real wood, but we've made them 2-ply for durability and versatility; they can be stained, painted, molded, glued, and layered.

Recommended Supplies

- ❖ Cricut Explore or Cricut Maker machine
- ❖ StrongGrip machine cutting mat
- ❖ Deep-Point Blade and housing
- ❖ Cricut Natural Wood Veneer
- ❖ Painter's Tape
- ❖ Brayer

❖ Broad-tip tweezers

Know Before You Go

❖ Because veneer is made from real wood, grain patterns and color will vary, making every project unique.
❖ Veneer thickness will vary between species. Walnut is thicker than Maple, which is thicker than Cherry.
❖ The characteristics of the veneer will vary between species. Walnut veneers, for example, have a more obvious grain and should be handled with extra care.
❖ Avoid bending veneers along the grain as this will cause it to crack or break.
❖ For best results use tweezers rather than a spatula to remove veneers from the mat.

Cutting Cricut Natural Wood Veneers With A Cricut Machine

❖ Place wood veneer onto StrongGrip Mat with the grain of the veneer running along the length of the mat.
❖ Use a brayer to create a firm bond between the veneer and the mat adhesive.
❖ Tape all four edges of the material to the mat within 1" of the corners (blue painter's tape is recommended).
❖ Select and size the image(s) you want to cut.
❖ Select Browse All Materials. Then, select Natural Wood Veneer from the list of materials.
❖ If you are using a Cricut Explore, ensure that the Smart Set Dial is set to Custom.
❖ Ensure the Deep-Point blade and housing are installed in Clamp B.
❖ Load the mat into the machine and press the flashing Go button.

Removing Veneers From The Mat

❖ Gently bend the mat slightly away from veneer against the grain.

- ❖ Work tweezers gently under veneer cut until it pops off of the mat. Take care with corners and be aware of a grain of the wood as you work the pieces off of the mat.

Tips

- ❖ Mold veneer cuts into shapes or curves using a technique called wet forming.
- ❖ Soak the cut in water to make it more flexible.
- ❖ Bend the cut into the desired shape, taking care not to crack the wood along the grain.
- ❖ Brace or prop the cut while drying too so it holds the desired shape.
- ❖ While veneers are real wood, they are delicate. They are intended to add a decorative finish to your project rather than provide structure.
- ❖ Keep dry and lay flat when storing.

3. Cricut Faux Leather: Cutting Instructions

Easy to cut, textured faux leather gives all the benefits of leather without the extra cost. Create fashion accessories, home decor, and paper crafting accents. Read on to learn about how to cut Faux Leather.

Cutting Cricut Faux Leather With A Cricut Machine

- ❖ Place Cricut Faux Leather face down onto Cricut StandardGrip Mat.
- ❖ Select and size images, and load the mat into the machine.
- ❖ Refer to Faux Leather Cut Guide below to adjust machine settings.
- ❖ Press the flashing Go button.

Tip: When using the Debossing Tip or scoring Faux Leather with the Scoring Stylus, place Faux Leather face up on the mat for best results. When scoring Faux Leather with Scoring Wheel or Double Scoring Wheel, place Faux Leather face down on the mat for best results.

Chapter 4 - Cricuit Joy

Cricut Joy is designed to be a companion machine to the Cricut you already own. Use it to make quick projects without having to break out your Cricut Explore or Cricut Maker, or having it running at the same time as your other machines when you're in the super-crafting model. The Cricut Joy is a small home cutter machine that allows you to cut and draw on various materials, including vinyl, cardstock, deluxe paper, etc. Due to its small size and ease of use, you can bring it to any area of your home and craft with ease.

What Does Cricut Joy Do?

Cricut Joy has a small blade that cuts paper, vinyl, and Infusible Ink materials to create endless projects using the simple Cricut Design Space software on your phone or computer. You can also swap out the blade for a compatible pen or marker to write or draw!, Whether you create your projects, or simply select pre-made ideas, it's the easiest cutting machine I've ever used. It doesn't even need any buttons or cords beyond the power cord.

Cricut Joy is simple. It has no buttons and is powered on when you plug it in. The cut width is 4.5" wide, compared to 11.5" on Cricut Explore and Cricut Maker. It has a single blade, a fine point blade. No fancy scoring tools or specialty blades. The housing can also use a pen, but you need to switch between the blade and the pen.

But then there are also never-before-seen features on Cricut Joy. My favorite is the Cricut Joy Card Mat, which makes it incredibly easy to make cards, as you'll see in an upcoming post. There is also matless cutting for adhesive Smart Vinyl and Smart Iron On (yes, that is cutting without a mat!). These "smart" materials have a thicker backing material that functions as a mat—meaning you don't need an actual mat to cut them.

The adhesive Smart Vinyl comes in several lengths, including a super long 20' roll in certain colors. Single cuts can be up to 4' long, and if you are cutting shapes smaller than that (think pantry labels or wall decals), you can cut that entire 20' of vinyl in a single go. Despite being a smaller machine, the matless cutting feature allows you to cut so many more images in a single go. Plus, no need to buy new mats! More information on this in an upcoming post, too!

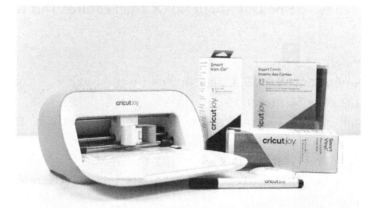

What Can I Make With Cricut Joy?

393

Easy projects are the name of the game when it comes to Cricut Joy! Think one color, one cut, one application. Perfect for simple ideas and brand-new Cricut users. You can create a little happiness in just minutes, including:

- ❖ Organization labels for the pantry, craft room, work, etc.
- ❖ Adhesive vinyl decals for mugs, tumblers, phone cases, and more
- ❖ Wall decals and borders
- ❖ Iron-on vinyl decals for simple shirts and baby bodysuits
- ❖ Cardstock cards, banners, and party decorations
- ❖ Cards for any occasion in less than 5 minutes.
- ❖ Personalize cubbies, school supplies, backpacks, etc.
- ❖ T-shirts with Iron-On and Infusible Ink

Cricut Joy Specifications

The Cricut Joy, although little it offers terrific things that even some of the bigger machines can't even do.

Are You Ready To Find Out About All Of The Features This Little Tool Has?

- ❖ Weight: 3.9 lbs
- ❖ Dimensions: 8.4 x 5.4 x 4.2 inches (In the box).
- ❖ Cuts over 50 materials.
- ❖ Built-in Bluetooth (You need a device with a Bluetooth connection to operate it)
- ❖ Cuts "Smart" materials without a Cricut Mat
- ❖ Draw on different types of materials, including "Smart writing vinyl."
- ❖ Cuts a single image up to 4.5 in x 4 ft long or repeated cuts up to 20 ft long.
- ❖ Use offline from a desktop computer or an iOS device.
- ❖ Portable and ready to go. You can take it to a friend's home and craft with ease.
- ❖ Make cards in as little as five minutes.

❖ Free Design Space app with the opportunity to upload your images.

Cricut Joy Accessories

The Cricut Joy has some cool accessories that go great together. Most of these accessories are vital, and you need them at all times.

Cricut Joy Blade

The Cricut Joy has one single blade called "Fine Point Blade.". This blade and housing are different from all of the other blades that Cricut has for other machines, and it's quite tiny. If you are new to the Cricut world, you need to know that the entire blade is made out of two parts. One is the blade, and the other one is the housing. The bade housing is what keeps the blade in place, and what you install on your machine. The blade is at the bottom of the housing. If your blade isn't performing as well as it was when you first purchased your machine, you only need to buy a replacement blade. There's no need to buy a new blade housing. To change the blade, you need to press the little plunge on the housing and remove it. Then carefully pick up the replacement blade and insert it.

cricut joy.

Cricut Joy Blade

- All-purpose, replaceable blade for Cricut Joy
- Long-lasting steel resists wear & breakage
- Cut a wide variety of materials

Cricut Joy Mats

Cricut Mats are sticky surfaces were you place your materials to keep them stable and secure while your machine cuts them. With the Cricut Joy, materials labeled with the word "Smart" don't need a Cricut mat. However, other materials like cardstock and regular vinyl need a mat to be cut.

Cricut Joy Has Three Different Types Of Mats.

1. LightGrip Mat – Blue: Use for thin materials like copy paper, adhesive vinyl, and iron-on.

2. StrandardGrip Mat – Green: Use for medium weight materials like glitter cardstock, Infusible Ink, glitter iron-on, corrugated cardboard

3. Card Mat: Use with insert cards. You can also use your paper and cut it the same size as the insert cards.

The tight grip and the StandardGrip mat come in two sizes 4.5 x 6.5 in and 4.5 x 12 in.

Cricut Joy Card Mat In Original Packaging

4.5x12 in light grip (blue) and standard grip mat for Cricut Joy

Note: When you're cutting with a mat (blue or green), your design can't be larger 4.25 x 6.25/11.75 in. And when using the Card Mat, your design can't be larger than 4.25 x 6 in.

Cricut Joy Pens

Cricut Joy Pens are specifically designed to fit the machine; therefore, they can't be used with any other of their devices. They have a wide variety of colors and styles, including:

- ❖ Gel Pens
- ❖ Glitter Pens
- ❖ Metallic Markers
- ❖ Infusible Ink Pens & Markers

All of these pens (except infusible ink) can be used on "Smart Writable Vinyl" to make labels for organizing your pantry, spice drawer, kids' toys, etc. I have a guide about Cricut Pens (when using the bigger machines) where you can learn the overall use in Cricut Desing Space. Also, if you are new to Cricut, you may want to read my Infusible Ink guide.

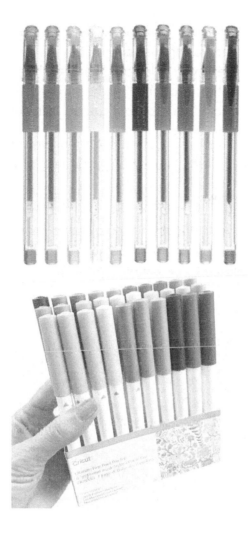

Cricut Joy Starter Tool Set

If this your first machine, I highly recommend you get a starter toolset to help you weed and lift your projects from your mat. This set has three different tools:

❖ **Weeder:** Essential for weeding (removing negative parts) vinyl projects.

- ❖ **Spatula:** Perfect for removing delicate cuts from the mat, especially when using the Card Mat.
- ❖ **Scraper:** A very versatile tool that can help you smooth out materials on the Cricut mat and clean it. The scraper is handy when trying to adhere to vinyl cuts to transfer tape.

There are other sets with more advanced tools for weeding. You should check them out if you are planning on working a lot with viny.

Cricut Joy Storage Bag

If you plan to take your Cricut on the go, so you can craft with friends and family, you may want to invest in their storage bag. It's not necessary at all if you plan on keeping your machine at home.

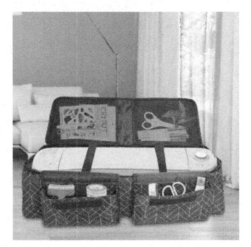

Pros And Cons Of The Cricut Joy

If you've read this article, you may already know some pros and cons of this machine.

Let's Start With The Pros

- ❖ Cut pretty cards in less than five minutes with the card mat
- ❖ Cut and draw on smart vinyl to make labels
- ❖ Cut up to 20 ft of vinyl (4ft continuos cutting)
- ❖ Take it to any area of your home with ease

- ❖ Simplify crafting
- ❖ Easy to learn when comparing the older machines.

Now Let's Move To The Cons

- ❖ It doesn't have a USB port (in case you don't have Bluetooth device).
- ❖ The width of the project is minimal only 4.5 in material and 4.25 on the actual cut.
- ❖ Expensive when you compare its capabilities and price of the Explore Air 2 (Check table on the FAQ section in this article).
  - ❖ Easy to outgrow if you want to cut larger or thicker products.

Chapter 5 - Cricuit Cuttlebug

The Cricut Cuttlebug manual dies cutting and embossing machine offers a simple, electricity-free option for cutting and embossing a wide variety of materials. The only Cricut machine that can emboss, the Cricut Cuttlebug gives professional-looking results with clean, crisp cuts and deep, even embossing. The Cricut Cuttlebug is a manual (read: no plugs, no internet, no electricity...just good 'old fashioned elbow grease) die-cutting machine that allows you to cut precise shapes from a variety of materials like paper, cardstock, felt, chipboard, fabric, and leather.

The Cricut Cuttlebug is a handy little machine used for embossing and dies cutting. The tool lets you do one or both, giving you a range of options and looks for your craft projects. Cuttlebug by Cricut is a compact crafting tool you can use to make cards, create unique scrapbook pages and enhancements, make die cuts, and add dimension to other projects you're making, even with other Cricut craft machines. This apparatus allows you to work with multiple materials: paper, tissue paper, acetate, cardstock, foils, thin metals, and light leather.

The Cuttlebug is user-friendly and straightforward. What you see is what you get: it's a mint-green and white device that stands on its own. When it's not in use, the embossing hand crank rests unobtrusively against the side of the machine. Grab it by its carrying handle to store it away or take your crafting projects with you on the go. This machine isn't electrical, nor is it computerized. You control it and operate it, and you are the designer of all its products. You're entirely in control of your craft projects from conceptualizing them to making them. It's easy to do with the Cuttlebug. Decorate your life and your memories. Add depth and expression to gifts you give to friends and loved ones. Cuttlebug makes it possible, effortless, and fun.

What Is a Die?

A die is a metal shape with a raised edge that cuts through paper/fabric/felt etc. when pressure is placed onto it. The Cuttlebug is a machine that makes it easy to put lots of pressure on dies so that they cut through whatever material you want. Dies come in a ton of shapes and thicknesses. Flat, thin, steel dies like THIS, or THIS is great for paper and cardstock. If you want to cut thicker materials, your best bet is the Sizzix Bigz Dies which are much thicker and go through chipboard, leather and felt like butter!

What Can I Make

The Cuttlebug will take you far. Just imagine being able to cut out precise shapes without fussing with scissors. Even something as simple as creating a bunch of paper hearts gets a lot easier when you don't have to do it with scissors. These days, my biggest reason for using the Cuttlebug is when I want to cut a lot of small shapes from special materials like leather.

What Comes In The Cuttlebug Box?

- Cricut Cuttlebug machine (3.69" tall x 16.10" wide x 7.30" deep. 5.25 lbs)
- A Plate – Spacer (approx.13mm - 0.5" thick)
- Two B Plates – Cutting (approx. 3mm - 0.12" thick each)
- One A2 embossing folder and two metal dies
- One 6" x 8" Rubber Embossing Mat
- (Approx. 2mm - 0.09" thick)

What Materials Can I Cut Or Emboss With My Cricut Cuttlebug Machine?

Many different materials can be cut or embossed using your Cricut Cuttlebug machine. Try using cardstock, thin metal, thin wood, some fabrics, thin felt, poster board, chipboard, tissue paper, and fun foam

404

just to name a few. The height of your cutting materials should not exceed 1/8". Attempting to cut through materials that exceed this height may result in incomplete cuts and may negate the machine's warranty.

What Brands Of Dies And Embossing Folders Will Work With My Cricut Cuttlebug Machine?

The Cricut Cuttlebug machine is compatible with most leading brands of dies and embossing folders. The B Plates - Cutting, A Plate - Spacer, and C Plate - Adapter (sold separately) are different thicknesses so that you can mix and match. Find stacking suggestions for a variety of dies here.

For certain dies, shimming with thin layers of cardstock might be necessary to get a clean cut. Simply add extra pieces of cardstock beneath the die until you achieve the right amount of pressure for your die.

Can I Use Cricut Cartridges With My Cuttlebug?

Cricut cartridges contain digital images that are used with Cricut electronic cutting machines; they are not compatible with the Cricut Cuttlebug. The Cricut Cuttlebug can use embossing folders and cutting dies to create elements that add dimension to your DIY projects.

Will Cricut Cuttlebug Dies And Embossing Folders Work In Other Die-Cutting Machines?

It depends on what machine is being used. Some machines will not cut the dies, while others will. Some machines will break the paper while using an embossing folder and other machines will not provide an even emboss. You will need to contact the manufacturer of the machine to ask if their machine is compatible with Cricut Cuttlebug dies and embossing folders and get suggestions for the best results when using Cricut Cuttlebug dies and embossing folders with their machines.

What Are The Features Of Cuttlebug Folders?

Multiple Sizes & Borders: , Cricut Cuttlebug folders were redesigned so that you can emboss a full A2 or 5" x 7" card or piece of paper. New folders also came with coordinating borders that are perfect for cards, envelopes, and other projects.

Folder Names: The names of new embossing folders are screen-printed directly on the folders for easy identification.

Continuous Embossing: Cricut released continuous embossing folders which allow you to emboss longer materials. These A2 and 5" x 7" embossing folders are specially designed with a gap in the folder hinge so that you can emboss longer strips of material.

Just place the material inside the embossing folder and run it through the Cuttlebug machine as normal. Then slip the embossed portion through the gap in the hinge. Align the embossed section with the design in the folder before running the folder through the machine again. Continuous embossing works best for folders that have a repeatable pattern.

The Cricut Cuttlebug Die Cutting and Embossing Machine are one of the most portable craft die-cutting machines on the market. It features a handle that makes it easy to take with you. You'll also get affordability with this one since it retails for less than $200. You won't sacrifice functionality, though, since the device can cut everything from tissue paper to thin leather.

How Does The Cricut Cuttlebug Work?

The Cuttlebug is a small, lightweight, portable craft tool. Its sleek design and carrying handle make it easy for you to take your projects with you almost anywhere you go. This means, of course, that it's unobtrusive at home, too, and doesn't require much space to use. Enjoy easy set-up and operation. Place the Cuttlebug on a table and pull down the platforms on each side of the machine. Doing so activates a strong suction mechanism which keeps the unit still and steady as you use it.

The Steps For Cutting Or Embossing Are Few:

- ❖ Place paper in the folder.
- ❖ Insert the folder between the two cutting plates and the spacer.
- ❖ Gently place the bundle of folder, plates, and spacer into the Cuttlebug.
- ❖ Turn the handle a few times.
- ❖ Remove everything and enjoy your embossed paper or your die cut.
- ❖ Challenge yourself and expand your skills by learning new techniques to add to your embossed work. Sanding and inking, for example, elevates your crafting even more. The Cricut Cuttlebug takes you to new heights.

What Makes Cricut Cuttlebug Unique?

The Cuttlebug possesses a unique balance of simplicity and sophistication. Further, Cuttlebug can be a part of anything you're crafting, or it can stand alone. Upon first sight, it appears to be simplistic. While it is indeed simple the Cuttlebug is low-tech, it is by no means unsophisticated.

This machine is the only Cricut machine that can emboss, and it does so sharply and with precision.

On its own, the Cuttlebug is basic, needing neither technology nor even electricity to operate. However, Cuttlebug can work with other Cricut machines to add richness and dimension in the form of dies and embossments. Other Cricut machines, such as the Cricut personal electronic cutting machines, can pair with an app called Design Space. Design Space is Cricut's free software you can use across devices to learn design and create projects. While Cuttlebug needs no technology, you can choose to use Design Space to plan what you'll create with it.

Public Perception: What Cricut Cuttlebug Users Are Saying

Crafters of all ages seem to enjoy the Cuttlebug thoroughly. Responses to Cricut's embossing and die cutting machine are positive. When reading reviews and another commentary, three themes emerge:

Cuttlebug And Kids

Parents and grandparents alike report that the Cuttlebug generates closeness and mutual enjoyment. Creating cards, ornaments, scrapbook pages, and decorative items is something that adults and children can enjoy doing together. Crafting with the Cuttlebug is a wonderful way to spend time together, making memories, passing along skills, and producing tangible evidence of shared fun. Letting kids design projects on the Design Space app encourages their budding creativity. Cricut's Cuttlebug is safe for children to use provided they are working with an adult. This is real craft equipment for adults; therefore, kids should always be supervised around the machine.

User-Friendly And Fun

The majority of people sharing their experiences with the Cuttlebug attest that the device is elementary to use. Once someone masters the straightforward steps outlined in the instruction manual, he or she can work as an expert. Embossing and die-cutting are effortless with the Cricut device, as are the set-up and tear-down. Thanks to its simplicity, you can grab it, place it on a table, and begin cutting or embossing. It's that quick. To put it away, you close the sides, pick it up, and store it. Because the Cuttlebug is so quick and easy, you'll have few frustrations. You'll spend your time and attention enjoying making crafts rather than on troubleshooting problems. Using this tool will be stress-relieving rather than stress-inducing.

Compact And Convenient

People love the Cuttlebug's small size. You can use it almost anywhere, and you don't need a huge work surface. The size makes the tool transportable. Take it to scrapbooking parties, card parties, a friend's house—almost anywhere you want to go, your Cuttlebug can go, too. This little machine is convenient. It's easy to store because it doesn't require much space. If you're in the middle of a big project and want to leave it out, go ahead. It's unobtrusive and won't clutter your living space.

How It Compares

The Cuttlebug isn't the only tool designed for embossing and creating die cuts; indeed, many embossing and die-cutting tools exist in the craft marketplace. All die cutters and embossers operate similarly, with plates that you push through the machine using a hand crank. Each tool has individual features that separate it from other, similar, devices. The Cuttlebug's outstanding characteristics include its compact size, portability, ease of use, and quality. This tool is excellent for those who have a small work or storage space. It's also an excellent choice for those who like to take their embosser on the go.

Like everything, the Cuttlebug has some drawbacks compared to other machines. Because it is smaller than most similar craft tools, it can't handle creating large die cuts or embossing big surfaces. If you want to make something big, you'll be out of luck with the Cuttlebug. Another possible disadvantage of Cuttlebug is the need to have different sizes of plates for the various projects you do. Some embossers and die cutter tools, such as the Big Shot by Sizzix, have a multi-purpose platform that works with anything you're making.

The different types of embossing tools can produce slightly different results. The Cuttlebug, for example, doesn't emboss the edges of an object it dies cutting. If you want your product to have embossed edges, you must do it in a separate step. Other tools, like the Big Shot, automatically emboss the edges of anything they die-cutting. Some people like this, but others do not. This raises an important point. Many of these differences are matters of personal preference more so than product quality. The differences are about your style, the crafts you're fashioning, and how you like to do what you do.

What We Think

Overall, we adore the Cricut Cuttlebug. It's proof that serious crafting tools can be both practical and fun. This sturdy machine embosses many different types of materials, and it dies cuts, too. Not only does it do one or the other, but it can also do both at once. This is a valuable feature that not every similar tool can claim. We also appreciate the fun we can have with the Cuttlebug. It's so easy to use that we can focus exclusively on enjoying crafting. It is a pure pleasure to use the Cuttlebug. And if we want to multiply the merriment by working with others, we can grab the Cricut Cuttlebug and go.

Overall, This Is What You Get With The Cuttlebug:

- ❖ Precise project results, clearly defined and striking.
- ❖ A chance to connect with kids, grandkids, friends, and groups such as scrapping clubs.
- ❖ A tool that is quick to learn and easy to use.
- ❖ Something that tucks neatly away, one less cluttered object in your living space.
- ❖ A machine that brings joy and removes stress.
- ❖ Fantastic décor, cards, scrapbook pages, and so much more.
    - ❖ Although the tool itself is tiny, the possibilities for your Cuttlebug are enormous and seemingly endless. Open the box and immediately experience its potential for both great product and enjoyable process.

Chapter 6 - Add-Ons And How to Use Them

Heat Press

This is the heat press I have. It's a 12"x15" Zeny 6-in-1 Combo that has attachments for two different sized plates, 2 different sized mugs, hats and then the clamshell heat press. When we bought it, I think we paid around $225 and at the time I was making 10-15 shirts each week. It was definitely worth the time and money I saved having a heat press vs. using an iron.

Short Answer: Yes, a heat press is a standard when creating items made with heat transfer vinyl. I'd advise against selling items using heat transfer vinyl that was applied with an iron.

Long Answer: Using a heat press when creating items with heat transfer vinyl is the standard if you are planning to sell them. Each brand of heat transfer vinyl is designed to be applied at an exact temperature and pressure, then peeled either hot or cold. Unfortunately, when you use an iron (even top of the line irons), you can't guarantee the temperature you are using, and you cannot replicate the even pressure that a heat press provides. Using an iron with heat transfer vinyl is fine for personal use items and possibly gifts. However, customers expect merchandise to last and design to not fall off after a few uses. It is better to offer a quality product that follows the manufacturer's application guidelines rather than opens your business to poor reviews, unhappy customers, or customers needing items remade or refunded.

What Kinds Of Heat Presses Are Available?

Heat presses fall into three different categories:

1. **Clam Shell:** These heat presses have a hot top platen that you pull straight down to press your items. Clamshell presses are often cheapest to buy and are readily available.

2. **Swing Arm:** The top platen on swing arm presses lifts up and down and swings to one side. Swing arms presses give you more space to work but take up a larger footprint in your workspace.

3. **Pull Out Drawer:** The bottom portion of this heat press pulls out like a drawer giving you more workspace. Pull out drawer style heat presses are often more expensive.

Heat Press Accessories

In addition to a heat press, you'll also need a Teflon sheet. An accessory that I can't live without is pressing pillows! They help level the area you are pressing, especially when pressing along collars, seams, buttons, or zippers.

Here Are The Pros And Cons.

Pros:

1. Easy To Use: You set the temperature and time, close the clamshell, press a button and the heat press does all the work for you.

2. It Remembers The Settings: When I turn on the heat press it automatically heats up to the temperature I originally programmed.

3. Evenly Distributes Heat: Compared to a regular iron the heat press gives equal pressure on all surfaces.

4. It's Much Faster: Shirts that were taking me 2-3 minutes to apply iron-on vinyl to now only take 30-40 seconds.

5. It's Much More Effective: The iron on felt and looked like it was attached better with the heat press.

Cons:

1. It's Heavy: Like 55 pounds heavy. It is a beast to unbox and don't even think about moving it around where you are working.

2. It Takes A Long Time To Heat Up: It takes about 7 minutes for it to heat up to 305°F.

3. Not only do the pads get hot but the whole machine gets hot. I was always worried about one of my kids touching it, even after it was turned off and getting burnt.

4. There Isn't A Lot Of Work Area: If you're working with designs that have multiple layers, you have to lay it out somewhere else and then move it on to the heat press. There have been a few times when the design got moved a little and the finished project came out slanted or distorted.

5. Limited On Space: Anything bigger than 12"x15" (and like 11.5" x 14.5") I couldn't do or had a hard time getting to line up with multiple presses.

Easy Press

Now let's talk about the EasyPress. Cricut released the EasyPress this last July during their Mountain Make-a-thon. As I said, I was a little skeptical at first because how could something so little pack as much power as my big heat press?! But after trying it on several projects I was convinced. It was just as well better than my heat press. There are still a few things I would change about it so let's get into the pros and cons.

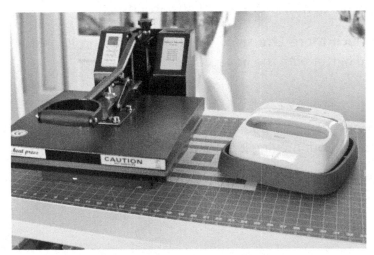

Pros:

1. It's small and lightweight. At 9"x9" and 5 pounds, the EasyPress is much easier to store and also move to do projects outside my craft room. My craft room currently doubles as my baby's room so before if she was napping I couldn't get my projects done. Now I can.

2. The EasyPress 2 comes in FOUR sizes and many different colors too!

3. The Mini is perfect for extra small projects like mugs, hats and stuffed animals

4. The 6"x7" is perfect for small projects like onesies or pressing Perler beads.

5. The 9"x9" is the most versatile in my opinion. You can use it for shirts, pillows, wood signs and more!

6. The 10"x12" is great for larger projects like XL shirts, table runners, pillows, and more!

7. It heats up fast. It gets up to heat (usually 305°F) in 2 minutes or less.

8. It's easy to use. With just a few clicks of a button, it's ready to go.

9. Evenly distributes heat. Just like the heat-press, compared to a regular iron, the EasyPress gives equal pressure on all surfaces.

10. It makes doing large projects easier. Unlike the heat-press, I can layout my designs on the counter and press them right there. This is especially useful when I make pillows and XL shirts.

11. It comes with a base to hold it in. This is convenient for not only storage but also when I'm using the EasyPress.

12. You can purchase tote bags for the EasyPress machines too that make crafting on the go even easier!

Cons:

1. You have to apply pressure to it. And not a whole lot but, unlike the heat press where you just press a button and pull down on a lever, the EasyPress you do need to apply pressure to.

2. It doesn't remember temperature settings. BUT Cricut does have this super useful guide on what temperatures and times for each type of iron-on (traditional, glitter, foil, etc.) and what type of material (cotton, polyester, leather, etc.).

Padded Squeegee

Squeegee

A tool possessing a wooden or metal handle to which is attached a thin, flexible rubber or plastic blade. A squeegee is used in screen printing to force ink through the printing screen and onto the substrate. The configuration of the squeegee handle is a matter of printer comfort and has a little direct bearing on the printing impression, but the shape of the blade is a factor that affects the thickness of the ink deposited and the sharpness of the printed image. The squeegee profile is a cross-sectional representation of the squeegee blade and is used to gauge blade shape. The most common shape for most general purposes is square and is used primarily for printing on flat substrates with standard poster inks.

A flat-point, double-bevel shape (essentially a cut-off triangle) is used for printing on uneven surfaces, especially ceramics. A general double-bevel without a flat point is useful for depositing a fine ink film, such as when the stencil contains intricate line art. Single-bevel blade shape is used for printing on glass. A square blade with rounded corners is used for printing lighter colored inks on top of dark backgrounds. A round edge is used for printing on textiles, such as T-shirts. When sharp blade edges are required, a squeegee blade sharpener is used to grind the blade to the proper profile.

Although the squeegee blade is generically described as "rubber" or "plastic," the specific chemical makeup of the blade needs to be compatible with the type of solvent and ink combination used. Blades designed for printing on vinyl or acetates, for example, are often water-soluble, and consequently, water-based ink cannot be used. Some blades are made of polyurethane, but neoprene (a synthetic rubber) is the most common all-purpose blade material.

A third important blade characteristic is its flexibility, described in terms of hardness or durometer. A general all-purpose blade has a durometer of 60, but a softer blade (i.e., having a durometer of 50 or less) will deposit a thicker ink film, while a harder blade (having a durometer of 70+) will produce a thinner but sharper ink film.

Screen frames and stencils can come in a variety of widths, and, consequently, the squeegee must be wide enough to completely cover the stencil image. A general rule recommends that each edge of the squeegee blade extend a one-half inch beyond the edge of the stencil.

The squeegee blade should be completely cleaned after a print run. Dried ink left on the blade with altering the blade profile, contaminate successive inks or cause other mechanical or chemical problems

Teflon Sheets

What Is Teflon Used For Cricut?

A Teflon sheet covers your design while you press. It is non-stick, so bits of heat transfer vinyl doesn't get stuck to your press and they help protect your design so it doesn't melt to your press.

What Is A Teflon Sheet Used For?

Teflon Sheet Uses in Screen Printing. Teflon sheets should be on your must-have list if you are a screen-printer. They are a great tool for protecting your shirts when using a heat press, and also for helping fix printing mistakes that might occur from too thick of an ink deposit or fibrillation from a tricky shirt

Teflon Sheet Uses In Screen Printing

Teflon sheets should be on your must-have list if you are a screen-printer. They are a great tool for protecting your shirts when using a heat press, and also for helping fix printing mistakes that might occur from too thick of an ink deposit or fibrillation from a tricky shirt.

Take a look at the blog below to learn about the different ways you can use a Teflon sheet in your screen printing business. Through each of these scenarios, you will want to make sure to clean the Teflon sheet in between uses.

Thick And Uneven Ink Deposits

When screen printing, it is inevitable that there will be times where a print will turn out with ink that is too thick or uneven. This is especially true with the thicker poly ink. An easy fix for this is to use both a heat press and the Teflon sheet. If you notice that the ink on your garment is too thick or uneven, you will first want to run the garment through a dryer to cure it. Then you can head on over to your heat press. Sleeve or place your shirt down onto the press, print side up with your Teflon sheet on top. Set the heat of the press to 320F and the pressure to a light to medium. Apply pressure for 8-10 seconds.

If you don't have a heat press, not to worry! You can use an iron. Place the Teflon sheet on the shirt and press with medium pressure until the print is smooth. You can get a matte or glossy finish with your print when using this technique with different textures of sheets. If you are not wanting a glossy finish, make sure to use the non-glossy side of the Teflon sheet.

Foil Transfers

Teflon sheets are also great for the foil transfer process. For the exact steps on how to do foil transfers, check out Get Your Prints Lit With Gold Foil Transfers. Essentially, the Teflon sheet is used similarly as stated above. In this case, after you print your design and cure it, you will place the foil on the print side of the shirt and then place the Teflon sheet on top of the foil and press away.

Heat Transfers

Doing heat transfers can be a great way to transfer designs onto shirts for onsite event printing and in a variety of other situations. It is also a place where a Teflon sheet is a must-have. When you are doing heat transfers you will want to place your garment onto the heat press and then place your heat transfer paper face down onto the garment. Place the Teflon sheet on top of this and press away.

Freezer Paper

What Is The Freezer Paper Stenciling Method

The Freezer Paper Method is a technique that allows you to make stencils that you can use to paint on fabric. Freezer paper has a unique property. It has a regular finish on one side, and it's coated finish on the other side; the coated side is what keeps food fresh when you store food in your freezer.

Materials

Must Have Materials

- ❖ Fabric Paint
- ❖ Paint brushes, or sponge
- ❖ Freezer Paper
- ❖ Cardstock
- ❖ T-Shirt or blank you want to use (Prewashed).
- ❖ Iron

Here's What You Need

1. Freezer Paper: I bought mine at the grocery store in the storage bag/foil isle but you can also get it on Amazon.

2. Fabric Paint: I used actual fabric screen printing ink. I found mine at Dick Blick but again Amazon is your friend. Just make sure you're buying ink for fabric, not paper.

3. Foam Craft Brush: I picked mine up at Jo-Ann's.

4. Standard Grip Cricut Mat: It's my go-to for cutting all things really

5. An Item To Print On: I got this shirt from Forever21 for $4 and it worked great! I've also used this method on canvas tote bags.

If You Have A Cricut

- ❖ Maker or Explore Machine
- ❖ Fine Point Blade
- ❖ Light Grip Mat
- ❖ Heat transfer carrier sheet (optional)
- ❖ Weeder (Optional)
- ❖ If you don't have a cutting machine
- ❖ Precision knife
- ❖ Cutting mat, or surface to protect your table.
- ❖ Printer

I encountered a lot of troubles with the paint, so make sure to read my disclosure on it.

How To Cut Freezer Paper Stencils

As I Mentioned I Use My Cricut To Cut The Stencils.

This method will work for other cutting machines also. And if you're loaded with patience you can cut them by hand with an Exacto knife. I also reused one of my heat transfer vinyl sheets for the freezer paper. (you know the top sheet you pull off after you've pressed on the vinyl?

Yes, save those!), So the first thing you want to do after your design is ready is to mirror the image on your cutting mat. I kept forgetting to mirror my image. It's a good thing freezer paper is cheap!

- ❖ We're going to pretend we're working with HTV even though it's freezer paper.
- ❖ Now for your cutting mat, lay down the heat transfer tape/sheet first. sticky side up.
- ❖ It's not the easiest thing to see in a picture but it's there, sticky side up. Make sure the heat transfer sheet is as big or bigger than your freezer paper.
- ❖ Next, cut your freezer paper slightly larger than your design. If you are also making the tea towels your design area is about 8"x12".
- ❖ Place the freezer paper shiny side up on top of the heat transfer tape. Shiny side up.
- ❖ That was one of my first fails. The shiny side needs to be up!
- ❖ Use your scraper tool to smooth down the freezer paper and remove any bubbles.
- ❖ On Cricut set your cut dial to custom and choose 'wax paper' from the menu.
- ❖ After your design is cut remove the HTV sheet with the freezer paper still attached to it from your cut mat.
- ❖ The best way to do this is to flip your mat upside down and peel the cut mat off of your design. This will keep the freezer paper from crinkling.

Weeding Your Design

When you're ready to weed, remember we're making a stencil. So you want to pull out the letters (be sure to leave the centers of your A's and e's etc.)

Weeding The Letters Out Of A Freezer Paper Stencil

Don't you just love the font Tonight's Menu is done in? I think it's perfect for kitchen towels and signs. It's called Jamish and it's part of the Fantastic Font Bundle over on fontbundles.net.

All Of The Fonts I'm Using Came From That Bundle

You can score 20 awesome font families for less than a buck each AND they all come with a commercial license (happy dance)

Applying The Freezer Paper Stencil To Fabric

- ❖ After the wedding is done we're ready to transfer the freezer paper stencil to your fabric.
- ❖ Make sure you pre-wash and iron the fabric you will be stenciling on for the best results.
- ❖ If you're making tea towels it's helpful to fold the towel first. And make sure the top of your design is at the fold. I made my first one upside down. (told you I made a lot of mistakes lol)
- ❖ The spatula in this design is part of my kitchen SVG set that is available in my resource library.
- ❖ And the fonts for eating it or starve are in the same family called 'Lick a Candy' It's also part of the super affordable Fantastic Font Bundle on fontbundles.net. (did I mention it's a steal of a deal?)

So Now You Want To Place Your Stencil On Your Fabric.

The shiny side of the freezer paper will be touching the fabric and your heat transfer tape will be on top.

Next Use An Iron (No Steam) Or Your Easy Press To Apply Heat To Your Stencil.

I set my easy press at 310 degrees and only left it on the freezer paper for about 5 seconds on each section. You just need long enough to melt the plastic coating on the freezer paper so it bonds to your fabric.

You can pull up the heat transfer sheet to test the bond. If it's not completely bonded simply lay the heat transfer sheet back down and apply heat for a few more seconds.

Painting With Freezer Paper Stencils

- ❖ So now that your freezer paper stencil is bonded to your fabric we're ready to paint!
- ❖ A huge mistake I made was painting this like a vinyl stencil. I just grabbed my brush and used back and forth strokes to apply the paint.
- ❖ Even though the freezer paper stencil bonds well to the fabric, you need to use a stencil brush or a sponge and paint it like you would a reusable stencil.
- ❖ So grab a flat stencil brush (or sponge) and dab the paint on.
- ❖ Be sure to place a piece of cardboard under the fabric you are painting. The paint will bleed through to the other layers of your fabric. (ask me how I know)

Choosing Paint

- ❖ I don't think it's necessary to use a paint specifically for fabric but you can.
- ❖ I mean if you've ever painted anything and got paint on your clothes you know it never comes out. Never.
- ❖ I use SeaPaint for everything. One it dries so stinking fast I can get projects done in a snap and two I love their colors.
- ❖ Plus it didn't end up super stiff, it flexes nicely with the fabric and it's survived many pieces of washing.

Pulling Off The Freezer Stencil

After your paint is dry you can pull off the stencil paper. It is much easier than pulling off a vinyl stencil. You don't need any special tools to get it back off, it just comes right up. I didn't notice any sticky residue on the towel either. This is the towel I made for my daughter.

Freezer Paper Stencils FAQ's

Can Freezer Paper Stencils Be Reused?

No, they are a one time use, but freezer paper is fairly cheap.

Can I Use Wax Paper Instead Of Freezer Paper?

No wax paper is coated on both sides so when you apply heat it will bond to your heat transfer tape or iron also.

What Font Is That?

I listed the fonts under most pictures. The fonts I used in this project are called Jamish, Lick a Candy and Intellecta Typewriter. They are all part of the Fantastic Font Bundle (with 17 more amazing fonts!) that you can grab dirt cheap for a limited time on fontbundles.net

How Do I Use Fonts With Cricut?

I have a whole post on uploading fonts, plus more text tips and tutorials for Cricut design space here.

Do I Have To Use Heat Transfer Tape For Freezer Paper Stencils?

You wouldn't have to if you are cutting the freezer paper by hand, or if you had a simple design. But if you are using letters and a cut mat for Cricut or Silhouette it will be a pain in the butt/near impossible without it.

Can't I Just Use HTV / Iron-On Vinyl?

Yes, you can, but after multiple pieces of washing, HTV starts to fade, crack and look like crap. The paint will last a lot longer (and it's more fun too!)

Can I Use Freezer Paper Stencils On T-Shirts And Bags?

Absolutely! Freezer paper stencils will bond to other fabrics, the possibilities are endless!

Where Can I Get Your Kitchen SVG Set?

I made an SVG set that will be perfect for adding design elements to your tea towels. Here's everything in the set.

Paper Trimmer

Portable Paper trimmers are perfect for going to crops. And also for keeping handy at your craft space when you need to make a few quick cuts instead of lugging out your big trimmer. I am very picky about the paper trimmers I use not every paper trimmer makes the 'cut' so to speak, pun intended.

This new trimmer has some great features you are going to enjoy.

- ❖ Easy Glide Cutting Blade Housing
- ❖ Precision cutting with an excellent cutting blade
- ❖ Inches and Centimeters marked
- ❖ Swing Arm allows for up to 15" measurement
- ❖ Spare Blade Housing underneath
- ❖ Cut and Score blades available

It Cuts Beautifully On A Variety Of Materials:

- ❖ Cardstock of various weights
- ❖ Patterned papers
- ❖ Glitter paper
- ❖ Specialty paper
- ❖ Thin chipboard
- ❖ And more

And The Price Is Right....

- ❖ Cricut Portable Paper Trimmer $14.99
- ❖ Cricut Portable Paper Trimmer Replacement Blade (2) pack $4.99
- ❖ Cricut Portable Paper Trimmer Cutting Blade and Score Blade pack $4.99

Best Guillotine Paper Cutters For Card-Making & DIY Projects

1. Fiskars Recycled 12-Inch Bypass Trimmer

With the global effort ongoing towards sustainability and eco-friendly development, you can now cut and design to your heart's content while making sure you've done your bit to save the environment. This 12-inch bypass trimmer gives you clean cuts, comes with a self-sharpening blade, and multiple safety features to ensure there's little chance of stray cuts.

Experience

Built from 100 percent recycled post-consumer (after at least a single-use) resins, this product stands tall in both quality and eco-friendliness. The other dimension of this product, which gives it immense value for money, is the self-sharpening blade. This blade would not need to be replaced for any foreseeable amount of time, as reports suggest. The side handle adds ergonomic value, and the safety lock gives you an extra sense of peace. While the lightness means it is very portable, the rubber feet ensure It doesn't move around while you're working. The blade can cut through several cardstock sheets at once and about a dozen or so sheets of paper at once. All in all, a wonderful product.

Pros

- ❖ Comes with a safety lock to ensure only you can use it
- ❖ Gives straight cuts with precise measurements regardless of thickness
- ❖ Compact and lightweight, useful for classrooms where frequent cutting is required

Cons

- ❖ Maybe a little tough to line up paper correctly due to the scale

2. Swingline Guillotine Paper Trimmer – ClassicCut Lite

If you're in the market for a dependable, useful paper cutter that can cut through hundreds of sheets of paper at once, you should probably consider the Swingline. It comes with an incredibly sharp blade that can deal with large scale projects like wedding invites and bulk cardstock with ease. Further, it's lightweight and attractively priced for all its cutting prowess.

Experience

With the best blade in business in your hands, you're unlikely to go wrong. Hence, if you're someone who deals with projects of a large scale and high frequency, but doesn't like the heft that generic guillotine cutters have, this should be on your list of cutters to look out for. This cutter states a ten-sheet capacity, but users report much higher volumes. The guardrail for protection purposes and the side lock for safety is appreciated, given the nature of the blade rest assured, you can have a safe and comfortable experience. Whether it be multiple layers of cardstock or different varieties of paper, getting a perfectly straight line takes minimal effort with this cutter. You can choose one out of three possible sizes as per usage.

Pros

- ❖ Delivers a wonderful experience
- ❖ Comes with several safety features to ensure your blade stays in the right hands
- ❖ Flexibility in size of the base and blade as per your specific requirements

Cons

- ❖ The blade has to be used very carefully to avoid injury

3. ClassicCut Ingenito Swingline Paper Trimmer

Catering to all sorts of users, Swingline has a version for those dealing with large-sized and high volume projects this one is recommended for most professional users. However, once you see it, you can probably guess its high-end nature. No plastic on this one it's made out of maple and comes with an 18 (!) inch self-sharpening blade.

Experience

While you might be wondering why you'd need such a large cutter, consider the bells and whistles that come with the product – a latch hook, a guard for your fingers, and a printed grid to adjust the alignment of the object you'll be cutting. It weighs in at a hefty 8 pounds, making it one of the most stable and hefty products on the market. It can handle any job you can throw at it. You have the ruler which is above the surface, which means you can measure all your dimensions properly without the paper covering them up – very useful for several applications. The grid still stays, so your alignments are proper. This has been on the market for a while and lasts for years – go for it if you want the best.

Pros

- ❖ Comes close to being the best overall guillotine cutter on the market, period
- ❖ The heft from the exquisite maple construction gives a solid feel, lasts for years
- ❖ Can handle large projects as well as cutting through the tissue paper and small chits

Cons

- ❖ Premium features and a premium look come at a not-inexpensive cost

4. Westcott TrimAir Titanium Wood Guillotine Paper Trimmer, 15"

If the prospect of an old-school cutter doesn't appeal to you, we present something equally sturdy and a part of our zeitgeist. It comes with a wood base, but the blades are finished in titanium – the stuff used in high-end sports cars and space applications. Yes, a piece of premium and rare metal, used in your guillotine cutter!

Experience

With arguably the best material possible being used for the blade, the Westcott TrimAir gives serious competition to the best in business. Although it comes in heavy at around 7 pounds due to the wooden base, it does not feel unreasonably large due to the compact 15-inch blade. You can use it for labels, small or large papers, any size of a greeting card or invitation. The plastic guard will make sure your fingers stay safe, while the rubber grip handle for the blade makes cutting quick, clean, and incredibly second-nature. Regardless of the material you're using, you'll find yourself making precise cuts in no time. The 30 sheet capacity makes for a truly versatile experience. Westcott has come up with an absolute joy of a machine here!

Pros

- ❖ Daily driver guillotine paper cutter – rubber grip makes sure you don't get tired easily
- ❖ Clean, safe, quick and easy cuts with the titanium blade
- ❖ Rough and uneven cuts are almost unheard of with this cutter

Cons

- ❖ The guide is somewhat unclear on usage instructions

5. Tonic Studios 808 8-1/2-Inch Guillotine Paper Trimmer

Let's face it, a vast majority of the guillotine paper cutters and trimmers on the market range between 12 inches to 18 inches. This product from Tonic Studios, however, is an iconoclast. With an 8½ inch long blade, and a small base for cutting with embossed grid lines, this 1 pound heavy cutter can match the bigger models cut-for-cut.

Experience

The fact that this comes with a blade and a base with grid lines and still comes in at a pound means it's a highly effective cutter for those who need to keep moving. The quality of cuts is as good as any blade on the market with durable high-end stainless steel materials. Further, you can easily chuck it into a drawer or a cupboard without needing a special workspace. The fact remains, with very few quality competitors, the 808 is in a league of its own. Incredibly well priced, with a guiding base to boot, it can easily cut through cardstock and small-sized papers. Another popular use case for this cutter is photos – several people report brilliant results after months of use. You will, however, need to keep it out of children's hands.

Pros

❖ Lightweight and easy to carry around for other settings as desired
❖ Bad cuts are very rare – unexpected from a cutter at this price point
❖ Comes with a carrying handle for better ergonomics

Cons

Lack of safety guards or other locks needs care and patience for safe use

Now that we're done reviewing the top five guillotine paper cutters on the market, we now come to the most important question: how do I decide which guillotine cutter is best for me?

Guillotine Paper Cutters Buyer's Guide

Though our reviews might have given you some idea on how to choose one that's best for you, we're outlining the major criteria you should keep in mind when investing in a paper cutter. There are many other small factors, but the following should be on top of your mind while checking out possible cutters:

1. Price: While most would consider this an obvious point, here's the catch. There are a large number of truly awful and issue-ridden paper cutters on sale today, and most of them are concentrated near the bottom of the price range. Hence, go in for something near the middle of the range they offer good quality and value for money.

2. Durability: The durability of the cutter should also be a prime consideration. The cutter should not move around when you adjust angles and take measurements, and it should not also have a cheap finishing. The materials on offer include metal, wood, and plastic — metal and wood are better.

3. Ease Of Use: The presence of a guide and adjustable rulers can make a world of difference when it comes to cutting precisely and when the margin of error is near nil. Even if not, most cutters don't come with a scale or grid lines.

4.The Sharpness Of The Blade: This is another important point. You should be, at a minimum, be able to cut through 10 pages with complete ease. The dull blades of several shoddily manufactured cheap cutters tend to break or bend or lose steam halfway. Hence, it should be able to cut a decent number of papers with ease.

This wraps up our list of considerations regarding buying a guillotine paper cutter. Whether it's DIY projects involving cardstock, creating several custom labels, or designing custom wedding invitations you are unlikely to go wrong if you buy any of the five products we've just covered. All offer reliability, quality, durability, and a certain peace of mind you get, and expect, from quality items. All have different uses and price points, however.

Chapter 7 - Practical Examples

How To Apply Vinyl (Wet Method And Dry Method)

Wet Methods

Wet Methods: Involves spraying water into a production process to reduce dust and other airborne particulate matter in the working environment, with the goal being to keep employees from inhaling polluted air. The use of these methods is often more economical and safe then requiring workers to constantly wear respiratory equipment. Wet methods are often used in large plants that manufacture fertilizer, cement, and other powdered products.

How To Apply Vinyl Instructions

Wet Method

Sometimes vinyl graphics should be installed "wet" using an application fluid to allow the graphic to be easily repositionable during installation. In warmer weather, wet applications will help prevent the graphic's adhesive from "grabbing" onto the application surface too quickly. A wet application is also useful in preventing air from getting trapped underneath the graphic during the installation process. The application fluid helps float the graphic onto the surface to prevent pre-adhesion (the vinyl sticking before you want it to).

Pre-Cautions Before You Start

1. Do not install your vinyl decal in direct sunlight. It is recommended you install your vinyl decal in a garage or building.

2. Room and installation surface temperature is recommended to be between 65°F and 80°F to reduce stretching or other undesired effects.

3. Do not install graphics outdoors if winds exceed 10 mph. Blown dirt, dust, or other contaminants can interfere with the bonding of the graphic adhesive to the vehicle during installation.

4. This-method is not-recommended for interior install (on walls for example). Please use your judgment when considering the wet installation method.

5. Do not store your vinyl decal in direct sunlight.

6. Do not use alcohol to apply – it will destroy the adhesive.

7. Do not touch the adhesive backing – oils from your skin will prevent sticking.

8. Do not point high-pressure car wash nozzle at the edges of the sticker/decal for a long time – may lift or break pieces. Car washes are safe.

Materials Needed

1. Spray Bottle.

2. Plastic Squeegee (obtainable in most hardware stores, purchase plastic spreaders used for applying "Bondo" Body Filler)

3. Application Fluid (Mixture 1/2 quart of water and 4 drops of liquid soap) Dishwashing Soap, Dawn, or similar.

4. Utility Knife

5. Scissors,

6. Rubbing Alcohol

7. Blue Painter's Tape %" (Need to Dry Application)

8. Tack Rag other Lint Free Towel

9. Roll of Paper Towels

What Surfaces Work With The Vinyl Wet Method

For example glass, stainless steel, certain types of plastic, finished wood, painted walls, sealed tiles and porcelain are all non-porous surfaces that are prone to bubbles when vinyl is applied.

That makes them the perfect candidates for the wet method because you squeegee out the water and the bubbles go with the water. Alright, let's get started. Cut your vinyl as you normally would and have the surface where you want the vinyl applied ready to go.

Surface Preparation

The surface must be properly prepared before the installation of the graphics. All surfaces MUST be cleaned before any application of vinyl graphic/striping products. Wash the surface with detergent and water, then thoroughly rinse the surface with water and dry completely.

Warning: Do not use any aromatic solvents such as acetone, M.E.K., toluene, paint thinner; lacquer thinner, gasoline, or ammonia-based Cleaners to Clean the vehicle surface.

Saturate a clean cloth with isopropyl alcohol and wipe the surface of the vehicle where the vinyl is to be applied to remove any contaminates such as silicone, wax, or adhesives.

Dry the surface with a lint-free paper towel.

Wet Installation

If the decal has no transfer tape, skip step

Run a squeegee over the front of the transfer tape to ensure that the transfer tape is stuck to the decal.

Spray surface generously with the application fluid.

Peel the backing from the decal exposing the adhesive. Spray the back of the vinyl as you peel it back.

435

Place the decal on the surface ensuring no part of the decal touches a trying spot! Maneuver the decal into position (decal should float on the surface because both decal and the surfaces should be wet). Once in position, use a squeegee or an old credit card, start from the center and work the water bubbles out towards the edge. (Don't allow direct contact between a plastic squeegee or a credit card with the vinyl as this will scratch it! at least you have the felt-lined Squeegee)

Let sit for 10- 20 minutes before removing transfer tape from the top of the decal. Remove the transfer tape by pulling the tape slowly at a sharp angle back away from the decal. It may help to put a squeegee behind-the tape to apply pressure to the decal holding it tight against the tape; this will help the decal from lifting with the tape. If the transfer tape starts lifting the decal, let it dry longer, before attempting to remove the transfer tape again.

Once the transfer tape is off, there still might be bubbles of air and water under the decal. At this point take the felt edge squeegee or a plastic squeegee/credit card, wrap it in the fabric so it does not scratch the decal. and work the bubbles out gently, starting from the middle working towards the edge.

Pros of The Wet Method

The advantages of applying the wet method are as follows:

- ❖ Fluid helps prevent pre-adhesion.
- ❖ It's easier and more forgiving for first-time users.
- ❖ It's ideal for flat surfaces.
- ❖ The fluid allows you to reposition the vinyl with ease as it gives you flexibility and won't damage the paint on your vehicle or the new vinyl.
- ❖ The process applies to graphics placed on the glass.
- ❖ The wet method is better for smaller applications, but not too little where it would soak the decal or film and ruin its adhesive properties.
- ❖ Wet wraps help you avoid problems like static.

Cons of The Wet Methods

While the wet wrap method is excellent for rookie vinyl installers, there are a few downfalls to consider before applying your film, such as:

❖ It's not ideal for curved surfaces.
❖ You must re-squeegee after 24 hours of installation.
❖ The film becomes more difficult to remove.
❖ The process takes longer for the vinyl to adhere to the car because the fluid must dry and conform to its surfaces.
❖ The wet method is recommended for specific vinyl materials and coatings.

Dry Method Application

In opposition to the wet wrap application, the dry wrap application method is the quicker and cleaner technique of the two. The dry process ensures immediate adhesion between the film and the surface of your vehicle. Because it creates an initial higher bond, you don't need to squeegee again after 24 hours or experience the hassle of the vinyl sliding around.

Installing vinyl with a dry technique often requires more skill. But as the saying goes, practice makes perfect. Once you perfect the wet application method, you will have a smoother transition in using the dry. You can hone your skills with each go-around to apply a vinyl to your car or even to other people's vehicles.

Using the dry wrap method depends on the actual skill of the installer as opposed to relying on a fluid to help you with positioning. The process is more difficult to handle because the vinyl can stick to the surface of your car immediately upon touching, so be cautious! If you find you need to reposition parts of your film, you will need to lift the film and move it. However, some damage may occur to the paint of your car or the vinyl if you have to reposition it several times.

The dry application method saves you time and money by using a firmly pressed squeegee technique. The method is also used for large projects and often requires two people to complete the job. It's the perfect DIY project for you and a friend who's a car enthusiast like you. With two sets of hands, the vinyl can remain taut as to avoid wrinkles and ensure a smooth application.

Because installers use the dry method for more significant sections of their vehicles, they are more likely to come across curves and divots. When dealing with curved surfaces, heating the film will allow it to conform to the shape of the vehicle, but be careful not to overheat the vinyl.

For example, crow's feet are unavoidable no matter how good you are as an applicator. When they appear, lift the film and apply a slight amount of heat until the wrinkles fade away. There is no doubt wrinkles will occur, so repositioning the film with tension will release the lines.

No matter the type of vinyl you are applying to your vehicle, the dry method is suitable. People often use the installation method for opaque vinyl wraps, but whether you are installing a camouflage film, matte black, or brushed aluminum, avoiding the wet process may be your best bet if your skills are up to par.

Pros Of Dry Method Method

The positive outcomes of using the dry wrap method are also why it's the more popular of the two techniques. The pros of the dry application are as follows:

- ❖ It is a more straightforward process when you apply vinyl around curves.
- ❖ It's a faster and cleaner technique.
- ❖ The dry method saves you time and money.
- ❖ The vinyl immediately adheres to the surface of your car.
- ❖ You don't have to apply extra squeegeeing after 24 hours.

Cons Of Dry Method

The negative possibilities of using the dry method include:

- ❖ If the vinyl touches the substrate before you're ready, you will have to lift it and reposition the film instead of sliding it around. It may raise the paint off your car or warp the pattern of the vinyl.
- ❖ The dry application method requires a higher level of skill.
- ❖ You can't rely on water to help you reposition the film.

Dry Method

- ❖ Clean and dry the application area. Make sure to remove any dirt, oil, or wax.
- ❖ Remove the paper backing slowly making sure the decal stays adhered to the transparent transfer tape.
- ❖ Carefully position the decal to the desired area. Once the decal sticks it will be nearly impossible to reposition without destroying the decal. Rub the decal from one side to the other, eliminating any air bubbles.
- ❖ Use a hard-edged object like a credit card to make sure the entire decal has fully adhered to the surface.
- ❖ Slowly remove the transfer tape. Making sure no part of the decal remains on the transfer tape.
- ❖ Check for air bubbles. In most cases, air bubbles can be worked to the edge of the decal, but if not, a pinhole will allow the air out and become virtually invisible, once the bubble is gone.

How To Use Cricut Iron-On

Everyday Iron-On Instructions

Cricut Everyday Iron-On works fabulously with the widest variety of base materials, including wood! Intricate designs are simple to cut with your Cricut machine, and you'll weed with ease to prep for flawless application. Find the cutting and application instructions and tips below.

- ❖ What you need
- ❖ Preparation
- ❖ Design, cut, and weed
- ❖ Apply
- ❖ Care

What You Need

- ❖ Cricut smart cutting machine
- ❖ Cricut Design Space on computer or mobile device, or Cricut Joy app
- ❖ Cricut Heat Transfer Guide
- ❖ StandardGrip machine mat
- ❖ Fine Point or Premium Fine Point blade
- ❖ Cricut Everyday Iron-On
- ❖ Weeder
- ❖ Cricut EasyPress, heat press, or household iron
- ❖ Iron-On Protective sheet (optional)
- ❖ Base material

Preparation

Pre-wash fabric base materials without fabric softener to pre-shrink and remove chemicals that may prohibit strong adhesion.

Recommended: To verify the cut setting, perform a test cut using a small basic shape.

Recommended: To verify application setting, apply test cut in an inconspicuous area on the base material.

Find Your Pressing Surface: If it's firm, flat, and around waist-high, you're golden. Be sure to avoid flimsy ironing boards.

Design, Cut, And Weed

Note: Everyday Iron-On can be used in multi-layer designs. It can be applied on top of other Everyday Iron-On, or you can use it as base layers for other types of Iron-On. Keep this in mind as you create your design.

Select and size your design in the software. Be sure to Mirror your mats before cutting if using Design Space. In the Cricut Joy app, Mirror is enabled automatically when you select a heat-transfer material.

❖ Select Everyday Iron-On from the list of materials.
❖ If using a Cricut Explore machine, turn Smart Set Dial to Custom.
❖ Place Iron-on sheet, liner side down, onto Cricut standard grip cutting mat.
❖ If using Smart Iron-On with Cricut Joy, it may be loaded into the machine without a mat.
❖ Load it into the machine and cut your design.
❖ When the cut is complete, weed your image.

Apply

❖ Preheat base material as instructed in our Heat Transfer Guide.
❖ Place the cut design on the base material with the shiny liner side up. Apply heat as instructed.
❖ Flip the base material over and apply heat to the back of the design as instructed.
❖ Use a cool peel to remove the liner.

Note: If using a household iron, use the Cotton/Linen setting (generally the highest temperature setting). Make sure the steam setting is OFF. Preheat the application area of your base material for 10-15 seconds. Place the weeded image, liner side up, onto the preheated material. Apply medium pressure with the iron for 25-30 seconds. Flip the material over and apply medium pressure with the iron to the back of the material for an additional 25-30 seconds. Use a cool peel to remove the liner.

Care

❖ Wait 24 hours before washing the embellished item.

- ❖ For the longest life, wash and dry the embellished item inside-out.
- ❖ If areas of Iron-On material lift after washing, simply follow the complete application instructions to reapply.

How To Cut Materials Using The Right Tools

Tools For Cutting Fabric And Basic Tools For Cutting Material

More Tools. More Materials. More Possibilities.

Let's start with the biggest difference between the machines, Cricut Maker's Adaptive Tool System. Cricut Maker has a completely different technology built into the machine, that we call the Adaptive Tool System, which allows us to expand the suite of tools you can use for several cutting and scoring applications.

The Adaptive Tool System can control your tools to cut from side-to-side, move up and down, and lift and turn, so you can cut more materials with more pressure than ever before. This is what makes it easy to cut through the fabric without a backer (right off of the bolt) using the all-new Rotary Blade. We'll talk more about the Rotary Blade below. Cricut Maker can cut hundreds of materials from delicate papers and fabrics to denser materials like leather, chipboard, balsa wood, and more.

Our Cricut Explore family of machines has a drag blade technology system that moves up, down, and cuts side-to-side. While you can still cut several amazing materials, they have to be stabilized otherwise the blade will get stuck in the fibers. It also makes it difficult to cut through dense materials like balsa wood, basswood, and leather because the Cricut Explore Family doesn't have the same pressure as the Cricut Maker. You can still cut up to a hundred materials like vinyl, iron-on, cardstock, and stabilized fabric, using the blades available with the Cricut Explore family of machines. To see the full list of materials the Cricut Explore family of machines can cut, follow this link.

What Tools Can Be Used With What Machine?

442

Now that we've explained the technology differences between the Cricut machine lines, we want you to know what tools you can use with what machine. All of the tools you love and use with your Cricut Explore family of machines also work with the Cricut Maker. This includes the Fine Point Blade, Deep Point Blade, Bonded Fabric Blade, Scoring Stylus, and Cricut Pens.

The new tools that were designed specifically to work with Cricut Maker, because of the Adaptive Tool System, include the Rotary Blade, Knife Blade, and Single and Double Scoring Wheels, Wavy Blade, Perforation Blade, Fine Debossing Tip, and Engraving Tip.

Rotary Blade

Rotary Blade brings infinitely customizable, precision fabric cutting to the home for the very first time. Use it to cut cotton, fleece, denim, and more. With its gliding, rolling action, it cuts virtually any fabric quickly and accurately – without backing material. Rotary Blade comes in the box with Cricut Maker.

Knife Blade

The extra-deep Knife Blade cuts through dense materials up to 2.4 mm (3/32") thick with unprecedented ease and safety, almost like an automated X-ACTO blade. It's ideal for thicker materials like balsa wood, matboard, and heavy leather.

Single And Double Scoring Wheels

Scoring Wheel makes a deep single-line score perfect for uncoated light materials like crepe paper, light cardstock, and even acetate. Double Scoring Wheel creates two deep, parallel score lines that are ideal for coated, heavier materials like poster board and cardboard.

Wavy Blade

The Wavy Blade adds a whimsical wavy edge to any design in half the time of a drag blade. This specially sculpted stainless steel blade is great for original decals, envelopes, cards, gift tags, and collage projects, or anytime you need fabulously finished edges and stylish design accents. Learn more about all of the materials the Wavy Blade can cut.

Perforation Blade

Get the perfect tear quickly and effortlessly with precise perforation cuts on a variety of projects. Evenly spaced perforation lines allow for clean, even tearing without the need to fold beforehand – especially great for shapes with curves! We love these projects in Design Space that use the Perforation Blade to create unique punch outs that allow you to interact with your project long after it's complete!

Fine Debossing Tip

Add professional polish and elevated elegance to papercrafts. To create crisp, detailed debossed designs, just snap this tip onto the QuickSwap Housing (sold separately) and tell your Cricut Maker to "Go!" Unlike embossing folders, which lock you into a specific design, this rolling debossing ball, powered by your Cricut Maker, gives you free rein to customize, personalize, and design with incredible intricacy. Make a dimensional wedding card, thank you card with your monogram, or add a flourish to gift boxes, tags, and more. Creates a stunning effect on foil cardstock, coated paper, shimmer and glitter paper, foil cardstock, and much more.

Engraving Tip

Make a lasting impression with Cricut Engraving Tip. To get professional-looking results, just snap this tip onto the QuickSwap Housing and tell your Cricut Maker to "Go!" Watch with awe as you write personalized text or create monograms, draw decorative flourishes and embellishments, or inscribe your favorite quotes on a keepsake. For an eye-catching effect, engrave Cricut Aluminum Sheets or anodized aluminum to reveal the silver beneath.

We know many of you ask why you can't use these new tools with your Cricut Explore family of machines. You can see at the top of the tools that were designed for Cricut Maker that they have the gold gear-like attachment. That is what directly connects to Cricut Maker's Adaptive Tool System so it can use the different controlled movements we discussed above. The tools aren't compatible with the Cricut Explore Air family of machines because the housing technology is simply different.

Brands

There are a few brands of fabric cutters that are popular for sewists and quilters, like Olfa, Fiskars, Dritz, and Clover. I've used both Olfa and Fiskars, and I'd have to say that I find them to be about the same in quality. Tip: The Olfa and Fiskars blades are interchangeable, so you can buy one or the other for your cutter, whichever is on sale!

Rotary Cutters

My absolute favorite tool for cutting fabric is not scissors, but my rotary cutter. Rotary cutters look a lot like pizza cutters, and they come in several sizes. The smallest is 18mm or 28mm, the most common is 45mm, and the largest is typically 60mm. On the packaging, the 60mm rotary cutters say they are for thicker fabrics or cutting up to six layers of cotton fabric at a time. The smaller blades are useful for cutting around curves.

If you can only buy one size of the rotary cutter, I'd say a 60mm is the way to go, but many people use the 45mm size. So did I, for a long time, and they work perfectly fine! You'll also notice that the styles of the handle are often different, which is another preference. Whichever you choose, you'll want to buy some replacement blades as well, which usually come in a pack of five. It's best to change out the blade when you notice that your blade is becoming dull and isn't making very sharp cuts. To use a rotary cutter, you'll also need a self-healing cutting mat and a clear plastic ruler or cutting template.

Mats

When you choose your mat and ruler, I recommend the largest size you can afford. This will save you lots of time when cutting a yard of fabric or more because you won't have to adjust the fabric as much on the mat. Again, this is a matter of preference on my part. The mat will also have markings you can use to line up your fabric. Smaller mats and rulers help travel with you to sewing meetings, but I don't find it necessary to have a smaller size. The mat I use regularly is 24 inches long, which is a great size for cutting a yard of fabric into charm squares, which I'll show you next!

Rulers

The clear ruler should have sightlines, or markings to help you line up your fabric. I use an OmniGrip ruler with a Lip Edge, which is great because it hooks onto the edge of the cutting mat to keep the ruler from slipping while you cut.

Types Of Scissors

Although I love my rotary cutter, sometimes I do use scissors to cut fabric. When you buy scissors, make sure they are heavy-duty and are meant for cutting fabric. Nothing will ruin your fabric faster than a dull, awful pair of scissors from the dollar store. Investing in a pair of quality scissors will make your sewing much more enjoyable!

A smaller pair of scissors, called point scissors or micro scissors, is also helpful for detailed cutting. Another tool you may find handy is pinking shears! Pinking shears have a saw-tooth or zig-zag edge for cutting fabric. You may wish to cut fabric charms with a pinked edge, for instance, to prevent fraying. Pinking the edge of fleece fabric along joined seams will make the seamless bulky. Or, you might use this edge on fabric scraps for a ticker-tape quilt. To "pink" the edges of the charms we cut earlier, look for a pinking rotary cutter blade and use it with your rotary cutter to pink the edges the first time around.

Caring For Scissors

To care for your scissors, make sure you only use them to cut fabric. Cutting paper with them will dull the blades. Also, try not to open and close the scissors unless you have the fabric in them because this will also wear down your blades. When your scissors aren't cutting very well anymore, you can often take them to a craft store for sharpening. Ask if your local craft store if they have a special knife or scissors sharpening day.

Conclusion

Together, We Make A Difference

Ever since we launched the original Cricut smart cutting machine, We have inspired us with their amazing creations. Today, they're on their way to making millions of face masks for friends, family, and communities everywhere. Step away from your inspiration board, and start making. This pint-sized powerhouse makes it easier and faster than ever to personalize your life with practical, everyday projects. Personalize, organize, or customize whatever your heart desires using hundreds of ready-to-use designs and fonts. Upload your designs for free. you'll always be at-the-ready to honor any event with a thoughtful card that says it all – and then some. Just choose the right design, put the pre-scored card on the mat, and let Cricut Joy do the rest!

Learning a new hobby or skill can be intimidating at first. I get it; sometimes we don't even know where to start because there's so much information out there and it's just overwhelming. For me, the best way to learn and master Cricut Design Space is from the beginning!, You see, when you have a clear concept of what every icon and panel is for, then you can truly dig in and start exploring further and further. Sometimes we are quick to jump from project to project but I think that knowing your work area will help you to take your creativity to a whole new level.

Investing in a Cricut is futile if you don't learn how to master Design Space because you will always need this software to cut any project. In my opinion, Cricut Design Space is an excellent tool for beginners, and if you have no experience with any other Design programs like Photoshop or Illustrator, you will find that although it looks overwhelming, it's quite easy.

Both the Cricut and Cricut Explore Air 2 require mats and blades which can be adjusted to cut through various types of paper, vinyl, and other

448

sheet products. The Cricut personal paper cutter operates as a paper cutter based upon cutting parameters programmed into the machine and resembles a desktop printer. Cricut Cake produces stylized edible fondants cut into various shapes from fondant sheets, and is used by chefs in the preparation and ornamentation of cakes.

Cutting & Writing Machine.

Personalize just about anything. Create a card for any occasion, custom labels to organize your pantry or a decal for your water bottle.

- ❖ **Works With Popular Materials:** Cuts iron-on, cardstock, vinyl, and paper and even works with materials you already have at home.
- ❖ **Draws Any Shape And Writes In A Variety Of Styles:** Customize your design with a variety of pen types and line weights.
- ❖ **Compact, Portable, Ready To Go:** Fits in a cubby look great on a counter, packs away easily, and sets up instantly.
- ❖ **Longer And Repeated Cuts:** Cuts one image up to 4.5 inches wide and 4 feet long or repeated cuts up to 20 feet long.
- ❖ **Bluetooth Built-In:** It's easy to wirelessly connect your computer, phone, or tablet so you can design anywhere.
- ❖ **Easy-To-Learn App For Desktop, Ios & Android:** Use the free Design Space app on your computer or mobile device to create, save, and share projects.
- ❖ **Works Offline:** Download images, fonts, and projects so you can design and cut even when you're not connected to the internet.
- ❖ **Flexibility To Upload Your Designs:** Use your images and fonts for free in a variety of standard file formats.
- ❖ **Inspiration Included:** Comes with 50 free projects online so you can start creating right away and learn everything the machine can do.
- ❖ **Support When You Need It:** With step-by-step help, FAQs, how-to videos, and extended chat & phone support, we'll be here whenever you need a hand.

Made in the USA
Las Vegas, NV
01 February 2021